THE BIRTH
OF
MILTON KEYNES

JOHN A. TAYLOR

THE BIRTH OF MILTON KEYNES

Published by Magic Flute Publications 2017

ISBN 978-1-909054-40-0

Magic Flute Publications is an imprint of

Magic Flute Artworks Limited

231 Swanwick Lane

Southampton SO31 7GT

www.magicfluteartworks.com

www.magicflutepublications.co.uk

A catalogue description of this book is available from the British Library

Contents

Acknowledgements   iv

A TWINKLE IN THE PLANNERS EYE
     HOW IT ALL BEGAN - THE CONCEPTION OF MILTON
     KEYNES NEW CITY   1
1963
     CONFLICTING VISIONS   7
1964
     THE MONORAIL CITY   13
1965
     THE DEMISE OF THE POOLEY PLAN   57
1966
     A DECISION IS MADE   91
1967
     THE BIRTH OF MILTON KEYNES   179
INDEX   225

Illustrations

The Pooley Plan for a "Monorail City."   16

The plan for the development of Milton Keynes   94

Acknowledgements

The source material for this book is mainly drawn from the archives of the Bucks Standard, which had published continuously from 1887 to 1967, when it became the Milton Keynes Observer. Subsequently this newspaper was taken over by the Milton Keynes Citizen, presently owned by the Johnston Press. The Johnston Press has kindly granted permission to use material from their titles.

The staff at Wolverton Branch Library and the Milton Keynes Central Library have, as usual, been most helpful.

A TWINKLE IN THE PLANNERS EYE

HOW IT ALL BEGAN - THE CONCEPTION OF MILTON KEYNES NEW CITY

Following the outbreak of WW2 a massive influx of evacuees arrived in the district. This was to escape the expected bombing of London, and although there had been an influx during WW1 this had been nothing on the scale caused by the Blitz. Thus as the war progressed it became increasingly apparent that once the hostilities were over, not only would there be a massive task of rebuilding but also, with the threat from the air now firmly established, it would be unwise to concentrate the increasing population of London in a central area. Even as Britain was locked in a struggle for survival during the war, Professor Leslie Abercrombie (b 1879), 'an expert on town-planning matters,' and a professor of town planning at University College, London, was asked by the Minister of Town and Country Planning to prepare a report on behalf of the Standing Conference on London Regional Planning. This was published in 1944 as the 'Greater London Plan' and called for a green belt to surround the metropolitan area beyond which new towns would be constructed. From the favourable transport communications it was suggested that to accommodate some of London's 'overspill' the population of Bletchley should be increased to 60,000. This was enthusiastically welcomed by Bletchley Urban District Council, not to mention the traders, and on Sunday, April 15th 1945 (the year in which Abercrombie was knighted) Mr A. Prince, the Bucks County Planning Officer, gave a lecture at Bletchley on Town Planning. He mentioned

1

that regarding the extension of the town, on the Abercrombie lines, it was possible that the council could purchase the whole of the land surrounding Bletchley for future development. As for the geographical situation, according to the Abercrombie Plan 'The exact location of an expanded Bletchley is a matter for careful consideration, the best site will probably be found on the north west or the north east of the present town, which is not residentially attractive and will require a good deal of rehabilitation and improvement in its shopping facilities etc.' In fact from Bletchley being earmarked as a 'reception' area for London overspill a local newspaper launched a novel competition. Every resident had the chance to help design 'the ideal town of the future' and there would be two prizes, one of £10 and the second of £5, awarded to those entries considered to have the best and most practical ideas based on the Abercrombie plan. Then by the New Town Act of 1946, (there would be several subsequent Acts) Parliament allowed the Government to designate suitable areas as 'new towns,' for each of which a 'Development Corporation' would be responsible for the construction. In pursuit of a 'Bigger, Brighter, Bletchley,' the town was providing increased accommodation for some of the London population and regarding the proposed 'new towns' at a meeting of Bletchley Council in May 1946 the newly elected Councillor, Mr. H. Price, suggested that a telegram might be sent to the Housing Minister saying that if Stevenage and Redbourne did not want to be 'satellised', then Bletchley would volunteer to be first. Yet Stevenage would be the first although at the council discussion reference was made to minutes recommending specific alterations to the 'Bletchley Master Plan' which, despite having yet to be revealed to the public, was duly approved. In spite of this the development remained slow and nowhere near kept pace with demand. In 1947 the Town and Country Planning Act set out measures to control urban sprawl into the countryside. Every area of the country was now to have a 'development plan,' and with all planning subject to local council permission in February 1947 Bletchley gained the official designation of an expanded town. Not however the New Town status. The eventual increase of population was proposed as 40,000 but this seemed somewhat optimistic in view of a studied report by the Great Ouse River Authority, by whose consideration such a community could not be adequately supported by water or sewerage services. Thus Bletchley now had a lesser target population than Abercrombie's recommendation. As for the estates to house the newcomers, those between Fenny Stratford and Water Eaton were among the first. Then at Far Bletchley in late 1948 new shops (now St. Mary's Avenue shopping centre) were planned to serve the 2,000 population of the Newton Road - Buckingham Road area. In 1951 construction of the Saints Estate began and within two years Harold MacMillan had opened the town's 1,000th council house. By November 1958 1,943 houses had been built since the war, with the 2000th, number 18, Kennett Drive on the Rivers Estate, opened in January 1959 by the then Minister of Housing and Local Government, Henry Brooke.

As for a new city in North Bucks in the first instance this was the vision of Fred Pooley, the Chief Architect and Planning Officer of Bucks County Council. He intended to include a monorail transport system, and this 'butterfly' shape, from featuring four wings, would be a 'linear city' based broadly on the development of Bletchley, Stony Stratford, Wolverton and New Bradwell. Much local opposition was aroused but it was hoped the plan - popularly termed 'Pooleyville' - would bring life to the 'Frozen North' of the county, a term applied since major development had been frozen through inadequate water and sewage facilities. Indeed there was much anticipation in February 1963 when speaking at Wolverton, Major Ralph Verney, chairman of the Radcliffe Trustees, said "I am convinced that within the next five years we are going to see enormous development in this area which will quite dwarf anything that Bletchley has so far been able to accomplish." His prophecy arose from the building of a vast new reservoir to supply Bedford, with Bucks Water Board intending to bring a large main up through the county to serve North Bucks.

Then with Sir Keith Joseph as the Minister of Housing and Local Government, on March 19th 1964 the South East Study was published, compiled by a group of civil servants from several departments. In ambitious plans for the south east of England this proposed amongst the recommendations the building of three new cities, one to be in North Bucks, with the study having been primarily undertaken due to the anticipation that between 1961 and 1981 the population of the area would significantly increase. Nevertheless in a statement in May 1964 Bucks County Council agreed to adopt the 'Pooley Plan,' rivalled in August that year by Bletchley's announcement, to national media attention, of a 25 year plan to create a town of 150,000. Involved in this scheme was Bernard Engle and Partners of London, but despite all these various aspirations, the Government remained uncommitted to any plan, not least until a technical survey of the area had been completed. Undaunted, in November 1964 Bucks County Council announced the site for their proposed new city, which was basically the original Pooley version but now on a different orientation. Then on February 3rd 1965 Richard Crossman as the Minister of Housing, having been appointed to the position the previous year, announced a Government plan for a new city in North Bucks; not as large as the Pooley Plan but still the largest since the war. In April he told a deputation of local farmers that the draft designation order would be made by the end of the year but it would be the following January that the issue was in fact made. Again many local objections were raised and in consequence a Public Inquiry was held in July 1966. Since there had been an intervening change of Minister, with Crossman being made Leader of the Commons, the outcome was somewhat delayed but in January 1967 it was announced that Anthony Greenwood, as the new Minister, had made an order under the New Towns Act designating a site in North Bucks; 'This includes the existing towns of Bletchley, Wolverton and Stony Stratford. He has decided to call the New Town "Milton Keynes" - this is the name of a small village within the area.' Responsibility for the construction was vested in the Milton Keynes Development Corporation, with 54 year old Lord Campbell of Eskan appointed as the head. Of the eight other people appointed to the Board four would represent local authorities, with one to represent the Greater London Council. Also appointed was Walter Ismay, from an engineering background, who as deputy to the chairman would be known as the Managing Director, and receive a salary of £10,000 a year. One of the initial decisions was to find a permanent headquarters within the designated area, and the situation chosen was Wavendon Tower. An interesting choice, for this had been familiar to Richard Crossman during WW2 in his involvement with the propaganda war, during which Wavendon Tower had been central to the spread of 'spin' and disinformation! Then in August 1967 with the telephone number Woburn Sands 3401 the Corporation moved into their new headquarters, having previously used the twelfth storey London office of Booker Bros. McConnell and Co. Ltd. The first meeting of the Milton Keynes Development Corporation Council Liaison Committee was held the following month at Wavendon Tower, and here the procedure was outlined to select consultants to prepare a Master Plan, which 'should first of all represent strategic objectives resulting from an environmental and land use survey. A broad concept - social and physical - with perhaps alternative proposals will be required before getting down to more detailed land use plans.' In fact the Board were now in the final stages of negotiations with the partnership of Llewelyn-Davies, Weeks, Forrestier-Walker and Bor, who had prepared the Master Plan for the new town of Washington in County Durham, and since the Milton Keynes Master Plan was expected to take two years an Interim Plan was prepared in the meantime. On completion this more or less met with local agreement and in due course after the relevant approval was superseded by the consultants Master Plan. Now the construction of Milton Keynes New City could begin in earnest. But that's another story.

1963

CONFLICTING VISIONS

On the evening of Wednesday, February 20th, at their annual dinner and dance at the Craufurd Arms, Wolverton, in speaking to some 140 of the town's traders Major Ralph Verney, chairman of the Radcliffe Trustees, said, "I am convinced that within the next five years we are going to see enormous development in this area which will quite dwarf anything that Bletchley has so far been able to accomplish.

"Equi-distant between London and Birmingham, North Bucks is the one area in the South East where there is really room for expansion."

"The difficulty over development since the war has been that because of the exigencies of the Bedford water supply there has been little development in Wolverton or Buckingham, Newport Pagnell or Winslow. Every new house that is built discharges its effluent into a sewage works which eventually discharges into the River Ouse - and it is the Ouse water that is drunk in Bedford. The Minister of Housing and Local Government has said this cannot happen and that is why we have got stories of decay in North Bucks."

However this was now going to change because of a vast new reservoir being built to supply Bedford. Indeed the Bucks Water Board intended to bring a large main up through the county to serve North Bucks, and, "In the next five years it seems to me as chairman of the Trustees that there is going to be enormous opportunity for development in this area. I don't believe that the future, despite any closure, is a grim one."

Later in the evening as chairman of Wolverton UDC Dr. J. Love mentioned during his speech that Major Verney was also chairman of Bucks County Finance Committee, and therefore he hoped his interest in North Bucks would be maintained. "Personally as chairman of the Council I have had a lot to do with the possibility of getting new industry in this area. Major Verney has given me greater hope to keep on persevering with this project."

In fact Major Verney's forecast of vast potential development aroused much local interest, and since the guest speaker was Fred Pooley, the County Architect and Planning Officer, it was 'with eager anticipation' that 80 local authority members, officers and business men from the North Bucks areas of Wolverton, Newport Pagnell Urban and Rural, and heads of local councils attended an augmented dinner organised by the Wolverton Round Table on Wednesday, February 27th. Here Mr. Pooley gave a talk on 'From Pompeii to Stevenage New Town' which was afforded polite attention until the last coloured slide had been shown, when in the hope of learning details of any future developments for their respective areas the members began an avalanche of probing questions. Yet despite members of Stony Stratford Chamber of Commerce and Dr. J. Love, chairman of Wolverton District Council, being in the front line, Mr. Pooley good naturedly gave no hint of any ideas that might be planned for the area. Instead he explained that not until the Government came forward in September with its 20 year master plan for the whole of South East England would he, or anyone else at the County Council, have any notion of what was intended for North Bucks. Major Verney might well be proved right, but it was no use the Planning Department coming forward with "airy fairy stuff on maps" until they knew everything was done 'legal wise,' and the master plan gave them something to work on - otherwise "it did not mean a bean."

"We have spent a Dickens of a lot of time over the past year or two trying to produce a solution for North Bucks but none of them are worth mentioning to you until we have the Government policy. We have more solutions for North Bucks than you can permutate on a football pool.--- I think it would be honest to tell you I can't give any solution because I don't know of one." He said that he and his colleagues had looked at many ideas towards solving the problem of North Bucks but until an overall plan was decided by the Government it would be nonsense for Bucks County Council to reach any final decisions; "After all. Anything we plan has got to be passed by the Minister so it is no earthly good my department setting out plans until we know they will be acceptable in Whitehall." Nevertheless he welcomed the opportunity to come along that evening and listen to their views on the matter.

Another person to be greatly concerned with the future development was Sir Frank Markham, MP for the Buckingham Division, who on the evening of Friday, April 26th when speaking at a Conservative meeting at Wolverton said one of the biggest tasks was to get the Government to realise that the problem of development of Bletchley and Wolverton is one. "There is something wrong with our Government planning if the new industries are going to be shoved into Bletchley and Wolverton is neglected."

"What we have got to see is that the development of this area is not just the development of Bletchley but does include Wolverton, Stantonbury, Stony Stratford, Shenley and Woughton."

Then, not least to the decline of the railway works, on May 14th he would raise the whole problem of the development, both of Bletchley and Wolverton, in the House of Commons on Adjournment, pointing out that whilst Bletchley had hosted 25 new industries in the last three or four years, Wolverton had only been allowed to have one small development, and this only employing a handful of men. He therefore urged that in no way should Wolverton's treatment be less favourable than Bletchley's, although not in any manner by which the development of the latter might be impeded.

Bucks County Council heard from the County Planning Committee on Thursday, May 16th that preliminary consideration had been given to the Government White Paper: *London - Employment: Housing: Land.* This had been presented to Parliament last February and primarily concerned the needs over the next ten years of the built up area of Greater London, extending, so far as Bucks was concerned, to the county boundary of Middlesex. Also it dealt with the impact of those needs on the 'outer metropolitan area,' and it was intended that the White Paper would be followed later in the year by the analysis and initial conclusions resulting from a review for a regional plan for London and South-East England. This would include the whole of Bucks, with the purpose being to match jobs, land, transport and housing in the region over the next 20 years. For both the White Paper and the regional analysis and provisional conclusions the Government's intention was to form a basis of discussions with the local planning authorities. Whilst the Government recognised that the Green Belt should remain as a permanent feature of the planning policy for London, consideration might have to be given to some changes. Yet where possible these should be on land with little amenity value, with local planning authorities asked to determine the additional areas suitable for housing. However any 'nibbling' into the Belt would not be permitted. In consultation with the Standing Conference on London Regional Planning, the Planning Committee said councillors had two questions to consider; Should provision for office development be made in any of the major towns in the county? And what additional allocation should be made of land for house building. Continuing, the report stated, "Further your Committee recognise that the concomitant of a strict Green Belt policy is a proper contribution to meeting the needs for the dispersal of industry and offices, and for the building of houses beyond the Green Belt." As yet they had not considered the extent of the contribution to be made, or the manner of making it. "This they would do following the publication of the analysis and provisional conclusions for the south-eastern region … when the problems not only of Greater London but of the region as a whole can be seen in proper perspective."

In consequence of Sir Frank Markham's concerns raised on May 14th, regarding Bletchley and Wolverton development, early on the morning of Wednesday, May 22nd it was stated in the House of Commons that there was 'no closed shop' policy regarding development in North Bucks. If Wolverton wished to participate in town development then it should begin talks with the County Council and the LCC, and in response Sir Frank said this gave "the green light for Wolverton's moderate and pleasant expansion." Indeed this was welcome news, for over the last few years the workforce at Wolverton railway works had declined from 4,200 to 2,800, and whilst there was no alternative industry in the town every time that efforts had been made to attract other industry the result had either been a direct refusal, or the threat of a refusal. In contrast 10 years ago Bletchley had been made an overspill town for London, with during that time a population increase from 11,000 to 19,000. Therefore it seemed hardly just that one part of his constituency should be afforded every encouragement, whilst another was snubbed whenever alternative employment was sought. He said on four occasions the LCC had expressed a desire to help Wolverton but they could do nothing without Government approval; "It makes you wonder how crazy our planners can get." However, Mr. F.V. Corfield, joint Parliamentary Secretary to the Minister of Housing and Local Government, thought some misunderstanding had arisen concerning the planning problems and procedures in the area. Unless an industrial development certificate was issued by the Board of Trade the Minister of Housing was not empowered to grant planning permission for factory development beyond a certain size. As for the Board of Trade's reason for refusing a certificate, this he understood to be almost entirely due to a sense that this sort of development should be channelled to a development district. Nevertheless any firm that wished to move to Wolverton could enter an application, which Bucks County Council would then forward to the Minister. There was no 'closed shop' on the subject and, "Indeed it is our anxiety that we should increase the contribution town development makes to the overcrowding and difficult land problems in the tight conurbation around London."

In fact efforts were being made to obtain an Industrial Development Certificate for Copperad Ltd., of Colebrook (Bucks), the largest heating and ventilating specialist, which with a need to expand had applied to build a factory in the town the previous year. This was turned down from it being alleged there was practically no unemployment in the area. As chairman of the UDC Dr. J. Love then asked Sir Frank to help and following many discussions on Tuesday, June 11ᵗʰ a meeting of Wolverton UDC was held to allow Sir Frank Markham to report on the progress, and for him and the chairman and managing director, Basil Turner, to answer questions. When the company had gone public the previous July its 5s shares had been placed at 9s 3d. They were now valued at 25s, which was perhaps a contributory reason for the Board of Trade announcing in August their agreement for the company to establish a new factory in the town. This followed high level discussions with David Price M.P. who told Sir Frank that Copperad could have an IDC for 100,000 square feet, but not the larger space they had asked for. Building would probably commence early the next year with the number of employees, not including clerical staff, to be around 150 by 1965. At a press conference in the UDC offices the welcome news was announced by Sir Frank Markham on the morning of Thursday, August 22ⁿᵈ, where he stated that on being offered an Industrial Development

Certificate of 100,000 square feet the firm in acceptance had received it that day.

1964

THE MONORAIL CITY

In a policy statement approved by the Bucks County Planning Committee, on Tuesday, January 7th a revolutionary plan to expand within 20 years the population of North Bucks from a present 80,000 to 350,000 was put forward. Preparatory to the review of the County Development Plan this served as a basis for consultation with County District Councils and others, and three of the more interesting proposals to achieve such a rapid expansion were:

1) The creation of an entirely new city of up to 250,000 people designed especially for the motor age, together with a modest expansion of each or some of the existing towns.

2) Major extensions to each or certain of the existing towns.

3) The expansion by housing only of the existing towns in the area and the creation of a new regional centre for the area as a whole and which would provide for shopping, commercial, education, hospital and other public services required by the area as a whole.

According to the report, 'The envisaged city is based on a free public travel monorail system, as it becomes even clearer that traditional cities and streets are now showing themselves incapable of handling the car. A new town must look beyond car saturation point and deal with the problem of alternative means of transport. The plan brings a new lease of life to North Bucks which has for long been regarded as the frozen and forgotten north, and has come about because the south of the county has almost reached saturation point.' The need to preserve the Metropolitan Green Belt and the need to safeguard the Vale of Aylesbury left only North Bucks as the area where any substantial absorption of new population could take place, and before proceeding with their own development plan the County Planning Committee had intended to wait for the Minister of Housing and Local Government's proposals for the south east region of the country. However, this should have been released the previous autumn. As vice chairman of the County Planning Committee, Councillor R. C. Horwood, of Loughton, said, "This is a scheme showing great imagination and foresight. At present it is little more than a basis for discussion. There will be fullest consultation with all the various local authorities before any implementation of the scheme takes place." As for County Councillor Walter Beesley, of Hanslope, who was another member of the County Planning Committee, he was of the opinion that, "Later on there will be individual difficulties which we shall have to consider, but the plan as a whole is well conceived and is a great forward-looking scheme. The influx of population to the south of the county has got to be stemmed and the only way to do this is to allow very much greater expansion in the north of the county. A scheme like this cannot be completed in five minutes. It will be some years before anything is really accomplished."

Entitled 'A City for the 70s', in an appendix to the draft policy the proposals for the new monorail city were explained, with housing and industry to be planned around the Monorail routes. No dwellings would be more than five minutes walk away, and high density housing areas, each of 5,000 people, would be developed around the Monorail stations. Between these areas light industry was to be accommodated with - in order to considerably minimise travel - heavy industry situated within its own areas. Open space would be enclosed by the monorail routes as an amenity, and also to provide sites for schools, clinics and hospitals. No dwelling would be in excess of a 10 minute walk from the school by which it was served, and these areas would be completely free from vehicular traffic. The monorail system would be free to passengers, with 15 minutes as the maximum journey time from outer terminus to city centre. Shopping facilities and the city centre would be built both over the main lines of communication and at the interchange point of the monorail system, and to offer the maximum choice all shops, except housing area corner shops, would be built in the city centre.

All this emphasised the current trends which desired larger, better shops, and would ensure commercial and social success. Grouped in the city centre would be all the civic, public and cultural buildings, thus recognising that only large communities could support social and cultural activities. Regarding other matters, multi level segregation of pedestrians and vehicles would be carried out, with car parking provided below the pedestrian deck. In addition the report contained that "The expansion and change of cities is part of their organism, provision would be made to expand housing areas and the city centre both horizontally and vertically." Dealing with the economics of the monorail the plan noted the difficulty of giving an exact estimate of the cost of building a town on these lines, where free transport and high density urban development were the essence. Indeed the cost would vary from other new towns in two ways:

1) The net density proposed is much higher than the existing new towns, leading to economy in land and services.

2) The monorail free transport system would be financed from the local rates.

'The cost to an ordinary ratepayer occupying a three bedroom house with a rateable value of £100 would be in the region of 2s a week. For that he would be provided with free transport for the whole of his family. This appears to be an acceptable burden and might well lead to a saving in the cost of living.' 'If a new city is to be successful people must be keen to go and live in it voluntarily; it must provide for the essential requirements of all kinds of people and a large percentage of the housing in the city would have to be available for letting. However a lot of people would welcome the opportunity of buying their own house and if it was possible to include such accommodation at an affordable price one would probably find that this would help to make the new city popular with people who would move there on their own accord as distinct from the great efforts that had to be made to get population to move into the older *New Towns*.' 'It is probably dangerous to speculate about "the ordinary man" but it is thought that the best hope of success in providing accommodation that most people would enjoy and afford would be to provide houses based on a patio type plan. This would offer each man a house with a small walled-in patio garden to give privacy and a garage within the curtilage of his own property. One could obtain in this way an urban development of about 15 dwellings to the acre, thus avoiding the open feeling of the earlier New Towns and the unacceptable likeness to by-law terraced housing

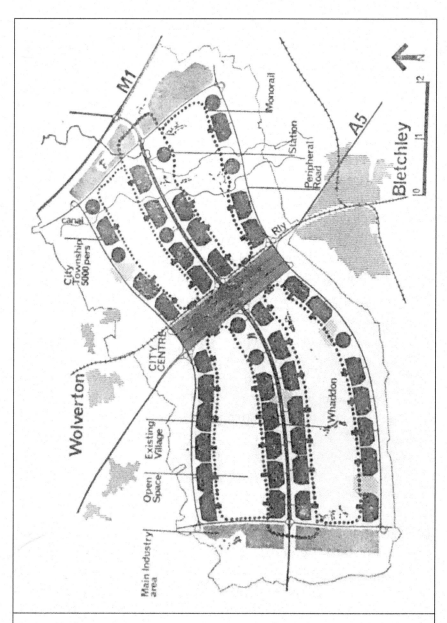

The "Pooley Plan" for the new city. In this scheme, Wolverton and Bletchley would be untouched (although not unaffected). Large blocks of high denisty housing, each with a population of 5,000, were to be connected by a monorail. In the early 1960s high density, high rise dwellings seemed desirable, and many towns and cities were busy pulling down 19th century houses to make way for the 'modern' phenomenon; nobody then understood the social consequences of these types of housing developments.

of some of the later examples of New Towns. The walled in patio garden would be useful as a living space in the summer months and help to meet the criticism that more living space is essential in housing accommodation. Experience shows that this type of house can be sold for £2,700 in areas where land costs something like £5,000 per acre. This selling price includes a proportion of the cost of major estate roads and services.' The report also stated the input of a large income derived from the industrial development, plus a considerable 'profit element' from the shopping and commercial centre. 'It is difficult to say exactly what this would be because the plan proposed for the City would not be comparable with one of the New Towns or with the rebuilt centres of the war-damaged towns. A conservative estimate of the profit from the shopping and office floor areas would not be less than £500,000 per annum.' All the other services required for the city, i.e. schools, health services, classified roads etc., were to be provided as normal national or local government services. Railway links were also important, and regarding the proposed closures of the railway link between Newport Pagnell and Wolverton, and also of the stations at Castlethorpe and Roade, a County Council objector, Mr. H. Astley, said at a meeting of the local Transport Users' Consultative Committee, called to hear protests against the probability; "It is our intention to bring new vitality to North Bucks, which has been lagging behind, and the city would cater for a quarter of a million people. We cannot say just what hardships there might be if the rail service is withdrawn, but we do ask you to take the possibility of this city into account."

On the day of its release the review was amongst the matters discussed at a meeting of Newport Pagnell Urban Council but several items were referred back to the committees until further details of the county plan became known. Then on the evening of Tuesday, January 14th the three ideas put forward by the Bucks County Planning Committee - to develop North Bucks, and increase the population by 250,000 - were the subject of a special meeting of Newport Pagnell Rural Council. The chairman, the Rev. H. Sparling, said they considered the best way to bring about development was to plan from the start, and the majority agreed that the best way was to adopt the suggestion of the Planning Committee to create an entirely new city. In the event two of the ideas put forward were accepted. Namely the creation of a new city designed for the motor age, and the expansion only by housing of the existing towns and the creation of a new regional centre for the area as a whole. This would provide for the needs of shopping, commerce, education, hospital requirements and other public services, but as for the other alternative, to carry out major extensions to each or certain of the existing towns, this was rejected. However, two councillors opposed the development, with Councillor M. Farrar saying that as long as it remained a dream it was alright, but if it ever came into being "God help them." As for Councillor E. Holdom, he was horrified by the thought of the additional population in North Bucks, particularly in view of the local road conditions. Yet forwarding the view that the idea to create a new city based on the monorail system must be accepted in its entirety, Councillor R. Parsons said "This magnificent plan should not be watered down." "The only way to do this is to go hook, line and sinker, otherwise we will end up with another Slough, or High Wycombe, coping with impossible traffic problems." Traffic was also the concern of Councillor A. Eley, specifically as to how the roads would cope with the heavy vehicles in the area during the construction.

Referring to shopping areas in the new city, Councillor Miss A. Chase deplored the layout of Bedford and Coventry; "In these two towns there are rows of small shops, which look cheap and are continually changing hands. I would like to see character, as in a town like Bristol, brought into the city." However, Councillor W. Beesley, as a member of the County Planning Committee, explained that Mr. F. Pooley, the County Architect, had formerly been Deputy Officer at Coventry, and he therefore felt certain they would profit from Coventry's mistakes. On the wider issue Councillor E. Holdom said he was surprised to see Councillor Beesley agreeing to a scheme which meant the loss of 10,000 acres of agricultural land, to which Councillor Beesley retorted "I would rather lose 10,000 acres than 20,000. We have to face this increase in population." Of the opinion that it was a "supreme challenge" to all local authorities in the north of the county to get together and support it, in summing up the discussion the vice chairman, Councillor R. Bellchambers, said he detected only one dissent from the whole plan, and he would rather see the creation of a new city than part development of villages and towns. "God help us if it doesn't come to pass. This sort of planning is needed in the country and Mr. Pooley had had the courage of his convictions." Before committing themselves to either the city, or the regional centre with satellite towns, the council would need more details, with the decisions mentioned having been proposed in a report from the Council's General Purposes Committee. This followed a meeting on January 10th attended by members of the General Purposes Committee, the Council's Planning Sub Committee, the Area Planning Officer and also the two council members who were County Councillors.

In the report was stated that the General Purposes Committee had asked the clerk to the County Council to convene an early meeting of representatives of all the district councils in North Bucks, suggesting that the chairman of the County Planning Committee, the clerk to the County Council and the County Planning Officer should be asked to address the meeting, such that further explanations could be made and further discussions take place. The report also stated that should either of the suggestions be accepted then certain conditions would be necessary.

1) Controlled expansion of some of the villages in the rural areas. Schemes similar to those already being undertaken by the Rural Council in selected villages might be one means of achieving this.

2) Very strict control in all villages to ensure that their basic character and charm was not destroyed.

3) No substantial industrial development in the villages. Nevertheless, with the changing pattern of family life, this need not rule out the establishment of some very small light industrial units to provide part time work for example women.

The adoption of the report would be proposed by the Rev. Sparling, who during the meeting said the development suggestions contained in the policy statement were "rather magnificent," and he congratulated those who had conceived the scheme. As to whether a city would mean an increase in the rates, speaking in the members' general discussion of possible problems Mr. R. Bellchambers said this wasn't a due concern, since he felt the finance of such a development would be so great that it could not be imposed as a burden on any existing rural, or even borough, authority. It would need to be paid with the help of Government funds, and he seconded the proposal to adopt the General Purposes Committee report.

Following the Rural Council, on Tuesday, February 4th members of Newport Pagnell Urban Council met for the first time since the release of Fred Pooley's plans for the proposed development in North Bucks. However, after considerable discussion it was felt premature to make any observations until they had met Mr. Pooley and, if possible, obtain further information. During the proceedings they were told of the discussions which had taken place on Thursday week at a meeting at Newport Pagnell between representatives of the various local authorities in North Bucks and, together with top officials of the County Council, the chairman and vice chairman of the County Planning Committee. Also the members were informed by Mr. F. Hall, clerk of the Newport Pagnell Urban Council, that his impression from the meeting was the County Council's favour of creating an entirely new city of 250,000 people. This was albeit on the basis of taking 10,000 acres of good agricultural land for building which Councillor F. Crawley, in strongly objecting to the scheme, thought to be a waste. He was of the opinion that the city should be built further south, where non productive land was available. Also not in favour was Sir Frank Markham, the M.P. for North Bucks, for during the month at a dinner of the Wavendon and District Conservative Association, held at Milton Keynes village, he said the taking of 10,000 acres of first class agricultural land for a new city would be a crime on the nation. As for the plan for a monorail super-city in North Bucks, in speaking of monorail systems he said "They have never proved to be an economic proposition anywhere," being only acceptable to "a government of architectural maniacs." Of Fred Pooley's three schemes he described the city proposal as "fantastic" whilst the option of a regional centre with 'satellite housing-only towns' "really gets my back up." Yet the suggested extension of existing towns he termed "very good" and the ideal solution; "This is the policy which I hope the County Council will decide to support." In fact he welcomed development in North Bucks, but it would need to be "graceful and purposeful and in keeping. We don't want development on Australian or American lines - let's be rational."

Indeed the idea of a new city was becoming increasingly divisive, for also during the month on the evening of Monday, February 17th at an 'Any Questions' session, organised by the local Conservative Association in the Unionist Club, Newport Pagnell, the chairman of the Urban Council, Dr. A. Clay, said he was 100% in favour of Mr. Pooley's new city. "Mr. Pooley is getting lampooned and castigated, but I hope to see his monument in the new city - many men have been laughed out of court. Many now stand with monuments as great men and the Pooleys of this world stand as great men." Emphasising these to be his own views he said Mr. Pooley was determined that the Stevenages and Harlows, which swamped surrounding villages, would not happen here. Meanwhile at Wolverton on the evening of Tuesday, February 18th Fred Pooley's proposals for developing North Bucks were debated by the members of Wolverton UDC, specifically to formulate observations to be sent to the County Planning Officer by March 9th. In opening the discussion Councillor Peter Cosford said "Someone has to launch into the deep end. I do feel that as an urban area we haven't received sufficient information to form an opinion on the proposals." For him there seemed to be a "lot of pie in the sky" about the plans, whilst as for the Chairman of the Finance Committee, Councillor D.E. Morgan, he thought the plan for setting up a regional centre for existing towns appeared completely artificial, to have no merits, and be the least desirable of the three. As the chairman of Wolverton UDC, Councillor Frank Atter described it as "a gimmick from start to finish," and following considerable discussion the members decided that if North Bucks had to house 250,000 more people then they favoured a city plan. In fact, had there been more frankness Councillor Atter said, he would be more friendly towards the proposals, but they had been told that, "it was a balloon in the air that could come down anywhere. This is the sort of nonsense I don't like very much," and he reminded councillors that once a scheme like the city started they would not be able to get a builder to build houses or factories within 30 miles of this development. Also, any city worth its salt would have a green belt, and if any Wolverton Urban District land lay within this Green Belt then a sterilisation of all industry would ensue.

Concerns were also being raised by Bucks farmers, on whose behalf the following observations regarding the proposed new city had now been submitted to the County Council by the County NFU:

'There is no mention in the report to the loss of good agricultural land, which is to be deplored. The time is not opportune, in the national interest, for such a scheme when non-viable land is available in other parts of the country for any proposed new cities.

Some revision of the area of the Green Belt is necessary to permit non-viable agricultural land to be used for housing development.

The area of North Bucks is one of the few parts of the country

21

which is unspoilt by housing and factory development and should remain so.

Thus the county branch feels it necessary to establish which is the most fertile land, and that such land should be retained for farming purposes and not lost to building development and thus production of food for the nation.'

In fact a resolution had been sent to NFU headquarters suggesting that a national soil survey should be carried out throughout the whole country by the Government, "so as to give positive proof as to which is good agricultural land."

On Tuesday, March 3rd regarding the proposals for expanding North Bucks it was stated by Councillor N. Hollis, chairman of the Housing and Developing Committee of Newport Pagnell Urban Council, that the councillors had met Mr. Pooley, the County Planning Officer, and, as mentioned in the Policy Statement, the three schemes issued by him several weeks ago formed the basis of a general discussion. During the meeting Mr. Pooley had explained that to expand five towns in North Bucks to each accommodate 60,000 persons would be bad planning. It would require a greater acreage of agricultural land than to create an entirely new city of 250,000 which, he said, would bring in its own industries, and be of a sufficient size to support a hospital and a couple of theatres and other amenities. As for the monorail system, on the question of noise it was explained that pneumatic tyres were now being used, whilst through the absence of tickets and fares there would be a cost saving, since these in a public transport system accounted for a third of the expense. Nevertheless not everyone had been won over by the proposals, and at the meeting of Newport Pagnell Rural Council on Wednesday, March 11th a vigorous protest against the 'dream city' for North Bucks was made by Councillor A. Snaith. He estimated it would take 10,000 acres of agricultural land and, with 2¼ million acres having been lost to agriculture in the first half of the century, he accordingly gave various statistics which, he said, showed that the type of land used for urban development was not marginal or poorer but nearly always of good quality. Moreover he told the councillors that between the years 1950-2000 it was estimated some 5 million acres would be lost. Thus, because "a community was not a matter of bricks and mortar and monorails" he was in favour on social grounds of expanding the existing towns. These were a collection of inhabitants, and spirits and attitudes really mattered. However, the vice chairman of the Council, Councillor R. Bellchambers, said he felt Councillor Snaith was very much mistaken if he thought a large number of people would be absorbed into new communities. The new community at Bletchley had not been absorbed by the old, and "If we have to have this increase let's start from scratch and build this new city with all the modern thought and science we know so that it will be the best possible for future generations." As the outcome of the meeting it was then agreed by the Council to inform the County Council that they welcomed the development plan for the north of the county (which envisaged an increase of 250,000 people) and favoured either a new city or the expansion of existing towns and the creation of a new regional centre. Of the third proposal, to deal with the expansion by major extensions to each or certain of the existing towns, the members were not in favour.

At a farmers' meeting on Thursday, March 12th Mr. V. Phillips, chairman of the Bletchley branch of the NFU, said that if the proposed new city was to be built then the North Bucks farmers must fight for adequate compensation for their land; "It's most unfair to think we will only get one year's rent as compensation. It is completely wrong and I think we should try and do something about it." Consequently a resolution asking for an investigation of the matter would be sent from the meeting to the County NFU. Mr. F. Woollard thought the idea of a city was so vast that he couldn't imagine it, but "Even so it's better than having all this sprawl of development on the outskirts of towns. And it takes up less room. It's inevitable, and it has to hit someone somewhere, and so we shall have to fight for compensation. You can't stop these things. The population of Bucks is going up more than any other county and so its quite reasonable it should be here." Adding that he thought the County Architect, Fred Pooley, should not be blamed by the farmers he said the city plan was called for by the Ministry, and so he was only doing his job.

Indeed, a new city in North Bucks then became more than 'a pipe dream' on Thursday, March 19th with the publication of the long awaited Government report (instigated by the Ministry of Housing and Local Government) on the future expansion of South East England. This listed the Bletchley area as a possible location for one of three major cities of the future, with the other two being the Southampton/Portsmouth area and the Newbury area. Preparation of the study had been undertaken over the past 2½ years and, including London overspill, examined the growth and movement of population in the area, plus the related employment and transport questions in the period 1961 to 1981. It suggested means to deal with the expected 3½ million population increase during the next 20 years of South East England (an area south of a line between the Wash and Lyme Regis) with a stated intention to provide a basis for discussion with local planning authorities in the South East. These would initially have to allocate land for houses, shops, schools, industry and all foreseeable needs over the 20 year period, and it suggested that "in the very long term" a city in the Bletchley area (a location chosen due to its proximity to the main lines of communication, to include the M1 and the main rail line between the West Midlands and London) might house 250,000 people. A new programme of new towns, plus expansions of existing towns on an unprecedented scale, was needed to act as strong counter attractions to London, and "In some ways it is easier to set out the requirements for a good new town site than for town expansion. … Good agricultural land has to be avoided as far as possible. It must be possible to supply enough water to meet the needs of the town, including its industries, and there must be adequate means of disposing of the sewage effluent." In the chapter naming the various places for expansion was included "It cannot be over-emphasised that the mention of a place does not imply a firm view that large scale expansion is necessarily practicable, or even, when the full facts are known, necessarily desirable. The list is intended simply to offer a starting point for discussion and consultation." Contained in the accompanying White Paper, which gave the Government's initial conclusions, was mentioned, "The Government, while not departing from their policy of channelling economic growth from the South East to other parts of the country wherever possible, accept the basic objectives of this study. Accordingly, they accept the need for new and expanded towns to accommodate one to one and a quarter million people, in ways which would provide effective relief for the pressures on London. Both private and public enterprise should contribute towards the programme."

In general the news received a positive approval and Fleet Street reporters circulated amongst the market day shoppers in Bletchley to gain impressions. Local civic leaders and officials were bombarded with questions, and despite the apparent view of Fred Pooley, the County

Planning Officer, that the present Bletchley would not form part of the proposed city, Councillor Harold Price, the 'father' of Bletchley Council, and chairman of Bletchley's Development Committee, thought the town would certainly be the basis. This was subsequent to his visit at the weekend to the Ministry of Housing, from which "I learned nothing which makes me want to modify my view." The vast expansion for Bletchley had been foreseen for a quarter of a century, and Robert Maxwell, the prospective Labour candidate for North Bucks, said he wouldn't support any suggestion for the city to be away from Bletchley. Yet soon after the report's publication Mr. Pooley had said he was convinced that Bletchley would retain its identity, with the phrase 'Bletchley area' meaning that the city would be near Bletchley but not on it; "I am very pleased with the report. It shows the Government is thinking along the same lines as we are." (ie a monorail city.) The exact sites of the proposed cities were avoided by the report although Mr. Price suggested that the development would be shaped like a figure 8 which contained two town centres - one being the present Bletchley centre. However, when this was put to Mr. Pooley he said "I only know what is in the report but I feel that Bletchley will be expanded but it will not play a part in the new city." In response Mr. Price remarked that should the Ministry go along with this view then it "could virtually be sticking a knife in the back of Bletchley, and one would expect a wholesale resignation of local councillors." He feared shopping trade and industry would be drained from the town, and holding the view that the proposed city had no connection with Fred Pooley's recent plan for a monorail city said of the new proposal; "I think this is a winner compared with a completely new town on virgin soil."

However, such a proposed city would have to extend beyond the boundaries of the present Urban District for "We could only go up to 60,000 at a pinch in the present area." Being in favour of city size expansion he said Bletchley was not like some towns which had a 'specific character' that might be destroyed. There was a need for modern development, at the start of which he thought there would be an acceleration of the existing programme over the next three years. This would thereby bridge the gap while new plans were brought to the drawing board, and a building force developed to cope with the requirements of such a large project; "In my view the Council will undertake control during the interim period but further major development would be done by something in the nature of a new town corporation - but probably improved in the light of the Government's experience of such bodies." Expecting borough status to be the first civic objective, he said that eventually a city status might well be desirable from the ecclesiastical point of view. As for Mr. H. Weatherhead, President of the Bletchley Chamber of Trade, he said, "... As far as the trading and commercial interests are concerned I think we shall be anxious to know about, and participate in, any decision regarding the positioning of the shopping centre. A lot of capital expenditure has gone into the existing shopping centre. I can foresee a lot of problems if it is decided to uproot the present centre and situate it elsewhere."

Contrary to a newspaper report, Robert Maxwell said it wasn't his view that if a Labour Government was returned there would be no new city in North Bucks; "What I do say is that I will not support the suggestion made by Mr. Pooley for a city away from Bletchley. The development must grow from Bletchley - it must be the key to the project." Then in a Press statement he said "This is a magnificent and exciting piece of social planning. It will bring a great deal of change, bustle and prosperity to North Bucks. It makes next month's local elections, to be followed shortly by the Parliamentary election, one of the most vital in the history of North Bucks."

Whatever the local views on Bletchley, on Wednesday, April 15th during the discussion on the South East Study, and the accompanying White Paper, the town was described in the House of Lords as "a very dreary sort of place" by Lord Taylor, Labour, who agreed it was just the sort of place to develop. Of the three proposed new cities - Newbury, Bletchley, and one adjacent to Portsmouth and Southampton - his main criticism of Newbury regarded the problem of a water supply from its situation in the Thames Valley. He then continued that "Bletchley is possible. Anybody who knows Bletchley knows that it is also a very dreary sort of place. It is a terrible place, and whoever has the job of redeveloping Bletchley has got his work cut out. It is a real stinker to do, but that does not make it less desirable to tackle: it is just the place to tackle." Not surprisingly in reply Lord Blakenham, Chancellor of the Duchy of Lancaster, said "I don't think the inhabitants of Bletchley will welcome Lord Taylor's remarks, but it is a town on the main lines of communication by rail and the M1 between London and the great industrial centres of the Midlands." As for patios, which were a feature of the 'Pooley Plan' city for North Bucks, Lord Taylor said "I have yet to meet an architect or town planner who has brought up his family in a high density area with a patio and no garden." However, as the debate continued he mellowed on his opinion of Bletchley, for it seemed his jaundiced view had arisen from his stay at the railway station on his way to school. In fact his last view of Bletchley had been from a boat cruise on the canal, and remarking that he'd like to make a tour, and so get a really true picture of the town, he admitted having been unfair by not really making a study of the place.

Convened by the Town and Country Planning Association, at a conference to discuss the South East Study the vice chairman of Newport Pagnell Rural Council, Mr. R. Bellchambers, said that Bletchley should become a full scale city. This was despite his feeling that it would overflow into the Newport Pagnell district, and "We have only given our support because we believe that the city can and should be something which shows that this country can plan and because we believe this is the way to set the pattern for a new England." His Council had reached the conclusion that the best method of developing the area was by a full scale city development, since it was felt that such a city with all the modern planning and design could produce the maximum social benefit with the minimal use of agricultural land; "There must be absolute planning consultation through from beginning to end." Also at the meeting was Mr. H. J. Price, Bletchley's Development Committee chairman. He spoke in support of the plan for a dual or triple centred city based on the present town, and on the need contained in the Study's recommendations for urgency said Bletchley was prepared to start developing the present town centre to a maximum. Mr. J. Ireland, a Bucks County Council representative, said his Authority welcomed the Study, and were pleased to see it supported the county scheme for a city in North Bucks.

Sponsored by the Bletchley and Newport Pagnell branches of the NFU, on Wednesday, May 6th a talk to a group of farmers at Newport Pagnell was given by Mr. Pooley, the County Planning Officer, and Mr. A. Comben and Mr. R. C. Horwood, chairman and vice chairman of the County Planning Committee. Presided over by Mr. D. Boulton, chairman of the Newport Pagnell branch, this concerned development in North Bucks, and with the reasons given for large scale development in the region the principles and benefits of the proposed monorail city were outlined. Mr. Comben explained that for a year or two there had been a Standing Conference on outer London Planning, which in considering the area from Brighton to North Bucks had studied planning and all its ramifications, such as transport, water, sewage, location of industry and education. "For 30 years we had tried to halt the drift of population from North Bucks. Now we seem likely to succeed. Increased population will reduce the area of agricultural land by two and a half percent, but agricultural efficiency has increased production of our farms by sixty per cent." Slides of the proposed new city were shown during the meeting by Mr. Pooley, who said that presently out of the half of a million people living in Buckinghamshire only 73,000 lived north of Aylesbury. Slides were also shown to illustrate new methods of construction, regarding which the county was currently building at a usual density of eight new houses to the acre. Edgar Lay asked why so little building had been allowed in Lavendon, to which the hope was expressed by Mr. Pooley of producing a positive plan for all the North Bucks villages. Indeed at present all applications for more than five houses had to be referred to the Minister of Housing. Since poor land and badly farmed land was available elsewhere several questioners asked why good alluvial land in Bucks was to be taken, to which Mr. Pooley said the matter of communications was important. They could not direct people as to where they should live. As to where the city would be, to laughter from some members he replied he had no idea. In response to whether dispossessed farmers would be given new farms, in the same arrangement that tenants of slum property were re-housed in new homes, he said the level of compensation would have to be the current market value, as the price agreed by a willing seller and a willing buyer. Of the £400 million project he said this would take between 25 and 50 years to complete and consist of four groups of 'villages,' each with between 4,000 and 5,000 people, some being housed in 30 storey skyscrapers. Industry and amenities would be centralised, and existing communities would have their expansion and development controlled. Mr. A. Cony asked what would happen to the effluent from the new city. Would it be discharged into the already polluted River Ouse, retorting that his question hadn't been answered when Mr. Pooley replied that the matter was 'receiving study.' Indeed it was felt by another member that the three representatives were side tracking questions. Another member asked for assurance that farmers would be notified as soon as possible of any plans which might affect their land. They not only had to consider owner occupiers but also tenant farmers, since as the law stood a tenant farmer could be deprived of the tenancy of a farm, which he had worked all his life, and receive only two years' rent as compensation. Mr. Horwood replied that on behalf of the County Planning Committee he felt an assurance could be given that the National Farmers' Union would be notified as soon as the Planning Committee knew of the proposals, and "I hope myself that within half an hour of that information being available to the Planning Committee, you yourselves will have the information." His inclination was that consultation with the NFU would be on three levels - national, county and local - and Mr. W. Snook, Bucks NFU County Chairman, said he was extremely pleased to hear Mr. Horwood's assurances. As to whether Buckinghamshire had "stuck its neck out" by offering to provide land for a new city, Mr. Pooley explained that the County was under an obligation to produce its five year plan, which was already overdue. By building at the density of eight houses to the acre they were losing agricultural land at the rate of 50,000 acres a year. By increasing the density, as in the new city, this loss would be greatly reduced. Acceptance of the proposals was then voiced by Walter Beesley, a well known farmer and a member of the County Planning Committee, and in conclusion a vote of thanks was given by the County Chairman, Mr. W. Snook, who said "Future generations may hinge on what is happening in the next few years. But the non-viable land must be sorted out or our future generations will hold it against use, saying in times of emergency 'Where are we going to get our food from?'" Carried unanimously, this was also the concern of a Newport Pagnell branch resolution proposed at the May meeting of the Bucks County NFU Executive by Mr. T. Bradshaw. He was the former chairman, and the wording urged the NFU headquarters "to do everything possible to impress upon the Government the necessity of building new cities and towns on the least viable land possible, as all good agricultural land will be needed to produce food for future generations." "To build this new city on the very best land that you can find is a very great sin."

On Thursday, May 21st members of Bucks County Council agreed to adopt the 'Pooley Plan,' for a new motor age city in North Bucks of a population of up to 250,000. This was provided that the modest expansion of existing towns in the area was not precluded, and it was felt that the construction of the new city should be undertaken in a partnership between the County Council, the Government and private enterprise. Regarding the Policy Statement, which had been issued earlier in the year on the proposed development of the county, their decision followed the receipt of a report (based on the observations received from the local Urban and Rural Councils) from the Planning Committee which, stating that it wouldn't be easy to have to start with the re-organisation of the centre of Bletchley as a major centre of a new city, rejected the suggestion of Bletchley Urban Council that the town should be expanded. In fact within the long report it was stated that Bletchley Council's desire for the town to be an integral part of the new city was, primarily, due to a fear that the construction of a completely new city in the area would be disastrous to the economic life of the town; "They fear that if a completely new city was built, trade would be drained away to it and that shops of this calibre would either leave or refrain from coming to Bletchley." Also mentioned was the choice being between an entirely new city or Bletchley's idea of expanding to 90,000 as a first stage of the new city. However, "To build a new city with Bletchley as an integral part would rule out the creation of a new city especially designed for the motor age, with all the benefits which would flow from it." Indeed, Councillor W. S. Johnson emphasised that it was described as a city for the motor age, and "after the appalling casualties over Whitsun I feel that in twenty years time the motor age may be halted considerably and small helicopters or planes will be available and there should be provision made for this." The Report continued "It is only your committee's policy statement and the South East Study subsequently published which have produced the probability of very substantial expansion in North Bucks. In these circumstances your committee feel that those who have come to Bletchley, whether to live or to invest their money, have done so in the knowledge that Bletchley would be a town of moderate size only, and that by creating a new city in North Bucks, your committee would be doing nothing to disappoint the expectations of these people as to the size of the town. Quite apart from this, your committee do not accept that the creation of a new city would be to the disadvantage of Bletchley: indeed they believe that the converse would be the case." Such was also the opinion of Alderman R. Verney, who thought the new city could bring prosperity to Bletchley and the surrounding villages. This was certainly the hope of the new 18 strong Bletchley Council at its first meeting on Tuesday, May 19th where, in his first speech since election as chairman for the coming year, Councillor J. Cassidy said "All of us, regardless of politics or creed, are resolved in unity to fight to expand this town into a great city, with all its amenities for work and leisure." As for the meeting of the Bucks County NFU Executive, with the land to be compulsorily acquired for the proposed new city fears were expressed that up to 100 farmers could be dispossessed within the next three years. Thus in a plea for common sense to prevail former County Branch Chairman, Mr. T. Bradshaw, urged that the city should be built on other non viable land. Meanwhile the County Branch was urging headquarters to take immediate measures to ensure that adequate compensation would be received by those who were affected. As to what form this should take, after considerable discussion a resolution was agreed demanding that where a tenant farmer was dispossessed by compulsory purchase order he should be compensated by either ten years' rent or a sum equivalent to his estimated profits over the previous five years (whichever was the greater); this money to be paid at the time he was forced to vacate the farm. Mr. Bradshaw's branch (Newport Pagnell) had originally raised the issue, and he told members that although within the past few days Bucks County Council had approved the plan to build a new city in the north of the county, it had as yet to be disclosed which farms might be affected; "Is it right and fair that we should be turned out of our farms, with no other compensation than one years' rent. We think that at least we should be found another farm, or given ten years' rent as compensation." "The County Council seems determined that this city shall be built in the north of the county although we have protested against it on many occasions and suggested it should be built on less viable land." As the chairman, Mr. W. Snook said the original resolution of the Newport branch had been considered immediately prior to the executive council, and the committee felt it better to delete the words "Having another farm found for him," since this might complicate matters when it came to getting the resolution onto the statute book.

Primarily as to how the Government South East Development Plan would impact on the village areas, weekend meetings around the beginning of June were addressed at Great Brickhill, Moulsoe and Woughton by Robert Maxwell, as the prospective Labour candidate for Buckingham. There was no doubt he said that the development would affect everyone in ways they might not anticipate, since the intention aimed to provide housing and jobs for 300,000 more people in North Bucks. When asked at Woughton if the Labour Party had a definite policy as to exactly where the new city would be he replied "No," since the opposition Party was not privy to all the necessary facts. However he thought that the Woughton area 'might not be far from the mark,' due in part to the relatively poor soil. Development in the 'declining areas' of the North etc. would be more actively encouraged by a Labour government, to thus curb immigration from those areas to North Bucks and further ensure that land for the new city would be acquired at its 'existing use price' by a North Bucks Development Corporation. This would then resell it to local authorities or private developers at reasonable prices, and also finance roads, services etc. He said the development of villages would be necessary although Labour would ensure that the character of the villages remained unspoilt, and that local people were properly consulted. As for the acquisition of land, the Labour Party would apply similar principles to the villages as would apply in the new city area, and so speculators who thought they were sitting on a pot of gold were likely to be very disappointed.

At Wavendon on Friday, June 12th the role that the village might play in the development of North Bucks was amongst the questions discussed at a Woburn Sands Labour Party forum. The panel included Mr. V. Jones, headmaster of White Spire School, Bletchley, Professor F. Norman of London University, a resident of Bow Brickhill. Also Mr. F. Watkiss, a member of Woburn Sands parish council and Newport Pagnell RDC, who said "We have got to look to the future and study traffic and housing problems. I back the Pooley plan," which, Professor Norman suggested, could be embellished by building skyscrapers in the new city, "… like some of the very beautiful ones in Chicago."

For Bletchley Urban Council, the beginning of July saw the intent for a firm of experts to prepare a plan for a new town centre and a new town map, providing for a very much larger population. This would be in support of how the South East Study should be implemented regarding the ideas of the Council, which, stating "most forcefully" its view that the existing town of Bletchley should be an integral part of the greater town or city proposed, had now submitted the requested observations on the Study to the Ministry of Housing and Local Government. This news was contained in a statement issued to the Press after the Council

32

had gone into committee at its monthly meeting, specifically to finalise the representations to be made to the Ministry. In fact to obtain the fullest publicity for their plans and proposals - namely for the further expansion of Bletchley in connection with the South East Study - on Tuesday, July 28th the Council would decide to retain the services of a public relations and publicity expert. However, whilst agreeing the need for full publicity Councillor E. Staniford said "We are not selling washing powder or petrol, or anything like that. I think it is a bit undignified. We have a good case and I am not very happy to have to employ anyone to put over our case …" Nevertheless in the Development Committee's preamble to the recommendation it was stated that the Surveyor, Mr. J. Smithie (having reported satisfactory progress on the Council's recent decision to draw up a scheme of development) had asked the Committee to consider the possibility of engaging professional guidance to secure the most effective presentation of the plans and proposals. This was supported by Councillor G. Clarke, who said he did so because this was a matter which concerned not the planners, nor the local government bodies, but the people of North Bucks. They would ultimately decide, and he hoped that all such plans for the future of North Bucks would be publicised to the people in the best possible manner. This could only be done by professionals, and if it was going to cost £500 they ought to be prepared to pay it, "so that the people who were going to live there should know what was proposed for them." For his part, Councillor Caldwell, the chairman of the Development Committee, said they would have to wait until the public meeting for the general discussion. Members could then "blow their tops or do anything except fight." All he was presently asking was for the recommendation to be approved.

Bletchley's development was certainly given approval by the employer and trade union members of the Southern Regional Board for Industry, who stated that from an industrial point of view it seemed 'sound' that a third of the anticipated growth of 3½ million in population by 1981 should be accommodated by substantial increases in relatively few places; "Of the places suggested as new cities, the members support the selection of Bletchley and the Southampton-Portsmouth area, but are opposed to the selection of Newbury, because of its nearness to London …" As for the style of the proposed new city it was disclosed by Mr. R. Horwood, vice chairman of the Buckinghamshire County Planning Committee, that this area might have a 'vertical village', differing completely from anything built anywhere before. As County Planning Officer the plans prepared by Mr. Pooley incorporated everything for modern living under one roof in an 11 or 12 storey building, set within a 20 acre park. This would contain high class residential accommodation 'and one would go up and down in a lift to the shops etc.' The reason was for an economy of land usage, and it would be a 'virgin village,' built in a completely open area wherever 20 acres of land was available. The scheme would require the co-operation of the County Council and one of the Rural District Councils in North Bucks, but Mr. Horwood said the Newport Pagnell RDC was very progressive, and he hoped their support would be forthcoming. The scheme would need to be funded from private enterprise, and through the provision of much needed housing such a 'village' would increase the rateable value of the area, thus easing other people's burdens; "To maintain our standard of living we must preserve our agricultural land as much as possible, and if we cannot go *out* then we must go *up*."

At noon on Monday, August 31st Bletchley's 25 year plan to create in two phases a town of 150,000, at an estimated cost of £195 million, was made public at a Press Conference held at the Park Lane Hotel, London. In conjunction with Bletchley's Engineer and Surveyor, Mr. J. Smithie, it had been drawn up by Bernard Engle, of Bernard Engle and Partners of London, W1, whose vision saw the "scar on the landscape" of the clay pits to the south east becoming a 'Marina,' to include artificial beaches of imported white sand. Together with the B.B.C. news and the television services nearly all the national papers and news agencies were represented at the conference, where Councillor Cassidy in presiding described Bletchley's presentation as "unique," saying they were "first off the ground" in submitting a plan directly arising from the South East Study. Being the first item in 'Town and Around' he was interviewed at the conclusion for B.B.C. television, with the 4½ minute feature to be screened at 6.10pm. Then at 7.30pm the Council held a special meeting at Wilton Hall, Bletchley, where amongst an attendance of over 500 were Mr. R. Millard, clerk to the County Council, and Fred Pooley, the County Architect and Planning Officer. The close of the event then saw overwhelming support for a resolution supporting the plan, with the Government to be urged to "take full advantage of the many advantages the existing town of Bletchley offers for substantial expansion under the terms of the South East Study, without being detrimental to the other towns and villages of North Bucks."

Obviously the proposed new city would greatly impact on the surrounding district, and at a press conference on Wednesday, September 23rd members and officials of Newport Pagnell Rural Council released the news that Olney would become a satellite town of the monorail city. With the impossibility of a precise forecast, it was anticipated that by the completion of development the population would be between 9,000 and 15,000, and as an amenity for the whole area the council in conjunction with the plans for Olney not only intended to develop the worked out gravel pits at Emberton, but had also agreed to offer facilities for the construction of a vertical village - 'the first in the world' - with this scheme being completely separate from the monorail city planned earlier by the County Council. The exact location of this 'village' was not made public, but was stated at the press conference 'to not be south of Newport Pagnell.' In partnership with Bucks Planning Department a plan had also been produced by the Rural Council showing how Olney could be developed during the construction of the new city.

Apart from the Rural Council, the Urban Council of Newport Pagnell was also investigating the impact of the proposed new city, and on Tuesday, October 6th announced that a target of 12,000 to 15,000 for the town was envisaged should the 'Pooley plan' city take place. The report had been jointly prepared by the Urban Council and Bucks County Planning Department but members stressed at their meeting that it was only a basis on which the town could be developed, and the plans were very flexible. Yet no firm decision had so far been taken on the development of North Bucks, and on Tuesday, October 27th Bletchley Council were told by the Chairman, Councillor J. Cassidy, that all depended on a technical survey of the area. This was to be undertaken for the Ministry of Housing and Local Government, from which he had received this assurance in response to his enquiry regarding County Council advertisements for technical staff in connection with a proposed new city. Indeed, in answer to Councillor Mrs. J. Ramsbotham he said he had been "terribly perturbed by the fact there had been public advertisements from the County Council for staff to be employed for the specific purpose of being engaged on the technical work involved 'with some proposed new city.'" This he felt was completely contrary to the earlier assurance received by the Council from the Ministry (that the whole decision on the future development in the area depended on a survey that had to be undertaken by a person from the Ministry) and, "… if the Ministry had made their minds up about the new city, I felt they should have let us know." However, "Their reply quashed my fears. The Ministry had certainly not authorised such proposals, and so far as they were concerned the position was exactly as we had been given to understand it - that the survey will be made and that, despite all the rumours, the decision on the development of North Bucks will be tied up with the technical survey of the area. I must say that seems the intelligent way to me." So did it seem to Mrs. Ramsbotham, who in reply said this statement "should stop some very unpleasant rumours that are going round." In other business, prior to Councillor Cassidy's announcement the Council had decided to seek an interview with the new Minister 'to put him in the picture' regarding Bletchley and its development problems, and also to ask the new M.P. for help in the matter.

That the new monorail city would mean a loss of trade to other towns was claimed at a meeting called of other Chambers of Trade in North Bucks by the Bletchley Chamber of Trade. This was held on Monday, November 2nd at The Bull Hotel, Stony Stratford, but although representatives from Newport Pagnell, Wolverton and New Bradwell, Stony Stratford, Winslow and Buckingham were present the fears were not reciprocated, it being the feeling that trade, as one example, would be increased by the expansion of Newport Pagnell due to the building of the new city. This was also the opinion of Buckingham.

By now interest in the proposed new development was not confined to national boundaries, for in a recent report the 'Toronto Globe & Mail' stated that Canadian designs and construction techniques were needed for the new city. Indeed the city received large coverage, with the article worded:

"Canadian designs and construction techniques are wanted for one or more neighbourhoods of 1,200 dwellings each in a proposed dormitory suburb in Buckinghamshire, England. The 1.2 billion dollar scheme being prepared by Buckinghamshire County Council would produce a city of 250,000 to relieve population pressures in the London area. A monorail system would provide mass transit within the city and steam for central heating could be carried in huge pipes built into the monorail structure, planners say. If the British foreign exchange crisis is of short duration, the surcharge applied this week to imported manufactured goods would be gone before the suburb is under construction. No date has been set for starting, but it has been described as a city for the Nineteen Seventies. F.B. Pooley, Buckinghamshire County architect and planning officer who has proposed Canadian participation in the development is with a British house builder mission completing a tour of Canada in Ottawa today and tomorrow. He wrote in a recent report on the new city: "From what we already know of Canadian architecture and building, we are convinced that such a unit would make a valuable contribution towards the design of the city itself and would help to prime the pump towards a continuous flow of ideas and materials from one country to the other. By retaining a number of architects, a variety of architectural design could be obtained and the monotony of other new towns avoided," Mr. Pooley said. "If one wants to attract a large number of people to live in a new city, then they must have the living conditions they enjoy and not necessarily those which the architectural profession feel are good for them," he added. Before the Buckinghamshire scheme was mentioned, the largest Canadian housing project proposed for the United Kingdom was 200 houses. A British mission that toured Canada last year recommended that six demonstration houses be built and that later 200 be built. The six were built last Summer and four of them were opened this week. One house in each pair is completely furnished, while the other is left open at certain points to show how it is built. The proposed new city would be developed in four sections, each surrounding a monorail loop. Each section would have about 60,000 inhabitants in a mixture of housing types both public and private. Suggested height for the apartment towers is 12 stories."

Putting an end to much uncertainty, during November the site of the proposed new £400m city for North Bucks was at last announced, and in a lengthy statement issued by Bucks County Council the development area of some 22,950 acres was stated to be in the urban districts of Bletchley, Newport Pagnell and Wolverton; the parishes of Beachampton and Thornton in the Buckingham Rural District; of Bradwell, Bradwell Abbey, Broughton, Great Linford, Loughton, Milton Keynes, Moulsoe, Shenley Church End, Stantonbury, Walton, Wavendon, Woolston-cum-Willen, Woughton on the Green in the Newport Rural District; and of Great Horwood, Nash, Shenley Brook End, Tattenhoe and Whaddon in the Winslow Rural District. The core of the city would be located on Loughton with the whole project, if passed, taking some 29 years to complete. According to the County Council's Chief Planning Officer, Fred Pooley, the proposals would go before the meeting of the whole County Council for their approval on Thursday, November 26th, and he emphasised that the city proposal was only one part of the County Council's scheme for developing North Bucks; "The expansion of existing towns in the area is also part of our scheme. They are as vitally important as the new city in our plan to solve the population problems of London and Bucks." As reported in the Press, 'The city will consist of a city centre, four series of small compact identifiable residential city townships, four main industrial areas, and large open areas all connected by a public transport system - possibly monorail - and a road system, pedestrian and motor traffic being separated from each other throughout. No airport is envisaged, those within easy distance being sufficient, but there may be provision for a helicopter or vertical take off service within, or close to, the city centre. The object of elevating the public transport system is to give free access to any point from the city townships to the open space within. The city townships will lie within the residential areas in the comprehensive development area. The residential areas run in continuous form between the public transport system and the peripheral road but the development is intended to take the form of small compact identifiable townships. These will be separated from each other by wedges of open space. Each township may be designed by a different architect and constructed in a different way to give each its own character and avoid monotony. The townships will vary in density but the average population will be 5,000 persons at an average net density of 50 persons per acre. The city townships are intended to be integral parts of the city and not in any way self contained. The residents will normally look to the city centre or the industrial areas for their work. However the townships will include some local shops and businesses, in selected areas light industry, primary schools, places of worship so far as not provided elsewhere. The four main industrial areas lie at the outer end of the series of city townships. The open space within the public transport system joining each of the four series of city townships will be used partly for agriculture, partly for educational, and general social purposes, and partly as public open spaces. The land to be devoted to public open space purposes, namely parks and public playing fields, in each area of open space will not be less than 8 acres per 1,000 persons but room is left for this to be increased.' Mr. W. Snook,

County Chairman of the Bucks branch of the NFU, said his branch had yet to be officially informed of the proposed plans for the new city, and were most concerned that consultation had not been made with all the interested parties before the plans were made public, particularly those who farmed the land; "Why spend all this money on various proposals - planning should be at National level. The NFU accepts the inevitable but good agricultural land should be saved. Building should be on derelict land according to NFU policy."

The area of land to be devoted to educational purposes was to be determined by the school population at any relevant time. This extent would also provide a large area of open space near high density housing for recreation and sport, thus enabling secondary schools, sports stadiums, swimming pools, concert halls and similar buildings to be centrally situated for the townships. Separated from pedestrians, restricted motor traffic would be allowed within the open spaces, with the city's main communications with the rest of the country being accessed via the M1, the , the London-Manchester main line and the Grand Union Canal. As for the main road system of the city, this would consist of a peripheral road and north east to south west spine road linked to the motorway and A5, 'and to other external roads on the one hand and city centre on the other.' 'The road system within each township will link each dwelling to the peripheral road while pedestrian access only will be provided separately from each dwelling to the public transport system, local shops, school and other buildings and the central open spaces including the secondary schools. The area between the outer road circling the city and the boundary of the comprehensive development area is intended in general to remain in agricultural use as a safeguard to maintain the entity and character of the city. The future proposed for each of the existing villages is as follows; Beachampton, Bradwell, Broughton, Great Linford and Willen are in the outer agricultural area and will remain much as they are. Any development will only be by redevelopment and infilling. Great Woolstone, Milton Keynes, Nash, Shenley Brook End, Whaddon and Woughton on the Green are in the open space areas within the public transport system. Except in the case of a village which may later be adapted to form the nucleus of an educational centre, these villages will remain much as they are, any development as previously mentioned. Little Woolstone, Shenley Church End, and Upper Weald are in residential areas and will be incorporated into the appropriate township as far as practicable. Loughton is on the city centre site and will be redeveloped for this purpose. However the Council may or may not adopt these recommendations. If they do the approval will only be for the purpose of consultation. No statement has been made by the Council as to where the money for the city will come from but the council say that investigations into this side of the project give no reason for recommending an abandonment of the proposals.'

The County Council's plan was the chief subject of questions at a Press Conference held at the County Offices, Aylesbury, on Monday, November 23rd. Here the comment was made that the officers seemed to have great confidence in the plan to which came the reply "That is because we are convinced this is the right plan, ..." from Mr. Pooley, who when asked about the open space within the city thought that about 1,000 acres could continue for farming. However Mr. R. Millard pointed out that even if the Government gave the go ahead there would be numerous delays for appeals and inquiries.

Yet the proposals did not meet with the favour of the Bucks County branch of the NFU, which in an announcement on Tuesday, November 24th stated "The objections of the Bucks NFU are that the County Planning Authority, by failing to consult with the Union, notwithstanding a promise which was given at a meeting of farmers recently by that authority, have brought out the plan in ignorance of the relative value of the agricultural land affected." It pointed out the wastefulness and continued "The statement made by the County Planning Authority that these areas in the centre and a belt of land right round the outside could be used for agricultural purposes, as well as for amenities for the people of the new city, is ill founded. In the opinion of the Union it would be utterly impossible to farm efficiently and economically in any of these areas, surrounded as they would be by 250,000 people. ... In the opinion of the National Farmers' Union, before projects such as this are undertaken more intensive use should be made of large areas of land where low density suburbanisation at present encroaches on farmland and that the congestion of the South East should be relieved, not aggravated by seeking to attract additional population, but by endeavouring to attract them to less favoured areas, especially those at present subject to depopulation." In fact by involving some 23,000 acres, and being comprised of four separate communities, with vast open spaces in the centre, the plan seemed extremely flippant of some of the best farming land in the north of the county, and Mr. W. Snook, as the chairman, said "If we are not satisfied after next Thursday with the County Council's report we intend to take this to the Ministry of Housing and the Ministry of Agriculture." In fact he had written a letter of protest to every member of the County Council.

As stated by Mr. Pooley, on Thursday, November 26th the proposals went before the meeting of the whole County Council for acceptance, with the formal recommendation given unanimous approval for 'the combined comprehensive development area map and designation map and all salient material for the purpose of consultation with the District Councils concerned and other interested bodies and persons.' Nevertheless Alderman S. Comben, the Planning Committee chairman, emphasised that the Council was not being asked for a final decision on the new city project. It was merely a move to open up consultations with District Councils in the county, farmers and other interested parties, and in the preamble came a hint that a semi independent body within the County Council 'machine' might be established to create the new city, with a separate fund to isolate the ordinary finances of the Council from 'unlimited calls.' As for the layout of the proposed city this was on the lines previously suggested by the county planners, and (expanding on the previous information) featured down the waist from north to south a multi level city centre, about half a mile wide. Across the nine miles from west to east a spine road would divide the whole area into four quarters each of which, with open space between them, but enclosed at the outer end by industrial development, would have on two sides of its length a series of 'city townships.' As for getting around, 'The object of elevating the public transport system, which might conveniently be a monorail system, is to give free access to any point from the city townships to the open space within.' With regard to the 'effect on surrounding towns and villages,' a section of the report stated 'The creation of the new city will stimulate the demand for housing and, to a lesser extent, service employment in many of the towns and villages in North Bucks and parts of the adjoining counties. Indeed, the controlled expansion of selected areas within the new city's sphere of influence is an integral part of the comprehensive proposals for North Bucks.' Relating to the cost of the new city Councillor P. Fry felt it was "only right that members of the Council and the general public" should be made aware of the problems specified by the County Treasurer.

However, in response Alderman R.B. Verney, chairman of the Finance Committee, said he wasn't prepared to report every matter of finance to the Council, and had not made any reference to the cost because "we don't know enough about it." The Committee had been told of the "approximate costs of construction" but there was much else to be entered into, and anything at this stage would be "misleading." Full financial discussions would begin at once; "And before you are asked for any final decision, these figures will be brought before you." Prior to the adjournment for lunch County Alderman A. Ward, the chairman, asked for persons having "any interests whatsoever" in the proposed city to "refrain from speaking or voting" on the subject, and thus after the break Councillor W.S. Johnson, Councillor Major J.D. Young and County Alderman F. Woollard duly complied. Councillor Comben then said that since the member for Bletchley had sought clarification of the phrase "modest expansion," he could assure him of no hindrance to the three towns in question in North Bucks because of the city proposals. Also he gave an assurance that all concerned with the city plans would be kept informed of future proposals.

That "Some members of the Council seem to have had a working lunch" was the opinion of Councillor P. Fry, in response to Alderman J. Ireland's enquiry, "Will you agree that in North Bucks this is the area?" He thought the proposals had been well received in the north of the county but Councillor Fry retorted, "We can't know where the first shilling or the last shilling is coming from 'til we agree where." We must start to think what we are in for." His view was that the venture was being pushed too quickly, and when the financial cost was reckoned many people would "want to go back." Councillor G. Moir expressed the hope that from being thus entitled a new city should give rise to a new cathedral. Yet according to the Reverend John Crisp, the vicar of Newport Pagnell, North Bucks already possessed one, for writing in the November edition of *The Country Churchman* he said that his parish church was often called the Cathedral of North Bucks. At the close of the hour long debate the comment that this was "the first step to put something on paper. We are embarking on four years of consultation and planning and perhaps 25 years of building," was made by Councillor Comben, who in reply to Alderman E. Colson's enquiry that "If this recommendation was passed that day and at a later date they wanted to retract, how much more difficult would it be?"

said "There would be no difficulty from this date." Councillor G. Moir remarked on the irony of discussing a new city while sitting in the "ruins of old Aylesbury" but he fully supported the recommendations, being convinced that the new development would "syphon some of the hideous and excessive pressure on mid and south Bucks." There was, he said, a movement abroad in Whitehall to regard local government and its members as "morons," and he hoped the new city would be a "noticeable monument to local government." However, Councillor J. Timberlake cautioned that the Council had no assurance of being the 'promoting authority,' and pointed out that the city might grow so quickly that it would become a County Borough, and therefore be of no benefit to the County. Until some directive was given on the promotion of the city he wanted funds laid aside to cover the initial stages. As for Councillor W. Beesley, he thought it "unfortunate" that the Council had received a letter of protest from the NFU although he understood their concerns from the potential loss of their livelihoods. Indeed since the farms of some 100 members of the NFU would be affected the main opposition to the proposals came from the Buckinghamshire branch, with the County Chairman, Mr. W. Snook, commenting that there seemed to be a total disregard for the farmer, "who appears to have come at the bottom of the list." "It seems that the city's open area is to be like Hyde Park without control. How can this land be farmed and still provide amenities?"

Uncertainty was also the concern of many constituents, and in response to enquiries by letter and telegram Robert Maxwell, M.P., emphasised in a long statement that no decision had been made by the Government on the Pooley plan. In fact without a Central Government decision to make the financial support available all the plans were merely pipe dreams. Further, he said George Brown's recent announcement that the Government was carrying out a general review of the South East Study confirmed that any decision about a new town was a long way off. In any case additional to the involvement of the Minister of Housing and Local Government consent would also be necessary from the new Ministry of Economic Affairs, and "I am doubtful, to say the least, whether our country could afford, over the next five or ten years, an investment on this scale. From what I have been able to gather of the financial and practical feasibility of the Pooley town scheme, I should be very surprised if the Government was to decide in its favour in its present form." Also he expressed surprise at the vast sums of ratepayers' money being lavished by Bucks County Council on planning for a new city that might never materialise, praising in contrast the excellent record of Bletchley Council in accommodating some of London's overspill. It was of course essential he said that expansion should take place in all the towns and villages of North Bucks, where people would welcome further development. Yet such communities must "retain their natural character and beauty," and "I anticipate that the Government will set up a North Bucks Development Corporation which will work in close partnership with the County, Urban and Rural District Councils and with private enterprise to ensure that we get value for money and a balanced development of the area whilst at the same time eliminating all profiteering by land speculators."

On Monday, November 30th at a meeting of Loughton Parish Council the Newport Pagnell RDC representative, Arthur Snaith, a retired local headmaster, severely criticised the proposals, saying "The city plan envisages Loughton to be redeveloped, but we could be bulldozed, and Loughton as we know it would not exist. We would have to go elsewhere even though Mr. Pooley has said they are playing a game of chess in the dark. Loughton, it seems, is the pawn to be sacrificed." "In this matter we are dealing with human beings, not bricks and mortar or monorails, but flesh and blood. I strongly object to thirty storey blocks of flats and monorails, which are interesting and exciting, but no good for a community in which to live. I feel the better citizens come from a smaller community." As a member of the parish council Mr. D. Foxley pondered the planners views on the Loughton floods; "Did they intend to build their new city buildings on stilts, or alter the rain clouds." As for 79 year old Mrs. W. Cox, saying she had been one of the original suffragettes she was against the plans for the village, and in conclusion it was decided to call a special public meeting the following Wednesday, such that the village could express an opinion on the 'Pooley Plan.'

During the last week of November, at the county NFU meeting the chairman, Mr. W. Snook, headed a team which passed a number of resolutions against the proposed scheme through the headquarters and the local M.P. Yet the *Architect's Journal*, 'the voice of the Royal Institute of British Architects,' supported the Pooley Plan, stating in a leading article of the contemporary issue their hope that the plan would result in the first 21st century city in Britain. However, the journal hinted that

'Fred Pooley's new city' could eventually finish up "well to the north of its present site in the Birmingham-London 'coffin.'"

Elsewhere, also hinted at was the possibility that any ideas for North Buck's proposed new city could be hampered by a shortage of sand and gravel in the area. At a public inquiry held at Newport Pagnell this concern was voiced on Tuesday, December 1st by a director of Hoveringham Gravels Ltd., regarding Bucks County Council's refusal to allow the company to extract sand and gravel from 145 acres of land at Quarry Hall Farm, Lathbury. The director, Robert Whiteside, said "Quarry Hall has a proved gravel deposit and if the developments that we have heard about in Bletchley, Newport Pagnell and Wolverton do take place, then the demand for aggregates is going to be more than quite extensive. If the postulated demand is to be met when it arises then it is essential that planning permission be given immediately. A gravel operator needs to plan forward." Defending their refusal the County Council said the question of gravel supplies in the area had been examined in 1960, with the conclusion that sufficient quantities would be available for the next 10 years. After the hearing the site was then inspected the following day, with the Ministry to announce the result of the appeal 'in due course.' Also regarding a Bucks County Council's refusal, a public enquiry due to be held in the first week of December had now been cancelled and the appeal withdrawn. This had been against the Council's denying permission for Brants Property Co. Ltd to build homes for more than 600 people on 15 acres of land at Loughton, with the reason being that the development "would not be in accord with the County Development Plan which proposes the retention of the existing use of the land." Supposedly the proposals would constitute a substantial departure from the Plan, 'and there seemed no evidence which would justify concurrence from the Minister being sought by the Council to depart from the Plan in the proposed manner.'

Being utterly astonished that local landowners hadn't made some representation to discuss the proposed North Bucks new city, Bernard Myers, a wealthy city business man, who was now resident at Walton Stud Farm, said "I have been waiting patiently for a fortnight, ever since the scheme was published, to hear something, but there hasn't been a word. I would like to see a North Bucks landowners' association, protection committee, or call it what you will, not necessarily to oppose plans for the new city, but merely to discuss its implications." Regarding himself as "a new boy in the district" he felt it would be presumptuous for him to take the first steps although he would be quite willing to associate himself with any such body and "hold the horse's head that brings victory." By distributing the costs he thought such a body would be able to engage top legal advisers for guidance through the problems, for "I feel sure that any representation to the County Council on an individual basis would get a person nowhere." Regarding the funding of the new city proposals he thought it possible that the money could come from private enterprise, since the Government might presently be unwilling to provide the finance. Also he thought that Bletchley from being already established should be developed further, since a new city "built in one lump" would only throw these 250,000 people together, "and they would be like sandpaper rubbing together, a sort of Mod and Rocker society." As for his interest in North Bucks he said this wasn't superficial. Walton Stud wasn't just a weekend place but his home, to be handed on to his son, and although the city scheme might eventually be a good thing, he was of the opinion that it had perhaps come a little before its time.

Yet if the city did become a reality then Loughton, a village of 403 residents, would be the core, and thus over 70 parishioners opposed to the proposals attended a special public meeting on Wednesday, December 9th called by the Parish Council. In opening the meeting Councillor E. Daniels said that over the last century Loughton had remained "very stable" and "a peaceful rural village." "Many old properties have been replaced with modern homes and at present we are in the process of expanding normally by approximately 40 houses for people who have decided that Loughton is an ideal place to bring up their families or in many cases, end their days." He said whatever the outcome of their deliberations they must, from being "in the centre of this contemplated lavish butchery scheme," ensure that their parishioners' views were totally supported, and he concluded by saying "Let us have expansion, yes. But surely this can be done in such a way as not to mean the annihilation of such a lovely and peaceful village which for centuries has enjoyed peace and harmony, true village life." Mr. A. Snaith, the Newport Pagnell RDC representative, said they had to tackle the problem immediately, for he felt sure that the County Council could commence the scheme straight away. Some people had said the Government lacked the finance for the project "But it is very real. The plans are so far advanced that they could go straight ahead if they had permission to do so." All that was needed was the "starter's pistol." Continuing, he said that the Architects' Department at Aylesbury seemed so pre-occupied with the city that they couldn't complete a school "which should have been open in September, which will not be open until the New Year and which will not be fully operational then." Regarding the recent County Council meeting he said he hadn't been allowed to speak or vote on the new city "simply because I own property in the area of the proposed city," but he agreed that North Bucks should take in more population, because the estimated population for the next ten years in South Bucks had already been reached; "The Government should do everything in its power to put people where there is a need for work. I know they have tried this in the North East and Wales, but they have the problem of getting the wives of workers to live there." "Industry should be taken where labour is plentiful and it can be done by training existing people living there. I feel that the best way for North Bucks to expand is by developing the villages as they are and infilling. If this is done all we need do is to expand the old to meet a modern demand, and done this way it is not unkind." Yet apparently the County Council thought this type of expansion wasn't sufficient and they had therefore been landed with the Pooley plan; "They have gone into a lot of things thoroughly but they don't say much about the cost. They have, however, got things to such an advanced state that they have even consulted a firm about building the monorail. All they are waiting for is the starter's pistol." As regarding the site for a new city, from proximity to Salisbury Plain he thought Southampton would be as good a choice as any; "A new city here, in North Bucks, will only choke the bottleneck of London more. The planners say that Loughton will be redeveloped, but to me this means it will be bulldozed. Our problem here is that we are overpopulated in the South East, but this can be eased by infilling. I object to agricultural land being wasted and to the uncertainty of Loughton. It is only right that we should try and preserve our community."

During the meeting Mr. Snaith and the parish council were asked by Mr. A. Herrington to try and seek an alliance with other neighbouring parishes, to which the chairman said support could be expected from Shenley Church End, where a meeting similar to their own was soon to be held. Referring to the 'starter's pistol' mentioned by Mr. Snaith, County

Councillor W. S. Johnson, the Loughton and district representative, said this was still some way off but it nevertheless meant uncertainty. On the question of costs he had received assurance that definite figures would be placed before the Council at its February meeting, but under a new Government ruling brought in last year he hadn't been able to speak on the subject from owning land in the designated area. From the floor Mrs. Greenwood, of the village Wheatsheaf Stores, then said that this was a worrying point, for if their own County Councillor couldn't speak it was a ludicrous situation. Indeed it meant in theory that many people would get no representation. Other views and questions then followed, including the pertinent inquiry "Has Mr. Pooley plans to re-house us? Could he not come here and tell us? He addressed the Round Tablers. I'm sceptical about whether he would have the time to come here." At the close of the meeting to the loudest ovation James Marchant, the youngest member of a well known family firm of solicitors, summed up the mood by saying he hadn't the slightest doubt that if the city came then Loughton, as they knew it, would disappear. Therefore he felt there should be a stronger form of opposition than a petition to the 'ludicrous' plan, and as a lawyer he considered that if the city came then the people in the village should know their legal position. They were really only tenants of the County Council, which could - if the proposal went through - compulsory purchase their homes and land. "But let our lords and masters at Aylesbury know that we b***** well aren't going to. We must fight them, we must argue, we must dirty our hands, but we must make representation as strong as we can and all the time. The Pooley plan city is merely part of a national disease at the moment, overpopulation." Now he knew what "insecurity of tenure" meant, and it was scandalous they could be faced with eventual eviction; "Compulsory purchase is one of the curses of civilisation, and procedure is arbitrary in the extreme." "Whatever have we done to deserve this? I'm blessed if I know." He then spoke of the various problems raised by the proposed project, adding "But the poor mugs in the way are no problem." If Loughton was to remain as they wished then the people would have to "lobby, nobble and get their hands dirty." It would be like canvassing for an election. There would be a lot of tedious work. They were outnumbered at the moment by the men at Aylesbury - "the little men with delusions of grandeur" - and if the city did come to Loughton "I am going to Australia for a start." At the end of the 70 minutes debate the villagers then lined up to sign a protest petition worded "We, electors of the above parish, wish to make the strongest possible protest against the proposed plan for a new city in North Bucks, as envisaged by the County Council, and especially to that part of it which designates Loughton to be 're-developed.' We are disturbed by such a plan which threatens our homes and our present way of life." This would be circulated throughout the village, and according to Mr. Daniels also be sent to all the bodies concerned with the new city - "No stone will be left unturned."

From having recently announced that the Government was to possibly form a North Bucks Planning Board, to look into local development and particularly the proposed new city, the Buckingham M.P., Robert Maxwell, now found himself criticised by local government officers, with the Reverend H. Sparling, chairman of Newport Pagnell RDC, saying "I think the board would be a delaying factor and a complete waste of time, if it comes. I feel that the County Council are so well manned that they can face any eventuality, and the best plan is to let them do it themselves. The thing I have found in the past few weeks is that people want a fairly quick decision on this question of development." On the subject of the new city he said "I think it will come, and I admire the conception as it is. Mr. Maxwell does not know the whole story here, and I think he is sitting pretty squarely on the fence." In referring to the proposed planning board, Mr. R. Horwood, County Councillor for Olney and district, and a wholehearted supporter of the Pooley plan, said "Such an announcement by Mr. Maxwell is disturbing in the extreme. This means that the district council's will lose half their powers and the county planning committee, presumably, will cease to exist. I was not aware that Mr. Maxwell had a mandate to end democratically elected local government, though there is another alternative. Such a board might uphold the decision of local councils but then this would be an unnecessary duplication, causing extra delay and expense."

Already perturbed by the proposals to build a new city, local farmers faced further concern when it became known that Bucks Water Board was considering flooding thousands of acres of farmland to provide not only one large reservoir in the next 10 years but, towards the end of the century, also a second one. Being in extent the largest man made lakes in the country both would be over three miles long, and in places up to two miles in width. With a 1¼ mile long dam at the Whitchurch end, one would reach from the edge of Stewkley to the edge of Whitchurch, whilst the other would be situated between Winchendon and Ashendon. Water would be pumped to them from the Thames, and investigations were presently underway as to which should be built first. In preparation, to determine the nature of the subsoil the Board had already applied to the Minister of Housing and Local Government for authority to survey the land and carry out experimental borings and other works. Also, warning notices had been served on landowners, the rural and parish councils and also the potentially affected farmers who, unsurprisingly said to be "hopping mad," were due to meet the Board's representatives on December 9th, together with the affected landowners and councils. The scheme had been outlined on Tuesday, December 8th at a Press Conference held by Mr. R. Pownall, the Board's engineer and manager, at Aylesbury, where it was stated that demands on the Board for water were going up "tremendously." Even without the new city 66 million gallons a day would be needed, and should the proposed development materialise then this would fast forward the requirement by five years. Whilst the second lake might possibly be deferred until the end of the century the first was of immediacy, being necessary for the development of Bletchley, Newport Pagnell, Wolverton, Aylesbury and also the new city.

Quite apart from reservoirs, a new city was the last thing needed by Major J. Young J.P. who as the Show Committee president said at the Fat Stock Show Dinner, held following the annual Bletchley Christmas show and sale on Thursday, December 10th, "I deplore it - it is the last thing I want to see, personally." He knew no more of the proposals for a new city than anyone else, but supposed that it would come some day. "It gives us considerable food for thought, and to put it mildly, worry." Then with reference to the South East Study he said the key phrase seemed to be "It would be difficult to find an area which would be more attractive to industrialists." However in view of the "history and fine agricultural background of this area of countryside, my own special personal wish is that this new place shall be called the Whaddon City."

Whatever the name, the building of a city was vigorously opposed by the farmers, for whom firm support was given by NFU headquarters on the evening of Monday, December 14th, when an eight man deputation from the county was received at London. Accompanied by Mr. L.

Barron, County Secretary, this was led by the County Chairman, Stanley Moss, who said afterwards; "We have been assured that Headquarters will be raising this matter, as a national rather than a merely local issue, at the highest level. ... We are not blindly opposed to urban expansion; we know that people must be housed and land must be taken. But the linear city concept is, in our submission, fundamentally unsound. ... It is based on the quite ludicrous assumption that farming will be possible within the grand loops encompassed by the three linear strips of urban development. ... It appears that the County Council is backing this concept for quite the wrong reasons - to milk it of rateable revenue. ... We are actively examining the whole complex problems thrown up by this proposal and, in due course, we hope to be able to come forward with alternatives which are more realistic, prudent and realisable." In additional opposition, on the evening of Tuesday, December 15th in the Reading Room at Shenley Church End a special meeting took place. Here, being addressed by both County Alderman F. Woollard and County Councillor W. S. Johnson, over 50 parishioners agreed to join Loughton in its protest over the location of the proposed new city, and as the outcome it was decided to invite Fred Pooley to a joint meeting of the parishioners of Shenley Church End and Loughton, as well as the people of Shenley Brook End. Still, it was perhaps possible that all this would be unnecessary, for in a letter to the Press a tongue in cheek solution was offered by 'Digger.'

"Sir. All this discussion going on about the proposed new city's location can easily be solved - why not put it underground. The farmers can continue to farm above it. There would be no climatic problems and if we are ever to be bombarded by atomic bombs it could be made as a large scale air-raid centre. The monorail would be a tube railway. Filtered air could be pumped in sans fumes. The excavated material could be used to fill in unused clay workings to become playgrounds. Food for thought?"

Food was certainly in the thoughts of Mr. T. J. Bradshaw on Friday, December 18th, when as president of the Newport Pagnell Young Farmers' Club he said at their 21st annual dinner, held at the College of Aeronautics, Cranfield, that during the last war North Bucks had played more than its fair share in growing food for the nation; "But today times are very different. Our fertile land in North Bucks seems to be of little importance to the planners, and in the near future we may lose thousands of acres in order to house the ever growing population of this country. We realise that development must take place, but I implore the authorities to build on the least productive land in the county or within the next century food will again be rationed. For once fertile land is covered with bricks and concrete it is lost for ever for growing food." Concluding, he said it was up to club members, as the farmers of the future, to ensure the preservation of the land. Regarding the recently announced plans to establish two massive reservoirs in the north of the county, preserving the land from the Bucks Water Board was now also an increasing concern. Heading the 'No Reservoirs' campaign at Westminster was Robert Maxwell, the Labour M.P. for Buckingham, who in the third week of December promised his full support in the Commons to a deputation of farmers from the threatened area. He had asked his legal advisers to probe the Board's actions to see if the scheme could be postponed on legal grounds, and was writing to Mr. Crossman to strongly urge him to refuse the application. Another equally important point was raised at the annual dinner of the Bucks branch of the Club and Institute Union at Wolverton on Friday, December 18th, where Mr. D. Dormer, a former secretary, asked if the planners realised that at least 20 working men's clubs would be needed for the proposed new city in North Bucks. People didn't want such amenities to be in the city centre and "We need to make representations now to ensure clubs will be built among the houses, so that people who want to go round the corner for a drink can do so. They do not want to ride on a monorail, or go into the city centre."

At the meeting of Newport Pagnell RDC on Wednesday, December 30th the chairman, the Reverend H. Sparling, was forced to use his vote as a councillor to ensure his Council's backing for the County Council's proposed new city. This came after the first vote showed a stalemate of 11 votes to each side. However, observers argued that theoretically there was still a stalemate, since one of the plan's staunchest opponents, Councillor A. Snaith of Loughton, whilst having been given a dispensation by the Ministry of Housing and Local Government to speak was not allowed to vote. Per the wording of the recommendation:

    a) "that the Council endorse its decision of March 4th. It considers that the construction of a new city is the best method of accommodating the rapid and substantial increase in population within the region. In view of the considerable impact that the proposed development would have on the district we give our support on condition that we are consulted on every possible occasion when the detailed plans are being made. We have in mind the particularly special problems of Loughton and Shenley Church End. The early stages of development could place special responsibilities on this Council and this we accept, but again there must be full consultation in all detail. We are very conscious of the fact that the growth of a new city in the area will mean temporary discomfort to some people, but we believe the construction of such a city could be of such national advantage as to outweigh any local difficulties."

b) "This Council would agree that the County Council should be the acquiring authority for land acquisition in this Council's district if the proposal for the new city proceeds."

In opening the discussion the Reverend Sparling said that the London Region, Hertfordshire and South Bucks all pointed to North Bucks and the new city for a 'hiving off' of their thriving industries and brimming populations.' Therefore "Concentration of these in a new city will help to preserve the character and charm of our villages, which would otherwise be swamped by an indiscriminate sprawl of houses and industries. The new city will happen whatever we say or do, and I think it deserves a name. My choice for it - Chiltern." "Chiltern is no pipe dream or fairyland but a first rate conception that our County Council is well equipped to carry out. The means and the money can be found though objections have been raised." As for his view of Councillor Snaith, comparing him to King Canute he said "If we liken him to that fond figure, standing against the tide of events, it is in no spirit of derision. His arguments are that a city would have no roots and would take up agricultural land, but the concentration of a city would be less wasteful of land than big bites in all directions by a vast expansion of existing towns. The Bletchley scheme, for all its drums and fanfare, is as dead as the Dodo. Agriculture is not the only consideration. The site chosen is just the right distance from the London Region and has direct road, rail and canal communications." 'Chiltern,' he said, would be a city fit to live in, and amongst his observations he included that "If I could be given a part in building up the life of it, there is nobody I'd rather have by my side than our good friend Mr. Snaith."

53

Regarding the efforts to oppose the new city by Mr. W. Snook, until recently the county chairman of the NFU, he said "He states as a fact that land cannot properly be farmed within the city boundary. And I most certainly state as a fact that it can. … I urge Mr. Snook to press for proper payment for the land, and even more for a generous compensation for farmers whose livelihood will be taken away. In all progress, there are those who suffer inconvenience and loss." Declaring his 'interest,' Councillor Snaith then said that following his own communication with the Ministry he'd been told that whilst not allowed to vote he could take part in the discussion, to which he duly contributed "I say that the County Council plan should be rejected, and that is the view of a parish meeting held in Loughton." This view he then emphasised by presenting a petition objecting to the development signed by 164 of Loughton's parishioners. During the meeting Councillor R. Bellchambers pointed out that when the matter was first discussed in March the only council to raise any objection was Bletchley. The city they were proposing to build would not be like London, Sheffield or New York, 'which had just been thrown together,' but was a city for 1981. Since there had never been such a fine project before the Council he said they were presented with a unique opportunity. Of the comments from other members, Councillors E. Holdom of Little Brickhill, R. Sharpe of Moulsoe, and A. J. Cony all supported Councillor Snaith in his objections, although Councillor F. Hawkins declared himself in favour of the scheme. In the press he had read the possibility of 'anti-city' councillors standing for election, which he thought wrong to be fought on a single issue. The observation that "If we do not have a new city, North Bucks will become a great urban sprawl like Bethnal Green or Camberwell, without a square foot of farming land left" was made by Mr. R. Horwood, County Councillor for Olney and district, who during the week referred to what he called the "mysterious silence" of Bletchley UDC regarding Robert Maxwell's statement that the Government intended to defer a decision on the proposed new city from "five to ten years." Such uncertainty he said would bring development to a standstill throughout North Bucks, and Bletchley in particular would suffer. However, speaking of the deferment Jim Cassidy, chairman of Bletchley council, said that the Government's decision was correct with regard to the country's financial situation; "No Government in their right sense would say, at this time, here is £400 million, go and build yourself a monorail city." Continuing, he pointed out they had an assurance that the town should develop at its present rate until a decision on the new city was reached, and "… I hope it takes a hundred years for a decision to be reached. Then Bletchley will be big enough to say 'who wants a new city now?'" This sentiment was echoed by the Liberal candidate defeated in the October election, who being strongly opposed to the new city plan believed that Bletchley should be expanded because of the existing development. A new city with no cultural or religious background could well become a breeding ground for crime and other vices. Also he was against the taking of so much farmland. His was the opinion that of all the industries farming should be expanded, and in other comments he said "I am in favour of expansion in Bletchley, Newport Pagnell, Olney and even dear old Buckingham, but I think that if the county should put all its eggs in the Pooley basket it will come unstuck." Then concluding the year Robert Maxwell said on Christmas Eve that no early statement would be made in Parliament about the development plans for the South East Region, including the proposed expansion of Bletchley. Such a possibility had been reported on December 16th but now he thought there would be no report until well after the Christmas recess.

1965

THE DEMISE OF THE POOLEY PLAN

At the annual general meeting of the Brickhill's Labour Party, held on Saturday, January 9th at Little Brickhill, Ray Bellchambers, of the Newport Pagnell Rural District Council, said the scheme by the County Council for the proposed new city was "far sighted and unexpectedly socialist in character," especially emanating from a body which might be considered 'conservative to the point of being reactionary.' His idea of a city was the best possible living accommodation in a limited area, and he had praise for the intention to fully utilise cultural and sports facilities, and also to minimise the time spent travelling to work and for recreation. Bletchley, he felt, would suffer less from being allowed to develop to 30,000 or 40,000, perhaps as a suburb of the new city, than if it was to be developed to the size of the new city in a piece meal fashion. As for the concern of developing on agricultural land, he said that unexpected agricultural use had sometimes been made of so called barren waste, and the intended site had the communications advantage of the M1, A5 and main line railways, plus the adequate potentials of water supply and sewage disposal facilities. This he said was the way to stimulate the economy, emphasising that the initiative and vision shown by the county planners was the kind which should be encouraged by the Labour Party.

On Monday, January 18th the position as secretary to the Newport Pagnell and Bletchley branches of the NFU was taken over from Mr. Michael Risebrow, who had now moved to Spalding, by 32 year old Mr. Raymond P. Furnival, of Lichfield, who being new to the area had for the last two years been a representative, covering four Midland counties, for a national feeding stuffs company in Staffordshire. Educated at Whitchurch, Herts., he moved to the Staffordshire Farming Institute until 1948, and on joining his father on their farm became a member of the junior NFU in North Staffs., with election as vice chairman in 1953. The following year he became a member of the senior union, and for two years served as a committee man and a member of the County Executive Committee. Then in 1958 on his own account he ventured into farming but due to poor health had to dispose of the holding after two years, then finding employment with the feeding stuffs company. Married, with an interest in swimming and cricket, he would continue to be assisted at his Newport Pagnell offices by Mrs. Patricia Cripps, of Tower Hill Cottages, Emberton, who having worked at the premises for some years was employed by the secretary and not by the Farmers' Union.

Support for the plan was given by Wolverton UDC on the evening of Tuesday, January 26th although this was in fact just a reaffirmation of an earlier resolution. At its monthly meeting Winslow Rural Council also gave approval but Councillor R. Bates, a former farmer, said the open spaces in the plan took up as much room as the development area, and it wouldn't be possible to use the land inside the plan for farming; "Instead of spreading it over so many acres, it could be confined to half that space." As for an alternative proposal from Bletchley, Councillor R. Davies said "Most of us have seen the proposals of Bletchley, but what they have to offer is very much worse than what the city has to offer. The densities they suggested would require rather tall structures, which would not fit into the landscape." In other comments Councillor C. Drabble said the Council knew the city would come. It was just softening the blow to let the council have its say - "But it is nice of them to let us have our say." Councillor N. Bevan was of the opinion that "If we have got to have a city, let's have a good one, well planned, on modern lines. Let's think of the people who are going to live in it. We are concerned with them. … We don't want to squash them up in slums." Therefore with the members in agreement the resolution read: "That this Council is in favour of the basic design of the city in the proposed designated areas. The Council regrets that there is no mention of Winslow in the proposals and feels that a modest residential and industrial expansion of Winslow should take place and that a Town

Map for Winslow should be prepared at an early date. The Council is in favour of the County Council carrying out the development in partnership with the Government and private enterprise, subject to favourable financial arrangements being made."

Then on the afternoon of Wednesday, February 3rd the uncertainties began to clear when in the House of Commons a statement was given by the Minister, Richard Crossman, regarding his Ministry's plans for accommodating the increasing population in the South East. The main point centred on a new town for North Bucks which, although not as large as the 'Pooley plan' city, would be the most sizeable built in Britain since the war. Housing some 150,000 people this, he said, would be in conjunction with major expansions at Northampton, Peterborough and Ipswich, with some 350,000 people to be accommodated by all the four 'development units.' As to the site of the development he said that since negotiations were still taking place with Bucks County Council they would refrain from committing themselves to one particular place. Included in the announcement was that "Immediate decisions are necessary if we are to avoid a disastrous gap in housing for Londoners. To prevent this the Government proposes, as an interim measure, to go ahead with a new town in North Buckinghamshire and with the expansion of Ipswich, Peterborough and Northampton. I will shortly be discussing with local authorities concerned the measures needed to implement these proposals, including the surveys that will be needed to determine the precise siting (sic) of the development. In particular, I shall be considering with them the desirability of using the machinery of the New Towns Act for these schemes."

For the realisation of the new town it seemed that two courses of action were possible - either to scrap the Pooley plan and introduce an entirely new scheme, or modify the Pooley plan to suit the development on a smaller scale, albeit without the monorail and other ultra modern amenities. However, already between £5,000 and £6,000 had been expended on initial planning for the Pooley scheme, which if scrapped would entail the re-recruitment of trained staff for the new project, an expertise which would be hard to find. Mr. Crossman's proposals would cater for the natural growth of the population as well as housing London's overspill, and in response to questions from Robert Maxwell, M.P. for the Buckingham division, he said it had still to be agreed with the County Council if they should build the new town, or whether it would require capital on such a scale as to turn to the new town organisation; "This is something that has to be discussed with the County Council, and I cannot make any statement about exactly what role Mr. Pooley will play or exactly what relationship will be between the county organisation and the new town organisation." Yet support for Mr. Pooley and his plan could be assured from an ardent advocator, Mr. R. Horwood, the vice chairman of the City Planning Authority and County Councillor for Olney and District, who being keen to see any large development in North Bucks said; "By concentrating development in one place, we shall be able to deal with the problems of water, sewage and highways, but more important still, we shall be able to preserve most of the villages in North Bucks. Our population is growing at such a rate that the only alternative to the new town would be an urban sprawl which would destroy the whole of our North Bucks countryside." Continuing, he mentioned that after this week's consent to the Pooley plan by Bletchley, all the local authorities now wished to see large scale development in the county. On the question of how long the development would take, with regard to Mr. Maxwell's words that the town would be built "very, very, quickly" he cautioned that considering all the necessary legal side, plus the other preliminaries, it seemed improbable that a start could be made within five years.

Yet the local farmers continued their determined opposition headed by Mr. W. Snook of Water Eaton, who at a special meeting on Monday, February 1st had been elected as chairman of a steering committee to lead the attack in their policy of fighting the Pooley plan. Then following Wednesday's announcement by Mr. Crossman the committee called a hurried meeting the next day at Aylesbury, where Mr. Snook said "Even if the Pooley plan has gone out of the window we will still resist any major development that threatens the farmer. Already one farmer had declared his willingness to go to jail, said Mr. Snook, who then outlined the argument of the steering committee; "We object if the proposed new town is on the lines of the Pooley plan, with its vast wastage of good agricultural land. We shall refuse to enter any negotiations pertaining to land until something satisfactory regarding compensation is on the Statute Book. ... We feel that some investigation should be made into the question of building upwards. This applies not only to houses, but also factories, in an effort to save valuable and ever decreasing farm land for the growing of food. We object to the uncertainty of Mr. Crossman's

statement in the House, and maintain that we should be told at once where the town is to be built, so that those farmers to be dispossessed can stop pouring capital into the farms, and allow those not affected to get on with their farming without this worry hanging over their heads ..."
This would be submitted to Bucks County Council, and at the beginning of the discussion Mr. C. Morgan, the vice chairman, had referred to a meeting of County NFU representatives with members of the County Council and the Country Landowners' Association. At this the County Council chairman with regard to compensation had assured the county branch of the Council's support in efforts to have the legal position satisfactorily settled. Questions about the proposed development had been answered he said by the County Planning Officer, Fred Pooley, after whose departure from the meeting came the agreement to form a steering committee comprised of Messrs. Snook, E. Gurney, G. Cowley and V.E. Phillips. This would deal with day to day matters, and draw up observations to be submitted to Bucks County Council. He then added that "The Steering Committee has already met and will be presenting its objections to the County Chairmen's Committee on February 12th, prior to objections on behalf of the county being submitted to Bucks County Council."

Replying to one of the members, the chairman, Mr. S. Moss, said "The Council submitted plans for our comments and we have not yet given our comments. Since this announcement yesterday (that the Government is to proceed with the new town) the council has been asked if it still wants our comments, and it does - and it should, because nothing was released yesterday to indicate favour or disfavour of this particular town, merely that the Government is favourable towards a development in this area." During the meeting Mr. E. Venn highlighted a lack of publicity in the national press about the way the farming community and others would be affected by the building of the new town, and also the reservoirs. "Getting publicity over to the general public is the only way to slow up this wastage of land, and the public will be helped in the long run if land is saved for growing food." In reply Mr. T. Blackmore, the London delegate, then said he would seek the co-operation of the Headquarters Publicity Committee in fostering an interest in the national Press about the situation in Bucks. Mr. T. Bradshaw said that during a meeting of his area, Newport Pagnell, a recommendation had been made for a new town or city site in Norfolk.

This would be closer to the port facilities on the East coast, and he added "But one can think further ahead than this. The amount of agricultural land which has been used in England for development purposes is absolutely staggering and I have heard suggestions that representations should be made to the Commonwealth to finance and build this city in Australia. This would be a far better proposition than building it in overcrowded England. Australia would welcome the suggestion with open arms." As for other comments the chairman said "We were told by the county council that full development of the villages and the towns had been taken into account, and it was still necessary to provide for a new city for 250,000 people on top of that."

In contrast to the farmers, no opposition to the proposals for a new town or 'city' in North Bucks had been voiced by Bletchley Council, who, subject to the Council's confirmation that Bletchley would be allowed to continue at its present rate until 1981, and that the Town Map would be adjusted accordingly, gave unanimous approval at a special meeting on Tuesday, February 9th. Here it was announced that almost complete agreement on these lines had been reached during informal discussions between the Council's surveyor, Mr. J. Smithie, and the County Planning Officer, Mr. F. Pooley, with the result being to continue the development of Bletchley to a population upwards of 40,000. As for the population of the new town, although no figures had been given in the Minister's announcement his Joint Parliamentary Secretary, Robert Mellish, had said at a Press Conference on February 5th that in the next 15 years one million people would have to find homes outside Greater London. With the addition of 70,000 each to Northampton, Peterborough and Ipswich, one third would be accommodated by a new town of 150,000 in North Bucks. "We have to make sure that every possible job is filled by a Londoner" and since 80% of people in the new towns were now Londoners he claimed success for 'the industrial selection scheme' - but "We aim to do better than that."

When invited by Bucks County Council to comment on the changes to the county development plan, as involved in this establishment of a new town, the Buckinghamshire branch of the Country Landowners' Association duly stated that, "If this new town is established as planned, all this farmland will inevitably be lost to farming, and a much greater acreage of agricultural land on the fringe of the town can be expected to become uneconomic to farm." Indeed, they did not accept that the county should necessarily give up such a large proportion of its agricultural land, and "will look for a complete justification for the taking of every acre. This unrealistic view is also indicated by the comment in the written statement that certain villages within the area of comprehensive development 'will remain much as they are at present.' In the view of the CLA economic farming would not be possible within a town of a quarter of a million people, nor could rural villages be retained as such within the town." Sympathetic to these comments were the farmers of North Bucks, who via their M.P., Robert Maxwell, were urging the Government to ensure that every effort should be made to find less valuable land outside the county for building this 'new city.' Should this not be possible then they would "reluctantly accept the expansion of Bletchley to not more than 100,000 to 150,000 - but not a free-standing 'new city.'" This had been agreed on Friday, February 19th at a meeting at Manor Fields Pavilion, Bletchley, where Mr. Maxwell addressed nearly 100 farmers on the points raised in Richard Crossman's recent 'new town' speech in the House of Commons. As chairman of Bucks NFU, Mr. S. Moss opened the meeting by saying that Mr. Crossman's statement in the House of Commons was a "masterpiece of ambiguity." Therefore an offer to come along and explain what was meant, and what the point of it was, had been made by Mr. Maxwell, who during his address said he was hoping to arrange for Mr. Crossman to tour North Bucks by helicopter, to see for himself what was involved. In explaining the Minister's statement he noted ambiguity regarding three aspects: The location of the new town, who would finance it, and who would control it. Yet there was no ambiguity about the arrival of the new town "The consequence is that it is no good any of you saying that you are going to fight this ..." Therefore the farmers, the local authorities and interested citizens should all concentrate their efforts on three things:

1) That they should lose the minimum amount of arable land.

2) That farmers should get compensation, either five years of expected profit or ten years' rent.

3) That they should find out quickly, precisely where the town would be situated.

Since the Commons statement he said Mr. Crossman had sent a team of experts to Aylesbury to discuss the financing and control of the project with the County Council, who he knew were considering co-operating with private enterprise if they were given control of the project.

However he had advised the County Council that a share of the huge profits to be made from the town should go to the ratepayers, and as part of the pressure being put on central government he was also receiving a delegation at the House comprising the chairman of Loughton Parish Council and four or five others from parish councils. There was also concern that apart from the farmers the Government should provide equitable compensation for, and the re-housing of, displaced persons, with the re-housing to take place in advance, and the compensation to be paid at market value prices at the time of acquisition. Emphasising "not from the buying of land," he said in answer to Mr. Cowley, of Calverton, that the huge profits from the new town would arise from the letting of buildings to industry and the letting of offices and factories to commercial concerns. As regards a public inquiry, he confirmed this would take place although the outcome would be a foregone conclusion despite this being an "ill-conceived plan." They may have survived the threat of starvation in two world wars but from being an island they would always face this vulnerability. In support Mr. Bradshaw said that good agricultural land was a number one priority, "But it seems to be bottom of the Government's list." Once built over it was forever lost to cultivation, and with an increasing population it was obvious that "every acre of good land is a hallowed acre." Thus he suggested that existing towns and villages could be infilled, supplemented by allotments and orchards. "There is no good reason why this county should take the overspill from London or any other areas." It was just the pleasure the planners were probably taking "in showing how clever they are." In fact he wondered had they considered building their new cities in Australia, where they were "crying out for Englishmen."

Re-affirming his stance against a new city of 250,000 people, plus the expansion of Bletchley, Buckingham, Newport Pagnell, Olney and other districts, Mr. Maxwell said if the County Council changed its mind, and agreed to expansions of natural limits, then once they had agreed that the size of the new town would be no larger than 150,000 he would cease his hostility. In fact he hoped it would be kept to 80,000, since this would mean less land and congestion. Yet he disagreed violently with Mr. Bradshaw's suggestion that people should be "exported" to Australia. If this was done then in the year 2000 'we would be a nation of old men and women.' Equally controversial he then suggested that both Wolverton and New Bradwell were areas of poor land. Perhaps unsurprisingly this was greeted with peals of laughter and shouts of "That's one of the best," and emphasising to Mr. Maxwell that land negotiations were not going to be opened by the farmers "until something is on the statute books," Mr. Snook pointed out that the land in question was "not just arable, but above the national average." As for Mr. Brown, the county secretary of the NUAW, he said that his organisation and the NFU had 'sat tight for too long.' Now they had awoken to what was happening, to which Mr. Maxwell said that both organisations should have taken an interest in the matter two years ago. This was met with shouts of "We did," to which he retorted, "You didn't take it quite as seriously as you might have done. You could have done more when the plan was only a dream." It was no use "hollering" when it was too late. Regarding farm workers he said to compensate people who were going to lose their jobs the Government was introducing a bill which would ensure their full protection, prevent any loss in their standard of living, and provide entitlement to the same benefits as tenant farmers, such as re-housing. Then in reply to a question from Mr. Unwin, of Bletchley, he envisaged that for completion of the "smaller city" in seven years a start on the project would have to be made very quickly. Yet where the construction would start was the '64,000 dollar question,' about which he was pressing the Government for an answer. Mr. Moss then said he was going to the House of Commons with Mr. Maxwell to see the Minister, and when told they were premature Mr. Maxwell replied that it was "never too soon," pointing out they were going to see him about the proposed reservoirs, which they hoped to prevent. Further to the matter of protests, Mr. Snook said "We hit this thing from the word 'go.' We objected to the County Council on the first day," but Mr. Maxwell countered that he hadn't read of any protests to the Ministry. They should have immediately got in touch with their M.P. who would have put their case. Nevertheless he assured them of his 100% backing if they still wanted to fight the new town. However he warned that if they diverted their time and money into these channels they could be labelled obstructionists. In that case the Ministry might not accept them as sensible advisors when questions arose such as compensation, regarding which he said he would press for obligatory payments – either five years' expected profit or ten years' rent, whichever was the highest.

In thanking Mr. Maxwell for attending, Mr. Moss said he didn't agree that hope should be lost because of Crossman, to which Mr. Maxwell pointed out that it was a Cabinet decision, and not one made solely by Mr. Crossman.

As with all other interested parties, at the meeting on Thursday, February 25th of the Planning Committee of the County Council, held at Aylesbury, the chairman, Councillor S. Comben, said the County Council would also like to know the "Where," "When" and "How Big" questions on the proposed new city. Then in suggesting that the city would be part of the arrangement to keep the green belt in the south, Councillor A. Bains, the member from Chesham, said "The north would be flooded with overspill to ensure the retention of the lovely stretches of country in the south." From living in the centre of the possible development Councillor W. S. Johnson said the people of the Shenleys and Loughton wanted to know something about their fate, and he urged the county to find out the financial aspects, since farmers and others wanted to know quickly about compensation. Councillor F. Monday said Robert Maxwell had been emphatic that with a population of 80,000 the city could be in existence in seven years, but the chairman, Alderman A. Ward, said no such information had been received by the county, and they shouldn't take much notice of such "guesses." Any major question would come before the Council - "it's not just a few people make a policy and tell you afterwards." For his part, Lt. Col. A. Matthews said "Isn't it another example that the electorate of Buckingham have a rather quaint Member of Parliament." As for the Finance Committee chairman, Alderman R. Verney said the question of whether the County Council would take on the job of building the new city, if invited to do so, would not be answered until they had the full financial picture before them, which he hoped would be at their meeting in May.

Endorsing the decision of the Steering Committee, set up under the chairmanship of Mr. W. Snook, that Bletchley should be extended to accommodate the proposed increase in population, on Thursday, March 4th a meeting of the County Executive Committee of the Bucks NFU further considered the proposals for a new town in North Bucks, as announced by the Minister of Housing and Local Government the previous month. Not endorsed however was that virgin farmland should be taken for a separate new town. Also, surprise was expressed at the observations made by Robert Maxwell, at the open meeting of farmers on February 19th, that the NFU and the NUAW should have been interested in the project two years ago. Not least with regard to the Bucks NFU, for at the first intimation of a new city plan in December 1963 (when consideration was given to the County of Buckingham Development Plan 1963) the County Council had been informed that the strongest objections would be made regarding the potential loss of good agricultural land in North Bucks due to a new city. Following this, resolutions were urged upon the headquarters of the Union to impress upon the Government and M.P.s the need to build new cities on non viable agricultural land, and also to press for legislation to provide the payment of adequate compensation to those tenants dispossessed from their farms. Further, strong opposition to large scale new town development in the whole area had resulted from a London conference in July 1964 of all the counties within the South East, with the Government urged to find sites in non agricultural land areas. Then subsequent to both a meeting during August at Newport Pagnell, when farmers heard the County Planning Officer explain his "new city" proposals, and the issue in November of Bucks County Council's detailed plan and proposed designated area, Bucks NFU once again made strong protests against the whole idea of a linear city, with its waste of good agricultural land. The Branch objections were duly circulated to all the County Councillors, and in order to enlist the help of the organisation at national level in December a deputation went to NFU headquarters. Their mission proved successful and during January 1965 those Councillors serving on local authorities were urged to oppose the new city proposals on the basis that too much good food producing farmland would be taken by a linear city. Then on February 4th the chairman of Bucks County Council and his officers met a small deputation of farmers headed by Stanley Moss, the County Chairman of Bucks NFU, to clarify the Council's proposals. That evening at a mass meeting at Bletchley the County Planning Officer explained in detail his intentions for a new city, and from this it was resolved to oppose a new city but to support the enlargement of Bletchley as the means to accommodate the population increase. Under the chairmanship of Mr. W. Snook, the past County Chairman of the Bucks NFU, a Steering Committee was accordingly set up, which from subsequently meeting on several occasions made recommendations to be forwarded to Bucks

County Council objecting to the new city proposals. Also it requested that in the near future a deputation should meet the Minister of Housing and Local Government, such that objections might be raised to the new town proposals.

Led by Mr. E.W. Daniels, chairman of Loughton Parish Council, and including Mr. A.G. Bass, clerk to Shenley Brook End Parish Council, in the first week of March a powerful deputation of councillors from three villages met Robert Maxwell at the House of Commons, this being to especially 'map out' a campaign to ensure that those North Bucks residents facing eviction from their homes due to the new city would receive fair compensation. Whilst there seemed little hope of halting the new city, the need to fight for generous compensation for the people affected was emphasised, and as the meeting's outcome it was agreed to pressure the Housing and Local Government Minister, Richard Crossman, into announcing at the first opportunity the actual location of the new city. Otherwise any delay would cause considerable hardship. Indeed, since hardship would otherwise be caused "Information as to the exact siting of this city or town should no longer be delayed," said Mr. Daniels, adding that the electors of Loughton "were greatly disturbed and frustrated at the uncertainty as to their future, not only as regards their properties and re-housing but as to their livelihood and ultimate effect on their way of life." Assuring the deputation that to press for comparable housing for displaced residents he would seek an early meeting with the Minister, Mr. Maxwell promised to do his 'very best' to make sure that unless they were offered similar property in comparable surroundings no one would be forced out of their home. Being told that 75% of the Loughton electors owned their own homes he also agreed that council houses or flats should not be offered to such residents who, said Mr. Daniels, were not immune to the fact that people needed homes. Nor were they against progress but the "real tragedy" was that Loughton faced complete annihilation. "We feel that careful consideration should be given to the retention of our village and we request the planners to think again of the city centre."

Mr. A. Snaith, of Newport Pagnell RDC, said the city would swallow up good agricultural land, and since the need could be met by expansion and infilling of existing towns and villages a new town was unnecessary. Alternatively he suggested Salisbury Plain as a site, for the present proposal would "destroy the most beautiful part of

Buckinghamshire." As the village representative for Newport Pagnell RDC, Mr. H. Hancock pointed out that the building of homes for old age pensioners at Shenley Church End had already been stopped due to the uncertainty of location; "We don't want this city but if it must come do not centre it on our village." Then regarding another aspect he said that "to move owner occupiers out of their homes into council flats or houses is damn degrading to say the least."

On the evening of Wednesday, March 10th the contest for the vacant seat on the County Council became a three cornered affair, when Tom Bradshaw, of Hardmead, announced his intention to oppose the Rev. H. Sparling of Sherington, chairman of Newport Pagnell RDC, and Ray Bellchambers of Old Bradwell, vice chairman of Newport Pagnell RDC. The position had arisen from the appointment of Walter Beesley, of Hanslope, to alderman, and with the election to take place on April 1st the nominations would close on the Tuesday of the following week. In contrast to his opponents, both of whom were strongly in favour of the new city (the Rev. Sparling contesting as an Independent and Mr. Bellchambers as an ardent Labour supporter) Mr. Bradshaw stood on an anti city stance, and of the opinion that some thousands of acres of good farm land would be lost had the unanimous support of the local NFU branch. Indeed it had been following the normal branch meeting at Newport Pagnell on the Wednesday that on being urged to stand by the Union he had made his decision to contest the seat. Bedfordshire born, he was married with three daughters, and for 21 years had farmed 300 acres at Home Farm. As for the present situation he said "I suggest that a better way of taking the increased population in the area is to build up the existing towns and by infilling the villages. ... If the Government want to build a major city reasonably close to London there is no reason why they should come to North Bucks. Thetford Common, or Salisbury Plain, where the land is of no agricultural use at all, is the place to put large scale development." Regarding a water supply for the new town he said the River Board were already worried about the effluent in the area, whilst at Thetford Common effluent could be discharged directly into the sea. "Out of loyalty to the NFU I am fighting for this seat to ask North Bucks people one question, 'Do they, or do they not want, the new town.' I believe the County Council were wrong in just going ahead with their plans, they should have come to the electorate first." As for the views of his opponents, Mr. Ray Bellchambers said he was in favour of the scheme but only provided that he could be satisfied on four major points:

1) That the new town would not be a heavy burden on the ratepayers of the Rural District Council and the County Council.

2) That fair compensation was given to those who would become involved.

3) That any benefits from the long term development of the town should be passed on to the ratepayers.

4) That this new scheme should not be done at the expense of normal improvements of existing towns and villages.

However, despite sharing the same views on the new city as the Rev. Sparling their political views were "poles apart." He was also poles apart from Mr. Bradshaw, of whom he would say in the run up to the polling "Those who say 'stop the new city coming to North Bucks,' cannot possibly stop it. And neither can I, for Ministerial plans have now been published that say Central Government wants a big new town in our area. But reasonable expansion of our villages will in any case take place, and I am actively engaged in planning them to preserve each one's identity and characteristic charm. ...."

Held by the Bletchley Central Branch of the Conservative Association, in early March the proposed new town was the subject of discussion at an Any Questions meeting at Bletchley Conservative Club. Comprising the panel were Mr. J. Speed, Ken Fuller, Miss Lane Fox and also Sir Frank Markham, who in reply to a question from Mr. M. Tompkins, regarding any justification for the new town, said "It is the North of England which should be developed. Any development here will only cause a greater influx of people from the north and abroad."

It had been the view of Beaconsfield Urban Council that the conception of the new city was originally intended to provide for the natural growth of population in the area, plus the county's own southern overspill, as well as the county's contribution towards housing London's overspill. Therefore, being surprised by the inference of the House of Commons statement that the new town would primarily serve Londoners they had corresponded in March with the County Council, stating that if this was correct then it seemed quite wrong that Bucks ratepayers should have to bear the heavy initial cost. This should fall on the Exchequer, with the proper agency for the new town being a

Government development corporation. In response the County Clerk, Mr. R. Millard, said he would pass these representations to the Planning Committee, adding that he should make two points clear:

"1) The conception of the new city in relation to the population for which it is to provide is not altered by the Minister's statement, and my Council's discussions with the Ministry are on the original basis; the point in these is that the higher the proportion of Londoners housed, the greater would be the amount of Government aid and, of course, the greater the assistance from the Greater London Council. If the Green Belt is to be preserved in South Bucks it is important that the provision shall be made for further housing not only for Londoners but for the future population of towns in the Green Belt and in South East England generally. The whole question is clearly one of proportions. My Council regard it as most important that the preservation of the Green Belt and the provision of additional housing in the new city and elsewhere should be looked on as complementary parts of a single policy."

2) "The preliminary indications are that the city should not be a heavy financial burden on the ratepayers, indeed it would be likely at some point to become a substantial financial asset which would assist towards the provision of county services for which the County Council would be responsible whoever built the city. What is required is some means of providing finance in the early years, and this is something which is being investigated. The County Council would certainly not wish to come to a decision one way or the other before all the facts, financial and other, are before them, and my object in writing this letter is to suggest that it would be a pity for other responsible bodies to jump to conclusions in the absence of this information. The Council will then wish to act in the best interests of the county as a whole."

Stating "They have been marked on the county map for a number of years for all to see," on Wednesday, March 31st Fred Pooley, County Planning Officer, emphatically denied rumours that Bucks county planners had overlooked the question of the extensive belts of brick clay, of an estimated value of several million pounds, when considering the purchase of land for the proposed new city. Further, he said the belts of clay straddling the proposed site were subject to mineral rights held by Flettons Ltd. and also possibly the London Brick Co. Ltd. In fact they had been obtained in perpetuity by the companies through agreements with local landowners, and when queried about the matter Robert Maxwell said "The Minister is expected in the next two or three months to designate the area of the new town. There will follow an inquiry when objections can be raised by people living in the area. They will be entitled to compensation as will the holders of the mineral rights." Acknowledging that the mineral rights presented a similar problem to the acquisition of 52 public houses in the area, Mr. Pooley nevertheless thought that regarding the proposed new city this wouldn't be a concern, saying "I know of nothing that will upset the general concept of the plan." As for the brick companies, prior to Mr. Maxwell's statement they'd understood that compulsory purchase orders were unlikely, since not only would the status of a multi millionaire be required to buy out the rights, but the brick shortage had now reached crisis proportions.

Having based his campaign solely on an anti city stance, on April 1st Tom Bradshaw gained election in the contest for the vacant County Council seat for the Hanslope and Sherington division. He polled 551 votes against 452 for the Rev. H. Sparling, and 395 for Ray Bellchambers, and in speaking of his victory said "I think that in electing me the people of North Bucks have shown in no uncertain manner that they are against the taking of a vast area of good agricultural land for the building of a new city. If it has to be built it should be built somewhere else in the south east where land is not so valuable, for the people from London who will make it up would be quite happy somewhere else. By returning me you have said, 'we do not want the new city here, put it where land is less valuable.'" "My next line of country (sic) is to attack this new city at County Council level, but we intend to fight every Rural District, Urban and other County Council seats if they come up on this issue. The result here tonight with me being elected is, I'm sure, just a forerunner to other things." Backed by the NFU he had fought the seat as an Independent, whilst as the nomination by the Hanslope Labour Party, Ray Bellchambers said that on the merits of the new city he didn't propose entering into an immediate debate with Mr. Bradshaw. But if he wanted one he would oblige at any time.

In London at a conference on Tuesday, April 13th Richard Crossman, the Minister of Housing and Local Government, told a deputation of local farmers that a draft designation order for the new city of North Bucks would be made by the end of the year, being separate from

Bletchley, for which there was a different development schedule. In view of this the Minister was then urged to ensure that the development took a minimum of agricultural land, with the deputation stressing the need for the development to take the form of expanding Bletchley, rather than constructing a new city on virgin land. However, it was the Minister's opinion that the needs of London's overspill would call for "new independent development," which he considered would "be better than a straightforward extension of Bletchley." Stating that he would hold a public inquiry if objections were raised to a city scheme - which he strongly inclined would have a population of 100,000 to 150,000 - he said any expansion plan would need to involve both Bletchley and other existing communities, such as Wolverton. Moreover, he told the farmers, headed by the County chairman, Stanley Moss, that the importance of taking as little agricultural land as possible would be borne in mind by the Government. With regard to the plans produced by Fred Pooley he said that whilst they were in no way committed to these they still had an interest in them. Comprised of Stanley Moss, of Chesham, William Snook, chairman of the steering committee, Robert Bullock, of Whaddon, Reginald Cowley, of Calverton, William Gurney, of Wolverton, and Victor Phillips, of Great Horwood, the delegation presented the Minister with a six page memorandum detailing the farmers' opposition to the new city scheme, and suggesting that the planners should not be looking to America for ideas but to Hong Kong and Japan, "or better still, develop our own school of super economy of land, combined with sound town planning." Another suggestion was that the Minister should promote a nation wide contest, thereby for town planners "to design developments specifically suited to this small island." Additionally the document included that the farmers had strong local support, and that an independent candidate for a seat on the County Council had recently won an election against "first class Conservative and Labour candidates by fighting on the sole platform of total opposition to the new city." The memorandum then concluded that if in spite of the good case made by the farmers the Government went ahead with the plans, then:

a) A speedy announcement designating the area of land to be required for the new city should be made so as to end quickly speculation and uncertainty.

b) An urgent and detailed public enquiry should be held.

c) An assurance that good and fair compensation and generous disturbances allowances will be paid.

After the meeting Mr. Moss expressed being "deeply disappointed that we could not dissuade the Minister from his plans to bring a new, freestanding city to North Bucks." Also in the aftermath, with the lack of satisfaction the farmers asked Robert Maxwell, who was present at the discussion, to arrange as the MP a meeting at the earliest opportunity with Fred Peart, Minister of Agriculture. This would specifically be to discuss practical ways of safeguarding the interests of the tenant farmers in the area of the new city, with particular regard to the question of compensation should their farms be taken for the development. Following the conference a joint statement was then issued:

"Mr. Richard Crossman, Minister of Housing and Local Government, today saw representatives of the Buckinghamshire County Branch of the National Farmers' Union to discuss with them the Government's plans for development of North Buckinghamshire. The NFU representatives urged him to take particular account of agricultural interests and to ensure that the development should make as small as demand as possible on land of agricultural value. They urged that the development should take the form of an expansion of Bletchley rather than a new city on virgin soil. The Minister said that he was strongly inclined to the view that the needs of London overspill would call for a new independent development providing for a population in the region of 100,000 to 150,000 in North Buckinghamshire. This, he thought, would be better than a straightforward extension of Bletchley, though it would, of course, have to take account both of Bletchley and of other existing communities, such as Wolverton. He hoped that a draft designation order would be made by the end of the year, and if there were objections, he would hold a public enquiry before finally making up his mind. He assured the NFU representatives that while the Government were interested in the plan produced by Mr. Pooley, of Buckinghamshire County Council, they were in no way committed to it. He said that the Government would certainly bear in mind the importance of taking as little agricultural land as possible. The NFU representatives raised the question of compensation for tenant farmers. The Minister suggested that they should put their views to the Minister of Agriculture and the Minister of Land and Natural Resources, which they said they would."

In his surmising of the meeting Mr. Snook remarked "The only quote I would like to give personally on this is that I assured Mr. Crossman that all the farmers in North Bucks were already committed to fighting to the bitter end on the question of compensation. We have said it before and to Mr. Maxwell and we tell you today that we shall continue to fight until you get fresh legislation on the Statute Book for fair compensation to the tenant farmer. Mr. Crossman seemed to agree that the tenant farmer would have a terrible crack of the whip on this unless something was done ... but we gathered that this question of fair compensation was one for the Minister of Land and Natural Resources rather than for Mr. Crossman."

As for the new city, Mr. Snook said he gained the impression that the Minister regarded North Bucks as probably the most suitable site, although not necessarily in the area envisaged by the County Council. "My impression was that the further expansion of Bletchley and Wolverton would probably be taken account of and also the infilling of villages, but that a town of 100,000 to 150,000 would be built on virgin land in addition. I also think the area will definitely be designated before the end of the year."

Yet despite all the local concerns regarding the new city, only six of the more than 400 villagers attended the annual meeting in April of the Loughton Parish Council, causing Mrs. J.M. Greenwood to comment that more people might have attended had the notices been in a different style from the usual. However, that they couldn't do anything about this was pointed out by the chairman, Councillor E. Daniels, who during the meeting said that regarding the development they had been promised that no one would be moved unless they could be transferred to the same standard of dwelling. For instance those now in detached houses would not be moved into flats. Yet for the present it seemed that accommodation could be in short supply for Mr. A. Snaith, the parish's rural district councillor, said that whilst the County Council had not stopped all building, the building societies were no longer prepared to advance money in the area. As for the proposed location of the new development he said the announcement that it would not be made known until the end of the year had come as a shock to him. The first date given for the disclosure had been the end of April, then it was May, and now it was the end of the year; "We shall have to put in a claim for disturbed minds."

The question of where the proposed new city would be situated was also disturbing members of Wolverton UDC, who heard from Mr. W. Houston, the area planning officer, that it could turn Wolverton into a trading backwater. In consequence at a special meeting called on Monday, May 3rd they decided to go no further than to grant formal approval to the comprehensive redevelopment of an area immediately west of Creed Street. Only when further details became known regarding the new city's location, its population, amenity values and other general knowledge, would the Council then decide to proceed with the complete third phase of East Wolverton's redevelopment, 'which is an impressive and ambitious scheme.'

There was no uncertainty as to whether there would be a new city, and in the first week of May a competition to provide a name was launched at the meeting of Haversham's Women's Institute. The judge was to be Mrs. Westcott, a VCO, but so many entries would be received that to choose a winner she decided more time was necessary, with the result to be announced at the next month's meeting. Then also in May it seemed that any name might soon be superfluous, for the possibility now arose that 'the proposals by Bucks County Council for building a new town in North Bucks, in association with the Government and private enterprise,' could well 'founder on the rocks of finance.' In fact from having charge of the matter the County Planning Committee would recommend that the County Council should drop the proposal, since satisfactory financial arrangements could not be reached with the Government. Nevertheless the Committee still held the conviction that the building of a substantial new town in North Bucks was an essential feature of solving the planning problems of this county and beyond. Also, that it was the counterpart of the preservation of the Green Belt, with this being a preferable alternative to the major expansion of existing towns. Thus with the future still seeming so indefinite it was of little surprise that Councillor W.S. Johnson, speaking in a short debate on the county's role in the new town development, said during the Bucks County Council meeting on Thursday, May 20th that people in North Bucks were sick of living with this "cloud of uncertainty." This had loomed over them since the beginning of the planning talk four years ago, and it was because satisfactory financial arrangements with the Government had not been reached that the Council had agreed to drop its own scheme for building a new town, as recommended by the County Planning Committee. Until more information was known about the location of the development he appealed for members to defer from voting on the recommendation, adding "This new town might well be too late to relieve the pressure at present on London." Nevertheless the recommendation was approved by an overwhelming majority, after which Tom Bradshaw, as one of the only two councillors voting against, said the loss of good agricultural land was an important point, and he advised the Council to build on the waste land in existing towns. Representing Shenley and Loughton, Councillor W.S. Johnson also spoke strongly against the scheme but from having an interest in the proposed project had not been allowed to vote.

Prefaced by a seven page preamble, which referred back to Mr. Crossman's statement in February that he would consider using the machinery of the New Towns Act for the scheme, the recommendation stated "That as satisfactory financial arrangements cannot be arrived at, the Council should not pursue the proposal that the construction of the proposed new town in North Bucks should be undertaken in partnership by the County Council, the Government and private enterprise, but should support the development of the New Town under the New Towns Act machinery by a development corporation." It went on to say that even if they gave approval the Council should still be consulted about any plans for the new town which could emerge from such machinery. Also that the Council should concern itself with the retention of the county's existing Green Belt. During the meeting, in his further comments Councillor Johnson remarked on the adverse effect being caused on the local property market by the uncertainty; "We are sick of living like this. I must refer to the expansion of the Green Belt in the south of the county and at the same time the spoiling of what is one of the most beautiful parts of the county, the north." As for the concept of a new town, Councillor S. Comben explained this would be cheaper than expanding existing villages and towns, namely because the deployment of county services would be concentrated, and therefore require less capital expenditure. Also building costs would be lower - "It is much easier to build on one site than spread it around several sites miles apart." Walter Beesley, of Hanslope, pointed out the dangers of flooding in the Newport Pagnell area when the new city came, and said that the water supply for the new development would be taken from the Thames Catchment Area. However it would still be discharged into the Ouse, and he therefore hoped that the River Board would start work as soon as possible to minimise the flood danger.

In the last week of May, Councillor J. Cassidy said at the annual conference of Bletchley Council that on Thursday, May 20th an assurance that Bletchley would be allowed to go on developing for two, perhaps even three, more years had been given by the Minister of Housing and Local Government, Richard Crossman, at his meeting with a Bletchley Council deputation. This had comprised Councillors J. Cassidy, F. Evans, E. Fryer, C. Head, and W. Caldwell together with officers, and also in attendance was Robert Maxwell M.P. and, as observer, County Councillor R. Haydock. With regard to the outcome Councillor Cassidy felt a lot more had been achieved - 'more than he had hoped for in his wildest dreams' - than during the meeting that a similar deputation had with the Ministry a year ago. Then they were told that the development of existing towns would be stopped should plans for a new town in the area go ahead. Yet from the recent meeting it seemed that the Minister had other ideas. In fact while the Ministry would push ahead with its plans for a new town built by a development corporation, with the Ministry making its own decisions as to the site, Bletchley would be expanded at an accelerated rate during the next two or three years. Further, Mr. Crossman had said that the Ministry would try to avoid any inconvenience to Bletchley in planning and location, saying they should now submit their proposal for a further two years' development to the County Council. At the meeting other members of the Council welcomed the decision although there were some heated exchanges at one stage between Councillor C. Clarke, who claimed that this latest position could have been arrived at much earlier, and Councillor C. Head, who said he had been impressed by the Minister's very high esteem for Mr. Pooley, the county architect; "That was very nice to know." Also very nice to know, at least by Councillor Mrs. J. Ramsbotham, would be if the Minister would again meet the Councillors, for at a meeting of the Council on Tuesday, June 22nd she urged that such an encounter should take place to clarify the new city situation. This she said had caused numerous projects to be halted, and "I am perfectly certain that if something is not done we shall wake up one morning and find that these amenities and necessities have been planned for some other part of the county, and Bletchley will remain a third rate town when we know it should be, and could be, the really go ahead centre for the whole of North Bucks."

In fact her comments had arisen from a Development Committee minute, reporting on letters from the Oxford Regional Hospital Board. This stated that although the maternity unit would be commenced in December, to be ready by mid-September 1967, the Board considered 'in view of the eventual decision to be taken by the Government as to the siting of the new town' there was little point in having a discussion on hospital provision in the Bletchley area. Mrs. Ramsbotham said they all knew the maternity unit "had been on the stocks" four years ago, but now it had been postponed because of the new city. "This is only one of the many projects which have been bedevilled by the new city. Bletchley was promised, and was due for, a new police headquarters and Magistrates' Court. The land is there waiting but we have been told there is no chance of having it until there is a decision on the new city. Then we were promised a College of Further Education. Again the land is there, but we have got to wait. The manufacturers and the traders in the town have been complaining about the telephone service. We know we want a new cable. I'll leave you to guess why we are not getting it. … Everything the town requires is being held back." In response Councillor W. Caldwell, the Development Committee Chairman, said he fully agreed with Councillor Ramsbotham, and revealed that his Committee had decided that the matter of the maternity unit should be referred to the M.P. for his information and "necessary action to assist clarification."

Elsewhere other delays were being caused by the uncertainty, with the report at North Bucks Education Executive meeting in July that the approved extensions and improvements to Shenley Church End Primary School were being held up until the site had been decided. Then at Loughton a decision was deferred on the future development of spare land on the corner of Pitcher Lane and The Leys, which the Newport Pagnell Rural Council had noted as possibly suitable for 'flatlet' development. This would be stalled until more information proved forthcoming about the future of the village and the location of the new city. Yet any forthcoming decision seemed unlikely, for having asked the Minister in the House of Commons on Tuesday, July 27th what the approximate location of the proposed new town in North Bucks would be, and what the population was intended to be, Mr. Boyd-Carpenter received a written reply stating "I am having the area around

Bletchley and Wolverton studied and expect to publish my proposals before the end of the year. My present intention is that the new town should provide for an incoming population of the order of 150,000." Not that there was any uncertainty for Louis Frederick Cribbs, a member of the United States Air Force stationed in Suffolk, for on Wednesday, July 28th he appeared in court at Newport Pagnell for having driven on the central reservation of the M1. When stopped he said he did so to "get into the city." A policeman duly gave him directions, and he was subsequently directed to payment of a fine.

Quite apart from the location of the development there were also associated concerns, for at a meeting of the Bucks County NFU Executive it was reported by Walter Beesley, Bucks County Council representative on the Great Ouse River Authority, that whilst the water supply for the new city would be drawn from the Thames Catchment area, the effluent would be discharged into the Ouse. Thus being proposed by Mr. H. Hull of North Crawley, and seconded by Jack Crook, a resolution was passed deploring the use of the Ouse as a sewage outlet for future development.

Then on Monday, September 20th regarding the location of the proposed new town development there at last seemed hints of progress, for in London at a press conference Robert Mellish, Parliamentary Secretary to the Minister of Housing, said that arguments about where a new town in North Bucks should go had been "largely overcome." He was making a statement about London housing and the house building programmes for local authorities during the next four years, and said "The problem of London overspill is now believed to be larger than was estimated in the South East Study and is put at above one million between 1964 and 1971. The Minister has already announced his plans to meet part of this need by the construction of a new town in North Bucks, estimated to house 150,000 people." When asked if any speeding up of the new town was envisaged he replied that he could only say that the site would be designated by the end of the year. North Bucks had been chosen as the obvious area but "There has been argument, as there always will be in a democracy, about where it should go but I think these are now largely overcome. But it will be for my Minister to announce details of the scheme." The necessary machinery for starting the new town - a new town commission - would be put under way fairly soon and he said an announcement would come from the Housing Minister. "I am determined this time that the right Londoners will go to these areas. We are improving the system of industrial selection. We shall improve the position so when we ask people to go outside they will be the sort of Londoners who should go. It was of the "greatest importance" to make much increased use of industrialised house building, and to dispel the idea held by some people that this system had anything to do with pre-fabs.

In view of this increased certainty, during September it was announced that a study was to be made by members of the Bucks Branch of the Country Landowners' Association with regard to the problems faced by those who would be involved when the site had been finalised. Towards this understanding the members would combine their annual meeting at Stevenage with a tour of Stevenage new town, and hear a talk on the problems faced by Stevenage from its beginnings to the present day. For presentation at the meeting, the annual report would refer to an invitation received by the branch from the County Planning Committee to comment on its proposals for a new city in the North of Bucks. However, since the receipt of their reply the control of the project had passed from Bucks County Council to the Ministry, with the total acreage of land deemed necessary to accommodate the city having now been reduced, as also the proposed population.

On Wednesday, September 22nd the view that he would like Wolverton to be part of the proposed new town in North Bucks was put forward by Robert Maxwell, Buckingham M.P. This was whilst giving a report on the recent Labour Party Conference to party members at Wolverton, where he said that the Minister, Richard Crossman, in hoping to shortly arrange the date had agreed in principle to visit the town to discuss its future. Members' views on his proposal were asked for by Mr. Maxwell but in the main it seemed they wished to keep the town as a separate entity, since, as one member said, there would be no hardship in travelling one or two miles into the new town for work. In fact some isolation from such a vast development might be an advantage. Nevertheless Mr. Maxwell retained his opinion that Wolverton instead of being just a suburb dwarfed by 'such a mighty colossus' should be an integral part of the new town, playing a vital part in its overall expansion. As for the location he could only say it would be "in the area somewhere." He was anxious that when the development took place the local authorities should be continually involved with the planning, for he was convinced that if a new town corporation was to be formed then this would save a lot of time and money, "and be a good thing for all concerned." The informal meeting then heard from Councillor F. Atter, of Wolverton, who said that although he was also in favour of local authorities being consulted about the development 'all along the line,' "Make no mistake, if any County Council candidate was to stand up now and say he is pro-city, he would be out with a bang."

On the evening of Monday, October 11th Wolverton was also the venue for a special meeting at which, with the press excluded, Wolverton UDC discussed the implications of the proposed new town. As the clerk, Mr. J. Harwood said no statement was being issued but that a meeting with Robert Maxwell M.P. had been arranged on Friday of the next week at the House of Commons. Thus speaking in late October to a delegation of more than 30 representatives from various councils, at a meeting at the Commons which he had arranged Robert Maxwell put forward two proposals to assist local authorities regarding the development of the new town for North Bucks. The first was for a Joint Consultative Committee, to make representations to the Government on behalf of persons affected by the plan. The second was for the setting up of an advisory liaison body for the New Town Development Corporation, when this was formed later in the year. Thereby such a body would be able to represent the views of all the local authorities, and the basic idea behind both proposals was to provide everyone concerned in the development with a chance to be heard, and for their views to be considered. He said the next phase in the new town plan would be in three stages, with the Minister to announce the designated area for the town between December and March. Local authorities could then make their representations, and probably in the Spring a draft order would be published. At this time formal objections could be made, to be followed by a public inquiry probably in the Autumn of 1966. A final decision by the Minister would then come near the end of the year, with building to commence during the next. After more than an hour's discussion his suggestions were given backing by the delegates, who were told by Mr. Maxwell that he would continue to press for the minimum amount of land to be taken for the new town, and that farmers who lost their land should be paid a more favourable compensation than was presently envisaged.

On October 26th Councillor J. Cassidy said that Bletchley Council and Newport Pagnell Rural Council had approved the setting up of a consultative committee between all the authorities in North Bucks. Then, dependent on the Government's agreement to the setting up of an advisory committee, the Minister would make appointments from the authorities, meaning that numerous objections which might hinder a development corporation could be dealt with and thereby save much time. "If, in fact we are to be part of the new town we shall react accordingly. We shall accept it and play our part. If Bletchley is outside the new town we shall equally accept it, providing it is not made the excuse for stopping growth in Bletchley. We can't be fairer than that. We are not burying our heads in the sand." "The Consultative Committee now being formed can only be a talking committee with no powers. But the Advisory Committee, if it is formed by the Government, would in fact have whatever powers the Government wished to give. It might even have the powers of hearing appeals."

At the meeting of the Bucks branch of the NFU, on Thursday, November 4th Robert Maxwell in emphasising his comments at the meeting he'd arranged at the House of Commons said "We have the new town coming here, and although it only concerns my part of the county, it is going to hit many of you very hard. I can promise you that I have fought hard to see that the quantity of land taken is kept to a minimum, and I am engaged in something close to the hearts of tenant farmers to see that trespass and interference by local and national government is kept to a minimum. And last but not least, if the Government is going to requisition land for community purposes, to see that the present niggardly compensation should be increased to at least five years' rent or ten years' profit, whichever is the higher."

The effects of the new city were also the subject of Mr. R. Dunbabin, clerk to Newport Pagnell RDC, when speaking to members of Newport Pagnell Young Conservatives on Tuesday, November 16th he said the North Bucks they knew today was unlikely to last much longer. He explained that since the war the Abercrombie Committee had devised the idea of a series of towns around London to take up the increase in population. However, the Committee had underestimated this growth and already most of the new towns had surpassed their envisaged number. By the recent South East Study it had been shown that this part of the country was somewhat overpopulated, and that over the next 20 years provision would have to be made for another 3 million people.

As this would largely mean a direction of labour - "something that was decidedly unpopular with the average Englishman" - he thought development on a large scale in the less densely populated areas would be unlikely to succeed, and therefore new towns would have to be built in the South East. Subsequently describing some of the effects the proposed new town would have on the area he said that amongst the many problems would be the provision of all services, and the housing of the huge labour construction force. Initially North Bucks would enjoy a boom but as the new development became established then trade would be drawn away from the other centres.

Regarding the new town development, Mr. Francis Whiting, the outgoing chairman of the Newport Pagnell branch of the NFU, claimed at the annual general meeting on Wednesday, November 17th that the farmers' stand against the proposed new town in North Bucks had not only killed the Pooley plan for a super city, but had also deferred the building of a smaller town. Addressing some 50 members he said "It is only by complete unity that strength to do the job in the future will come." When lobbied by the deputation of 100 local farmers at the House of Commons, the local M.P., Robert Maxwell, had been made to realise the strength of feeling of the branch about the new town plans, and Mr. Whiting continued that "After a meeting with the Buckingham M.P., Mr. Maxwell, about the implications for such a development, a steering committee led by Mr. W. Snook, of Water Eaton, had been formed. The climax of the committee's efforts was a meeting with the Minister of Housing and Local Government, Mr. Richard Crossman, who they left in no uncertain terms as to their feelings on the new town. The Pooley plan is dead, and a smaller town has not yet been built. Not only has this so far been achieved but should the building come then we want better compensation for the farmer who is dispossessed." He then congratulated Tom Bradshaw, of Hardmead, on having won a County Council seat for the Union by standing purely on an anti-city platform.

In responding to representations from Robert Maxwell, requesting the approval and loan sanctions for building as many houses as possible for the North Bucks area, Robert Mellish, the parliamentary under secretary, said that for the time being priority for building would still be given to the larger towns. However, Mr. Maxwell felt that having suffered so long from this mistaken policy a rural area such as North Bucks should now be given some fairer treatment, not least from accommodating a great many inhabitants moving out of London and other conurbations. Nevertheless, in a lengthy written reply Mr. Mellish included "Obviously it does not mean that the authorities in your constituency are not getting anything at all, but it does mean that they cannot expand their programmes as fast as they might wish." Not that Olney was greatly concerned for in the wake of a special meeting in the town, held on Friday, November 26th, one of two main points in a statement issued the following Tuesday by Newport Pagnell RDC was, albeit early in the New Year, that the townspeople would have the chance to discuss and find out what type of proposals were contained in plans to boost the town to a community of over 10,000.

For those residents of North Bucks who would be affected by the new city scheme, some of the uncertainty was dispelled on the morning of Friday, December 3rd, when the two recommended sites for development were made public in a Ministry of Housing and Local Government study. In a foreword the Minister pointed out that whilst decisions had already been taken on the expansion of Northampton, plus the building of a new town in North Bucks, he was not committed to the details of these projects. Nor to the present recommendations of the planning consultants, for the report merely provided a useful 'working document for the consideration of the local authorities and others interested in the proposals.' Assessing the inter-related growth of the three areas the 86 page report was officially a 'study' of Northampton, Bedford and North Bucks, and urged the Minister to choose the site nearer to Bletchley (on more than one occasion the document referred to 'the city of Bletchley') since if the site centred on Hanslope was chosen (extending as far south as Wolverton, and to the north to Paulerspury and Grafton Regis) the immediate relocation of the Diplomatic Wireless Station would be entailed. The preferred site was therefore suggested as being centred some three miles north of Bletchley, and comprising some 25 square miles would seem to be bounded to the south by Bletchley and the Bedford branch rail line, to the north east and north by the M1 and Wolverton, and to the west by the main Bletchley/Wolverton railway line. Bringing relief to many, 'Loughton, for so long fearing itself as the new town centre, escapes almost unscathed and will become merely a suburb.' Also the Shenleys and all the villages to the west were excluded but those of Wavendon, Walton, Woughton on the Green, the Woolstones, Milton

Keynes, Broughton, and possibly also the Bradwells found inclusion. The report stated that of the two areas that nearest Bletchley not only offered a more suitable location for the new city but from being more open would be easier to develop, and have a better relationship to the existing pattern of towns. Therefore it was recommended that this should be the site chosen. The form of the city would be such as to allow expansion beyond the initial population figure, with the system of transportation capable of a phased construction to meet the increasing number of journeys consequent to the growth of the city - 'This should include a conception of public transport which allows changes in form to suit current levels of demand and to embody the latest techniques.' In fact many observers took the last sentence as reference to a monorail service. With the site well located for road and rail traffic the report viewed the attracting of a range of industries to the new city as posing no difficulty, albeit with acknowledgment of an initial serious absence of public facilities. As for the farming community threatened by the new development no reference was made, merely the observation that the site was 'an undistinguished, slightly undulating clay area, fairly open and undeveloped, except for about ten small villages dispersed throughout.'

Regarding one of these 'small villages', at Walton the property tycoon and race horse breeder Bernard Myers had spent a great deal of money building up his farm, and being unimpressed after seeing the report said from his London office "It's a pipe dream, at least I think it is, and I hope it is; just like the South-East Study and the Pooley plan ... For a start where is the money going to come from? They would do much better to expand the existing towns to give them more character and to bring more people in this way." Asked of his intentions if later during the month Mr. Crossman accepted the site recommendation he said "I shall fight him with all the means at my disposal." On being told of the study's recommendation Ray Furnival, as secretary to the Newport Pagnell branch of the NFU, said it came as "a bit of a surprise," revealing that on the evening of Friday, December 3rd a meeting with the half dozen members of the steering committee and himself had been arranged by Robert Maxwell, the local M.P. Here, presumably timed to coincide with the report's publication, they would go fully into the question. In the final general summary was stated "Particular attention should be paid to the role of public transport in the large settlements proposed, its effect upon town form and its phasing with the development of the town. In the implementation of these proposals, consideration should be given to the advantages resulting from the setting up of Development Corporations working in conjunction with the local authorities and also to the planning of towns and expansions in advance of designation of the sites." Yet despite the mentioning of the two sites it seemed almost certain that when the formal announcement in Parliament of the site was made by the Minister his choice would be the Wavendon - Little Woolstone area. This announcement was supposed to be made later in the month, and in the first week of December when speaking at the annual dinner of the Bucks branch of NALGO, Ray Bellchambers, chairman of Newport Pagnell Rural Council, said he expected to hear the Minister announce the designated area in the next few days. As for the repercussions on local authorities of the proposed new town, these he said would be tremendous; "It would mean vast new chances for people with local government experience to use their ability and knowledge to create a town of credit not merely to the district and the town corporation, but to the whole country." The venue for the dinner had been Wilton Hall, Bletchley, to where the Prime Minister, Harold Wilson, arrived with his wife on a Saturday to report to the Northern Home Counties Labour Party Rally on how the Government had been faring with the job of building the New Britain. Of great surprise he made no mention of the new town, despite having been urged to name the site in a letter from Robert Maxwell. Nevertheless hopes were high on Wednesday 15th, when it was learned from his office that Mr. Maxwell had tabled a Parliamentary question asking the Minister to name the site. However, with many observers viewing the publication of the recent North Bucks Study as a delaying tactic, it was then generally recognised that the site would not be named on Friday, but that the area would be revealed the next Tuesday, when Mr. Maxwell's question was due to be answered. Then on Thursday, December 16th it was learned from Mr. Maxwell that he had withdrawn the question, for the reason that the Ministry of Housing and Local Government was "not yet ready to commit itself." Yet he still intended to press the issue and would present a rephrased question when Parliament reassembled after Christmas. Whilst he didn't expect the Minister to name the site he thought he would probably issue a map, showing his proposal for the designated area.

All this did little to placate Ray Furnival, who said "This appears to be still more dilly-dallying. We want to know where it is going to be quickly, so that we can get rid of all this terrible uncertainty." Indeed, when told of the latest position Mr. Snook said "The Minister has broken a written promise. In June, when we met at the House of Commons, he promised us that the designated area would be made known by the end of the year, and now he has gone back on it. We shall make immediate representation through Mr. Maxwell, or direct to the Minister, to try and get the matter settled quickly once and for all, for although we know that this new development is coming, we think it only fair to the farmers concerned that we know who is going to be dispossessed at the earliest possible moment so that they might make adequate alternative arrangements." Mr. R. Dunbabin, clerk to Newport Pagnell RDC, said that with regard to the issue of a map, showing the area for the new town, the Minister under the New Towns Act 1965 was obliged to this course, and after producing the map and observing the comments of interested parties there would be the necessary public inquiry. Only after this could the Minister then officially designate the area. As for the North Bucks Study, recently published by the Ministry, and known to the local authorities as the Wilson Report, the only difference from the Pooley plan, prepared by the County Council, was the population being squeezed into a smaller area. For his view on the latest position Frank Hall, clerk to Newport Pagnell UDC, said "My Council received the Northampton, Bedford and North Bucks Study on December 3rd and the Minister asked for local authorities views when they had examined the study. As my Council and other authorities could not have had the time to study the report and forward their views to the Minister, I am not surprised to be told that the Minister will not be making his statement this year."

Protesting about the lack of firm official information on the new town, and how official silence was causing hardship to thousands of families in his Parliamentary Division, just before Christmas Mr. Maxwell wrote to Mr. Crossman, and in response on Wednesday, December 29th received a reply worded; "I well appreciate how important it is to get out the area to be designated for the North Bucks New Town. I had hoped to do this, as you know, by the end of the year. It will in fact be early January, and I shall be glad to make this clear on the Question you put down for Tuesday, and which has now been deferred until 25th

January." Then again on the Wednesday Mr. Maxwell contacted the Ministry, to be told that in two weeks time the Minister would send out a letter plus a map indicating his proposed location for the new town. This would be sent not only to Mr. Maxwell and Bucks County Council but also to all the local authorities in the area, including the Parish Councils and statutory bodies such as the Electricity Board, the Gas Board etc. The Minister would next invite the recipients to forward their opinions about his proposed draft designation area. If convinced that his suggestions were unlikely to be helpful he could then change his mind. In fact on January 25th regarding the location of the new town he would be answering a Parliamentary question put down by Mr. Maxwell, who in the light of the consultation with local authorities and public opinion in North Bucks would thereby be provided with an opportunity to ask questions about his proposals.

By approximately February 15th the Minister would officially publish his draft designation order, followed in the summer by a full public enquiry at which all the objections would be heard. Next the Minister would receive a report from the inspectors, and in consideration of their recommendations duly publish towards the end of 1966 the final designation area for the new town. However on Tuesday, December 28th it was the general feeling at the meeting of Wolverton UDC that the recently published Northampton, Bedford and North Bucks study, which outlined the two sites for the proposed North Bucks new town, merely added further complications to an already complicated and uncertain issue. Limited copies of the study would be made available to Council members, with Councillor H. Dewick, chairman of the Planning Committee, wishing, "the best of luck to you when you get it. It is a rather weighty study." Also, at 25s a copy, a rather expensive one, said Councillor D. Morgan. As for Councillor J. Love, he asked what had become of the proposed visit of Richard Crossman, as the Minister, to the Wolverton area. In reply the Council Chairman, Councillor F. Cornford, said that since the site of the new town was still in abeyance there seemed little point in pressing him to visit Wolverton, pointing out that the clerk, Mr. J. Harwood, had been instructed to write to the Minister asking both for an early designation of the site and where the Council now stood in the matter.

1966

A DECISION IS MADE

On or about February 15th the Draft Designation Order locating the site of the new town was to supposedly be published by the Minister of Housing and Local Government, Richard Crossman, and thus during the first week of January all local authorities, from the County Council to parish councils, plus statutory bodies such as the Electricity Board and the Gas Board, could expect to receive a map and an informal letter outlining his proposals. This would then allow the local bodies a month to forward their views and objections, which, if sufficiently convincing, might lead to his change of mind.

During the first week of the New Year, on Monday, January 3rd, at a gathering of the Conservative 106 Supper Club, held at Newport Pagnell, guest speakers offered conflicting views of the proposed development: Dr. A. Clay, a member of Newport Pagnell UDC and a fervent supporter of the new town, and Stanley Moss, chairman of the County branch of the NFU, and an anti city man.

Speaking first, Dr. Clay said that eight years ago after the sharp rise in the post war population the Tory Government had begun a series of studies as to how to house this population. This was undertaken with a team headed by Sir Keith Joseph, whilst as for locations he said "The fact is that you can get anywhere quickly from North Bucks …" and since "there were not many people who would want to go back to an agricultural state of living" industrialisation and development was the obvious choice for North Bucks. "You have got to put 250,000 people somewhere, and if no town is built you will merely have a sprawl, with no cohesion, a mass, like - if they forgive me - Slough. The Pooley concept was that we should have a new town surrounded by villages which would not lose their character in a sprawl, and this is the idea." Of the existing communities he said it was pointless building a new sewerage system for Newport Pagnell if that of the new city could be adequately used. "The development of North Bucks is here, whether we like it or not." "The key to success is for the new town with the tradition still going on in the villages outside, but if Bletchley and Wolverton keep shouting for their own, then you will have chaos." Concluding, he said that since the war agriculture had seen an increase in production of 86% with only about 2% of its land taken. Sir Keith Joseph's recommendation was that only 3% of land would have to be taken over the next 20 years to fulfil the planners needs, and the quality of land developed could not be taken into account when considering the efficiency of the industry.

Stating the opposite view, Mr. Moss said he wasn't opposed to building as such but when agricultural land was developed it was destroyed. As with most farmers he would prefer to see the redevelopment of slums and badly developed areas in contrast to a huge new city, which would take up good agricultural land. For every acre lost to building there was 30cwt less of wheat and "I am not wholly satisfied that the need for a city exists, for I can't help feeling that people's judgement is clouded by the need to build a monument to Pooley or Crossman." His vision was to see North Bucks kept for North Bucks people, and when the time arose for a new town he would prefer far more research to be undertaken than had presently been done.

As a body set up by local authorities to keep in touch with the proposals for the new development, the North Bucks Joint Consultative Committee agreed in principle to the establishing of a new city in North Bucks but not to the concept of linear development interconnecting the towns in the region. Thus at a meeting at the offices of Newport Pagnell Rural Council on Tuesday, January 11th the committee agreed that its collective view, as well as observations from individual councils, would be submitted to the Minister of Housing and Local Government. A letter had been received from Robert Maxwell M.P. stating his willingness to co-operate with the committee in every way, and mention was made that as soon as they had considered the Minister's letter and map, showing his proposed designated area, he would no doubt welcome meeting a deputation from the local authorities in North Bucks. If such a meeting could be arranged it could either take place in the near future, when Mr. Crossman visited the area, or in London. Either way endeavour would be made to persuade the Minister to meet the full consultative committee. After receipt of the Minister's letter and designation proposals, the next meeting of the consultative committee would be convened as soon as possible in the offices of Winslow Rural Council, from being a member of the committee.

Regarding the date of the Draft Order, in December 1965 Robert Maxwell had sent a letter to the Minister protesting about the continued lack of firm official information. Then in consequence on December 29th 1965 he received a reply stating, "I well appreciate how important it is to get out the area to be designated for the North Bucks New Town. I had hoped to do this, as you know, by the end of the year. It will in fact be early January, and I shall be glad to make this clear on the Question you put down for Tuesday and which has now been deferred until January 25th." In fact there wasn't this long to wait, for at a special Press Meeting at Whitehall on Thursday, January 13th the Minister announced that comprising some 27,000 acres the £400m new town would envelop Stony Stratford, Wolverton and Bletchley. In fact the whole area would be split almost down the middle by the A5, with the newly electrified main railway line from Bletchley junction to Wolverton running through the middle of the site 'like an axis.' The M1 would form one of the boundaries and the concept stood the County Council plan on end, so as to include Bletchley and Wolverton. However very little of the Winslow rural and Newport Pagnell urban districts were affected. By the proposals, within some 20 years the Minister envisaged a quarter of a million people living and working in a multi centred town scattered in the area now occupied by Bletchley and Wolverton, with a six mile wide strip of land between the two places. This he hoped would be achieved by the intensive use of industrial building, special incentives and propaganda for the movement of industry and population out of London. The appointment of a Development Corporation would be made with which the existing local authorities, who regarding the proposals had now been sent letters, were expected to afford 'enthusiastic collaboration.'

The Minister's letter to the MP, local authorities, the Railway Board, and United Counties Bus Company stated that the area was very much

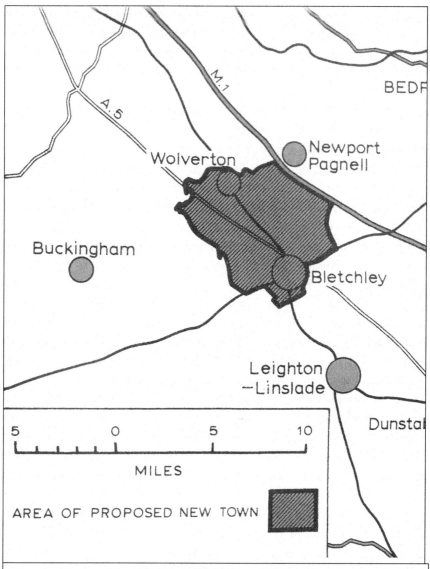

The new plan incorporated the pre-existing towns of Wolverton, Stony Stratford and Bletchley. The recently-built M1 formed the north-eastern boundary, and therefore Newport Pagnell was excluded.

Outside of the 19th century developments of Wolverton and Bletchley, the entire area was under-populated, and mainly comprised farmland supported by scattered villages. The concept of a large town, or 'city', as some called it, of a projected 250,000, was alien to most residents and was strongly resisted by many interest groups. Even large, well-established towns, such as Northampton and Bedford, were under half that figure at the time, so this was a novel enterprise indeed.

larger than in any of the earlier new towns because of four main reasons:

1) The proposed new town will be much larger in population than any previous new town. It is proposed to provide for an incoming population of about 150,000 over 20 years, and this together with the existing population with its planned increases and further growth by natural increase is likely to result in the long run in a total population of about 250,000.

2) The Minister believes it right to plan the town from the start with a capacity for expansion to this total population. This means taking a bolder and more forward view of the ultimate shape and size of the town.

3) A new town of this size is bound to introduce new principles of structure and design. The traditional centralised form of town based on a radial pattern is not likely to be satisfactory for this new town designed for the rapidly changing circumstances of the late 20th and 21st century. A more dispersed pattern of development is almost certain to be needed even though the individual components of the town such as the housing areas will be built at economical densities so as not to waste land.

4) It has been decided to include Bletchley, Wolverton and Stony Stratford in the proposed designated area so as to integrate their growth into the new town in a constructive and positive way. The area the Minister has in mind to designate lies within the areas of Bletchley, Newport Pagnell and Wolverton urban districts and the Newport Pagnell and Winslow rural areas.

The local authorities involved were asked to submit their observations within one month, and in the light of these the Minister would then consider whether to prepare a draft order designating the area and the site. Opportunity would be given to anyone affected to object, and if objections were received and not withdrawn he would order an Inquiry to be conducted by an independent person. Explaining his proposals at an informal meeting at the Ministry, Mr. Crossman firstly pointed out that this was a much larger area than had been suggested for previous new towns. "Quite simply, I looked at the first round of new towns and it seemed to me a mistake to have new towns and later to double their size and then have to decide on the further area required. There is something to be said for getting the area right first time." "A second point is that we were very grateful to Buckinghamshire and to Mr. Pooley for all the work they had put in. But when I looked at it I felt it would be in every way - economic, sociologically and politically - unwise to think of a new town as pushing out Wolverton and Bletchley. The only sane way was to bring Wolverton and Bletchley within the total area. A further point is that we are therefore obviously not thinking of a single centred new town of the traditional pattern. ... Bletchley has been extremely concerned to get an assurance that their development will not be blighted for years and years by a new town. They felt there was a great danger that it might stop dead. We have given them those assurances. They are doing useful overspill work now, but I want to let them go ahead and their present overspill can be integrated into this non single centred new town." If the scheme was approved a Development Corporation would be appointed later in the year. The master plan would then take a year to 18 months to prepare but this would not preclude building in the meantime. "We have a plan to anticipate the master plan and this is where the existing developments of Bletchley and Wolverton are important."

Not surprisingly the immediate reaction focussed upon the amount of land to be taken, being far greater than envisaged after the scrapping of the Pooley plan. However at the meeting Mr. Crossman stressed his sympathy with the farmers' claims for better compensation, and said he would do all he could under the present official structure. Indeed in the light of recent meetings between his Ministry and that of Agriculture he had done his utmost to take land of a poorer quality, and in the initial stages little of the virgin acres would be taken up. For a town of this anticipated importance a high standard of industry, shopping, public services, recreation and other amenities would be the intention, with the Development Corporation during the preparation of the plan being instructed to liaise closely with the County and District Councils concerned, thereby to ensure from the outset their inclusion in the planning process. When submitted to the Minister the plan would be made available for inspection, with an opportunity for him to be made aware of the public's views.

Responding to a question from the Press, Mr. Crossman said the Ministry was grateful for all the help given by Frederick Pooley. As for the proposed new development, for which a name had yet to be chosen, from being multi centred he said it would be "the biggest and most ambitious development we have ever tackled," novel in many ways and with the feasibility of a monorail transport system. Yet by the comment of one consultant "a large amount of water would have to be made available close to the new town" (the inference being the proposed reservoirs near Aylesbury) and it was admitted that both sewage and water for the town was still a problem. As for the Master Plan, the Minister's advisers assured the meeting that preliminary work had been undertaken. Saying that he wouldn't give the new town any priority over industry for the North East, Mr. Crossman thought some heavier types of industry would come to the area, pointing out that in the past this had proved a minor problem with other new towns, where industry had been attracted without the need to offer incentives. He was anxious that although primarily for the London overspill the town would be made up of 'a fair cross section' of the community.

Only hours after the plan's announcement an informal discussion was held by Bletchley Council, and although from the short notice five members were not present they were provided with copies of the policy. Despite their absence, and in anticipation of their acceptance, four points were agreed for discussion at the Council's next public meeting on January 25th. Namely:

1) That we ask Mr. Robert Maxwell, MP, to continue his good work and arrange for an early meeting with the Minister.

2) That we assure the Minister of Bletchley's willingness to co-operate 100% with this scheme for North Bucks.

3) To assure the Minister of our willingness to continue with developments at Bletchley up to our Urban District boundary and to do everything in our power to facilitate assimilation in the general scheme for North Bucks, whatever he may have in mind later on.

4) To assure the Minister of our willingness to provide for mixed private development within our scheme.

A committee comprised of Councillors W. Caldwell, E. Fryer, C. Head and Mrs. D. Ramsbotham was appointed to meet the Minister lead by Councillor J. Cassidy, who in the aftermath of Mr. Crossman's announcement said "The designation, of course, rectifies the fantastic errors in the County Plan, which narrowed in at the middle to exclude Bletchley and Wolverton. The fact that the new designation brings them in shows how right we were and how successful Mr. Maxwell's efforts have been. I am sure I speak for everyone in Bletchley, including industrialists, traders and the townspeople, when I say how grateful we are to him…" As for Mr. Maxwell (who had always considered that the plan put forward by the County was harmful and a threat to Bletchley, Wolverton and Stony Stratford) his view on the news took a political stance when he spoke at the Brickhills Labour Party annual meeting on Friday, January 14th; "People sometimes say that politics do not matter, and that who you have as MP doesn't matter - yet here is a classic example of a colossal mistake that would have been made had the Conservatives been in. We should have had the county plan, and no matter how badly it would have affected Bletchley, Wolverton and thousands of others, they would have said, 'Never mind it is a beautiful plan. … Now, under the Labour Government not only will Bletchley be encouraged to go ahead under the vigorous leadership of its Labour council and become a pulsating centre for the big new city, but Wolverton, Stony and other places will go ahead too. …" However he thought too much agricultural land had been taken, and having 'in perhaps an unorthodox way' brought this to the Prime Minister's notice at the public meeting at Bletchley said the matter was now under discussion at the Ministry of Agriculture. Indeed to a sympathetic reception he had raised the subject with the Minister on Thursday, with regarding the question of better compensation to tenant farmers a suggestion being made that the money could come from the Land Commission who, through the improvement tax, would be collecting something like £80 million a year - 'cash which would have otherwise have gone into the pockets of the land speculators.'

As chairman of Newport Pagnell RDC, Councillor R. Bellchambers said his first impression was of the total area being larger than first anticipated. Ultimately since 80% of the proposed area was in Newport Pagnell Rural District this would mean a drastic reorganisation for the Council, and, emphasising the need for the newly formed North Bucks Consultative Committee to be adequately informed on all aspects of planning and negotiation, he hoped future consultation would take place on the detailed use of the land. Mr. F.A. Hall, clerk to the Council, said "It does, in fact, embrace the area included in the Pooley plan and yet it is larger. However, I feel sure that the fact that only a very small part of Newport Pagnell is included in the area will please many of the residents." As for property tycoon Bernard Myers, of Walton, he said that even if his farm was affected he was pleased that the Minister had included Bletchley as an integral part of the new town, something which he'd always advocated. Yet from a personal point of view he didn't see how he could continue his stud farm next door to continuing urban development; "You can't have 40 pregnant mares in fields right next door to major building, it's just impracticable." Of those not impressed by the Minister's announcement, when informed of the proposals Mr. W. Snook, chairman of the NFU steering committee (set up specifically to look into the new city question) said from his home at Slad Farm, Water Eaton, "We will fight to the bitter end, with our MP who has already given us considerable help, for fresh legislation to be in the statute book for better compensation for the dispossessed tenant farmer on the basis of ten years' rent or five years' profit, whichever he cares to choose. No land will be released until we can achieve this, and it is a bitter blow to find the suggested site of such a vast acreage. A meeting of the steering committee will be held on Monday to discuss the present position and next Friday all North Bucks NFU members are invited to a meeting at Water Eaton Hall, when Mr. Maxwell will be available to discuss the whole situation." Nevertheless he went on to say that he agreed with the Minister's decision to expand Bletchley, and was pleased to see that the "blighted" areas of agricultural land near the town - land where vandalism or trespassing was rife - would also be included in the proposals. Stating that the steering committee was now being inundated with letters 'from all types of people' about the question of compensation, support for Mr. Snook's comments was given by the secretary to the Bletchley and Newport Pagnell branches of the NFU, Ray Furnival.

On Tuesday, January 18th, at their meeting at Winslow the North Bucks Consultative Committee asked Robert Maxwell to ask whether the Minister of Housing and Local Government, Richard Crossman, would receive a deputation from all the local authorities in the North Bucks constituency. This was for the purpose of discussing the proposed designated area, and whilst the committee welcomed the issue of the preliminary proposals they intended to urge the Minister's consideration of allowing existing districts to expand, thus to remain as viable units 'in the changing circumstances'. At the same time the committee was expected to ask the Minister to ensure local representation on the

Development Corporation and to press for adequate compensation for the dispossessed tenant farmer.

With regard to the Minister's proposals for the new town, in a statement issued on Wednesday, January 19th Alderman R.B. Verney, chairman of the Development Plan Sub-committee of Bucks County Council, said in a statement; "The site which the Minister now proposes is, save that it includes Bletchley and Wolverton, basically that which the County Council chose for their proposed new city though it omits the Beachampton-Nash-Whaddon triangle. The Minister says that the new town should be designed for the rapidly changing circumstances of the late twentieth and twenty-first centuries. This is what the County Council have always striven for. They will, therefore, I am sure welcome the Minister's proposal but naturally they would like further time to consider the details. So far as Bletchley and Wolverton are concerned we have always realised that that they must be planned in relation to the new town, but we do not think it necessary when preparing our new city plans to include them in the designated area with all the implications for compulsory purchase which that entails. So far as Bletchley is concerned, we have already approved a plan, which we gather is likely to be acceptable to the Ministry, for expanding the town up to a population of 40,000 in a manner to fit in with the new town, and of course we shall make sure that the future interests of Wolverton are safeguarded. We hope it will now not be long before the Minister approves our green belt extension proposals in the south of the County, which are a corollary of expansion in the north."

At an informal meeting on Tuesday, January 25th members of Loughton Parish Council decided that a public meeting to discuss the plan should be held on February 3rd at the Memorial Hall, with the attendance of local county councillors expected. "We were the people who protested against the original plans as we are against the village being demolished" said Councillor E.W. Daniels, chairman, "And we are not proposing to alter our opinions at this stage until we know more of the designation of the new town. We shall probably take a vote at the meeting as to what are the views of the people." Similarly Walton Parish Council would meet to consider the plan on January 26th and then Woburn Sands Parish Council on January 31st.

At Water Eaton on Friday, January 21st more than 200 farmers from North Bucks made a last 'defiant stand' against the Minister's proposals to build a city of 250,000 population in the area. A call for farmers to try and save every possible acre of land from inclusion in the proposed new city was made by the Bletchley NFU chairman, Vic Phillips, who said "The cloud under which we have been living for so long in this part of the country has now broken. We who farm are deeply conscious of the responsibility which now befalls every one of us to see that every acre of land must be fought for to ensure that our duty to feed the nation is not overshadowed by those whose duty it is to house it." By the meeting it was decided to make the Minister aware of their opposition but if the development went ahead then to make certain representations to safeguard their interests. County Councillor Tom Bradshaw, who farmed at Hardmead, proposed that especially in view of the envisaged world food shortage in the year the meeting should oppose the development on the grounds that it would take valuable agricultural land. All hands were raised in the hall and the proposal was seconded by Charles Head, a Bletchley Urban District Councillor, who said there was no sense in taking good agricultural land when there were acres of sites 'growing stinging nettles' in the present towns and villages. Present at the meeting was local M.P. Robert Maxwell, who having pledged his support to the farmers' cause said he would take their view to the Minister. However, he pointed out there was little hope of reversing a cabinet decision. Nevertheless the Steering Committee of the Bletchley and Newport Pagnell branches, which was also present at the meeting, hoped to see the Minister within three weeks and present him with a seven point draft. Claiming their opposition on the grounds that too much good agricultural land of above the national quality would be taken, this was to be presented by the Steering Committee chairman, Mr. W. Snook, with the request that farmers should be told as early as possible when their farm was likely to be possessed. As for other points, if part of a farm was taken then payment should be for the whole farm, since that part might well be the most productive, and as such compensation should be awarded as though all the farm had been claimed. That in view of Mr. Crossman's statement of the necessity to take 6,000 more acres than originally planned, an appraisal of the specified acreage should be undertaken, with towards the preservation of good agricultural land consideration made of both building 'upwards' rather than 'outwards' and high density housing. On the subject of compensation for tenant farmers Mr. Snook said, "This is now far more important than when we raised the issue some two years ago. I have stated to the Minister himself that we will not give up an acre of land until there is fresh legislation on the statute book. The discretionary payment by the local authority is not mandatory or obligatory and why should we be paid such a niggardly compensation?" "There should be as much pressure as possible for compensation on an equal footing for the owner occupier." As a final point he emphasised that the Minister must be made to carefully consider the question of those farmers whose homes and land would be on the boundary of the conurbation. Regarding their efforts to obtain a square deal Mr. Maxwell then congratulated the Steering Committee, before launching into 'a fierce attack' on the present system of compensation paid to the tenant farmer. Being "A grave injustice to human liberty and a national scandal," he pointed out that this currently totalled only one year's rent plus the ex gratia payment made by the local authority. Continuing he said he additionally wished to see the Minister grant full compensation to the man who lost only part of his land, pointing out the difficulty many tenant farmers, many of whom knew no other form of employment, would have in finding new premises. However he advised that the newly formed North Bucks Consultative Committee, comprised of all the local authorities, would aid the farmers in their fight. Many questions were 'hurled' at the platform and Mr. Francis Whiting, the immediate past chairman of the Newport Pagnell branch, wondered if he could be convinced by anyone present that North Bucks was an ideal site for the new town. Ample land of less viable nature lay within the same distance from London, and in other views Councillor Charles Head suggested that many derelict sites in towns and villages should be infilled. Councillor Bradshaw then put forward his resolution, which receiving the unanimous support of members brought the meeting towards a close.

At Walton on Wednesday, January 26th a public meeting was called to give the views of the parish - comprised of 722 acres and a population of 116 - on the Minister's proposed site for the new city. George Hooton was elected chairman, and apart from some 30 parishioners also in attendance were Newport Pagnell Rural District Councillor, Councillor F. Hawkins, whose home was close to the Wavendon Parish boundary, and Mr. M.R. Scanlon, a property developer. Also present was another property developer, millionaire Bernard Myers, who, with it being his greatest wish that the farm could reach 'the peak of perfection' by breeding a Derby winner, told the meeting that his Walton Stud Farm, described as a £300,000 project at its open day in June, could not exist if a new town came. He then concentrated on the Newport Pagnell RDC chairman, Mr. R. Bellchambers, and the clerk, Mr. R. Dunbabin. Both were primarily attending to assist the parish in formulating any protest it wished to make to the Minister, but in addressing them Mr. Myers alleged that the Council seemed content "to sit back, accept the coming of the new city, and leave it at that." Everyone seemed to be looking after their own interests, and he viewed the struggle for survival against the development as becoming a free for all. Indeed he could not envisage Walton Stud remaining a viable unit in the midst of urban development, and directing the remark to Mr. Bellchambers said "If we are to be like King Canute and say to the town 'go back' and it doesn't, just how is the Rural Council going to help us. It is simply that if the town comes we cannot farm. I ask is each person uprooted or disturbed going to receive the help of the Council? It is not for me to tell you where your duty lies, but I always imagined that the Council was the servant of the ratepayers, not the other way round. My wife and I have worked hard for everything we own and I want everyone to be protected by the Council. It seems to me that the Council is just doing a hand washing act of the whole affair." As for other comments he included "As far as Walton is concerned I am against a new town. I have fought the new town and done everything in my power. I came to Walton five years ago, it took three years to get the place ready. It was the place to which I was going to retire. ..." He then said that any area abutting a new town became a mere appendage of it, "excluded from its amenities and having all the disadvantages of being severed from it." He couldn't continue to run such a farm, not least while it was being constructed with all the traffic on the road. His stud groom had told him it was impossible - "We have got to go."

Replying to Mr. Myer's concerns Mr. Bellchambers explained that the Council was not unmindful of personal feelings. Its job was to observe the district as a whole, and to do whatever it thought best for the whole area. He pointed out that every member of the Council lived in the Rural area because they liked it, and probably everyone of those Council members did not want the new city. Yet the Minister had decided on the building of a new town in North Bucks and nothing could alter that. However, it was the Council's wish that with the aid of the North

Bucks Consultative Committee of which, together with seven other authorities, it was a member, all the ratepayers were assimilated into the new town 'without undue stress.' Mr. Myers then asked "When is the next Council election," to which Mr. Bellchambers replied "I don't think that is relevant to what we are discussing." "It is," countered Mr. Myers, "For next time we should elect a Council which is fully mindful to the needs of the ratepayer. We must consider the people now, not the people of Newport Pagnell area twenty years from now." Responding, Mr. Bellchambers assured him that the Consultative Committee had the matter in hand, with Mr. Dunbabin adding that through the Consultative Committee they spoke for eight authorities, which he considered carried rather more weight than Newport's "voice in the wilderness." "We have put the points of ample compensation to the Minister, not only for the organised people, like the farmers, but also for the individual. We have also asked the Minister to receive a deputation from the Consultative Committee to discuss these points, for all eight of the authorities do not think the compensation is enough. The question of when villages like Walton will go, if they go, is a matter of programming. The Minister has to consult his various planners for this. However, if it will help you, I can give you an example of a new town programme at Bracknell. Here a new town was built around the existing properties, and the project began fifteen years ago. Hardly any of the old properties in or around the town have yet been pulled down." These remarks seemed to partly allay some of the meeting's fears, and the Council reclaimed further approval when Mr. Bellchambers added "I think the development company concerned would be obliged to find alternative accommodation for the farm worker whose home is taken." Saying "I'm glad to hear it," Mr. Myers then broached the question of the alleged green belt around the new conurbation, and wondered if it would be best for Walton to be inside the city limits, thereby to enjoy the benefit of compensation, rather than just outside, with farming affected and getting no benefit. "One thing I had hoped would emerge from this meeting," he said, "was a firm resolution with some leaders - but there aren't any. We are being pushed around like a lot of sheep. If there is going to be a new town my stud farm cannot exist. In these circumstances, provided the Council will agree to use its best endeavours to help everybody in this parish and secure the best possible compensation, they should go ahead and accept the designation." Yet this was the hardest decision of his life, and Walton could never be recompensed by the amount the State was going to pay. Pointing out that he couldn't of course commit his Council, Mr. Bellchambers said he was nevertheless completely in line with their trend of thought, and after the hour or so discussion Mr. Myers proposed a resolution worded; "If this new town has to come, we ask the Newport Pagnell RDC to protect the interests of all people in Walton and especially on the questions of compensation and re-housing." "This resolution," he said, "supports the Council and I would like to think they support us. If they don't we should elect a new Council who will." With the proposition seconded by Mr. P. Joy, a farm worker living in a tied cottage, and with only Mr. Hawkins voting against, it would be sent to the Minister and the RDC. Winding up the meeting Mr. Hootton considered there was little redress whatsoever. He had been to many meetings and felt that whilst they could complain and offer alternatives it would do no good. Then concluding on a humorous note he remarked "Some time ago I sold Mr. Myers three fields; that makes it look as if I knew all about this town all the way along …"

At their monthly meeting in the last week of January by a unanimous decision Bletchley councillors gave whole hearted support for the new town proposals. This was given in the form of a seven point resolution which, submitted by the Development Committee Chairman, Councillor W. Caldwell, included the suggestion of setting up a Town Development Committee with plenary powers. Yet at a meeting of Newton Longville parishioners on Wednesday, January 26th they said no to the proposals to include their village in the new town.

It was now halfway through the period of grace granted by the Minister for local authorities and other statutory bodies to forward their observations on his proposals. With others expected to soon comply a number of councils had already made their decisions including Bletchley Urban Council, with their unanimous agreement to the proposals. Then meeting on Friday, January 28th also in agreement was Winslow Rural Council, albeit with the larger rate paying part of Newton Longville to be left out of the designated area. It was hoped to put this to the Minister, with Newton Longville representative Councillor R. Davies saying his parish would "rather be on the border outside the new town than on the border inside." As for Buckingham Rural Council although not territorially included in the scheme it nevertheless proposed that the new town should be called 'The City of Buckingham.' The members agreed with Councillor T. Mitchinson that the town should not be referred to merely by a 'tag' and it was decided to suggest the name to the Minister.

Following the annual meeting of the West Bletchley Conservative branch, in reply to a statement by Robert Maxwell M.P. Mrs. Elaine Kellett, the prospective parliamentary Conservative candidate, said whilst speaking at an 'Any Questions' session that if the Conservative government had been in power they would not have had the Pooley Plan for the new city. "What we should have had was a decision 15 months ago. ... It is this dreadful uncertainty which has been so damaging."

By a parish meeting at the Institute on Monday, January 31st, it was the feeling at Woburn Sands that whilst a new city was welcomed in principle as a means of easing the population problem in the south, there was apprehension that if the boundaries of the proposed conurbation were to stay then the community would become an isolated unit, adrift from the rest of the Newport Pagnell Rural District. Therefore it was decided to ask the Minister to move the present boundary running along the M1 slightly to the west, thereby to border the A50. Woburn Sands and Wavendon would then link with Moulsoe and the rest of the rural district, with a natural corridor to Newport Pagnell provided by the A50. However a suggestion was put forward by the vicar of Woburn Sands, the Rev. M. Meakin, that the boundaries should remain as they were, with Woburn Sands, Aspley Guise and Aspley Heath becoming a separate and self contained Rural District, probably included in Bedfordshire; "We could band together in a unit with the same RDC. We have a common interest and lovely countryside, and we can look after ourselves which we can't do if we are swallowed up by the new town." Despite not being adopted this had the support of Aspley Guise resident John Macario, an official of the Woburn Sands and District Preservation and Protection Society, who asked Councillor Ray Bellchambers how the development would begin. Would a bulldozer start at one end of the designated area and level everything in sight? In reply Councillor Bellchambers confirmed that it wouldn't be done in this way, for he envisaged initially Bletchley and then Wolverton being allowed to expand. Reminding that until firm plans were announced no one would know how the development would take shape, he had earlier asked the meeting not to become embroiled in detail but to consider the question in broad terms. Also he said that two points had been put to him before the meeting: 1) that the boundary be moved to the A50, and 2) that Woburn Sands should come within the city limits and so enjoy the benefits of the conurbation. Mr. K. Lewis was of the opinion that Woburn Sands should stay outside the conurbation, for his experience of living in both villages and towns was that the latter could not offer such services as regular refuse collection, road gritting in bad weather and other amenities, which Woburn Sands now enjoyed. This then sparked a discussion about towns in general, with the overall impression being that the villagers visualised another Birmingham, Manchester or Stoke on Trent on their doorstep. Yet Mr. Bellchambers was quick to correct this impression, saying of the designated area, comprising some 27,000 acres; "Just think what you can do with such a vast area. You can really plan properly and it will include open spaces within the development. This is the whole idea, and once it is born I think it will be the finest example of building we have ever seen." Being unconvinced, Mr. Lewis used "soul-less" as the term to describe any new town, saying in newly planned Coventry he knew of one large chain of chemists which, from a commercial viewpoint, bitterly complained that the planners had paid insufficient attention to detail. During the meeting Mr. M. Eakins, an official of the Woburn Sands and District Preservation and Protection Society, asked how long it would take to see a large population in the area, to which Councillor Bellchambers replied that the present plans allowed for 60,000 to 70,000 to be accommodated in North Bucks by 1970, with this to be almost doubled by 1980. Indeed such a large area had been designated by the Minister such that in many years time the natural increase of this incoming population would allow for the town to accommodate 250,000.

In principle, on Monday, January 31st Wolverton UDC approved its incorporation into the proposed North Bucks new city, albeit with an emphasis that the interests of local people should in no way be neglected. As chairman, Councillor F. Cornford said there were five points they wished to make to the Minister.

1) That the designated area was satisfactory.

2) That there must be a plan to anticipate the master plan for the area so that development could take place within the interim period.

3) That there must be consultation with the Development Corporation by local authorities and the County Councils.

4) That there must be a limit to the development of conurbations in the South East as no one wanted to see an urban sprawl into the rural heart of England.

5) That there must be a statement by the Minister on both the immediate and long term plans for the future of local government in the designated area.

Opening the meeting Mr. Cornford appealed to the Minister to provide them with more information, since with the scheme now fairly certain it would achieve very little to come out in 'cold opposition' against the plan. If the meeting accepted the proposal as being inevitable then the only thing they could do was to try and slightly alter it. They had to consider what was best for the urban authority. Beginning a hard hitting speech Councillor Frank Atter, vice chairman of the Council, said this was the most important meeting they'd ever had, since everything they had planned for the last 20 years would disappear. There must now be an entirely new conception of the town's future development, "and before the invasion started" it was the plain duty of the Council to defend the interests of local people. Pointing out that he was a Londoner, as could be told from his accent, he said he wouldn't see local people disadvantaged. As from where this overspill would come he said there seemed a wide divergence between the contents of the Minister's letter and, particularly in the larger daily papers, what had appeared in the Press. His concern regarded the serious social effects, for in some towns where overspill had been accommodated friction had occurred due to a preferential treatment of newcomers; "If we are to receive overspill we want money for it. We must find out what the Minister wants us to do in the interim period." As to what to preserve in the area, he said that frankly there wasn't much worth preserving in Wolverton or New Bradwell. However, Stony Stratford had a wealth of old world charm and from being an integral part of the town's character the Market Square and High Street should be conserved. Concluding he said that "We should contact the Minister and tell him his plan is agreeable. It is better to be inside the new city than just outside. Those just outside will be frozen stiff. They may not think so at the moment, but they will and it is important that representatives of the Council should be consulted with the Development Corporation in drawing up the Master Plan."

For his input, Councillor J. Brookes said the inclusion of Stony

Stratford in the New City had been received locally with mixed feelings, for whilst the farmers and the older generation were against it the younger generation were for it. This was where they would have to live. Pointing out that over the last ten years the town's population had declined, and that the school was shortly due to close from a lack of pupils, he concluded by saying, "Unless the town becomes part of the new city it will be dead. It will become like Markyate, a town similar in many respects to Stony Stratford, but dead except for the incessant roar of passing traffic."

On Wednesday, February 2nd, when speaking at the Constituency Annual General meeting, held at Padbury, John Cornwall, the prospective Liberal Parliamentary candidate, alleged that Robert Maxwell by promising the farmers his "root and branch" opposition to the new North Bucks town had been discourteous to the North Bucks Consultative Committee. Also he attacked the Tory candidate, for "Mrs. (Elaine) Kellett has been pottering dutifully round the constituency mentioning everything but this topic of universal interest ..." (the new town.) The situation had now crystallised and "The big issue in this Constituency is the new city. We could see that with the rapid increase in regional and national populations, we were bound to be called on to play our part in this area. Indeed, the local authorities were making progress even before the South East Study and the County Council's development plan indicated the Bletchley area as suitable for a major expansion or New Town scheme."

After a week of Parish and Parish Council meetings conducted throughout the Rural district (at which RDC representatives were mostly told by villagers that they didn't want the new city) Newport Pagnell RDC, in whose area lay 60% of the proposed development, firmly rejected the whole idea of a city being built in the vicinity. This was decided at a special meeting on Thursday, February 3rd where the voting totalled 15 against. Only 6 were in favour with this being a complete reversal of the council policy some months before, when the original Bucks County Council scheme for a new town, drawn up by Fred Pooley, gained Council consent by one vote. The other three authorities in the area - Bletchley Urban, Wolverton Urban and Newport Pagnell Urban - all welcomed the Minister's plans, in principle. In the course of the meeting the decisions of the parishes were outlined by Councillor Bellchambers, with Great Linford being against, primarily for the protection of its architectural features. How compensation would be paid was the concern of Woolstone and Willen, with the RDC to be asked to try and set up a bureau for 'personal problems.' Castlethorpe agreed with the city, Woughton wished to be left out, whilst Little Brickhill wanted its area preserved for amenities. During a three hour debate, as the leading objector Councillor A. Snaith, of Loughton, clashed both with Council chairman Councillor R. Bellchambers and with other Councillors, and began by saying they shouldn't act as though the new city was a foregone conclusion. It wasn't and he demanded that a flat "No" should be given to the Minister's proposals, viewing the taking of so much land for population expansion as unnecessary. The need could be met by infilling existing towns and villages, and if the plan went through there would be a complete dislocation of landowners, tenants and householders in the designated area. Quite apart from this upheaval he doubted the social wisdom of transporting thousands of people to a new city with its "monorail gimmicks." Declaring that large cities often meant sick cities he pointed out that if the city was built then the industries would need raw materials, with the consequent export of the products causing increased congestion at London's docks. Elsewhere lay large areas of unproductive land more adjacent to a port, and he quoted the example of Southampton, which had "acre upon acre of waste land." "Why not build it there?" However, Councillor Bellchambers pointed out that a new city was going to be built both there and at Ipswich. Whilst some of the villages near to the proposed designated area had expressed their approval of the new city, primarily because of the extra amenities they stood to receive, Councillor Snaith said "I suggest there won't be much of an amenity on the fringe of a new city," and he appealed to all parishes outside the designated area to help those who were inside it. Everyone would be affected, not least by increased rates, since the administration involved would expand. Also the city would just become a base for hordes of commuters travelling to London everyday. People were still pouring into the South East from other parts of the country, and this drift should not be accentuated but reversed. Since they were already "half finished" he agreed with the expansion of Bletchley and Wolverton but said "We must beware of jumping on the bandwagon, lest it becomes a hearse." Also in favour of rejecting the proposals were Councillors R. Sharpe and E. Holdom. As farmers they said that no amount of compensation would suffice to those who had been 'pitch forked' out of their farms but Councillor Bellchambers replied that the question of adequate compensation would be taken up when they saw the Minister. Regarding the sewerage and water supply Councillor W. Beesley thought these would be insufficient, although Councillor H. Sparling, who had always pressed for the development, said the new city was doubtless a certainty. Therefore it was essential that the Council should have a hand in its shaping. By including Bletchley and Wolverton he thought the Minister was beginning at the wrong end, and suggested that the RDC should merge with Newport Pagnell UDC to protect both their interests.

Then within an hour of leaving the Council chamber Councillor Snaith and Councillor Bellchambers again met at the Loughton Parish meeting, where to applause Councillor Bellchambers admitted that Mr. Snaith had "come out on top," and he would of course abide by his Council's decision. Following an address by Councillor Snaith the meeting then passed the resolution: 'That the people of Loughton say "No" to the Minister's proposals.' Stating their opposition to the city, albeit whilst recognising its 'near certainty,' during the proceedings 'hard hitting' speeches were made by Mr. J. Chapman and also Mrs. J. Greenwood, who claimed that the uncertainty of the draft area was placing a "dead hand" over property dealing. Thereby those people who wanted to move because of the threat of the city were prevented from doing so. Therefore she suggested the formation of some form of Householders' Association, by which the interest of the owner-occupier could be catered for. As for Mr. Chapman, in noting the inevitability of the new city he thought the best policy would be to plan rather than have an urban sprawl; "It is no use living in cloud cuckoo land, we must just do the best we can for adequate compensation." The inevitability of the new city was also considered at a meeting at Great Linford during the week, with Calverton and Little Woolstone to ask the Minister for their exclusion from the proposed area.

After a meeting the previous day between a deputation of the North Bucks Consultative Committee (the body composed of the eight local authorities whose territories would be involved) and the Minister of Housing and Local Government, Richard Crossman, it was announced on Wednesday, February 9th that in connection with the Government's programme to develop a new town he would visit North Bucks in early March. Lead by Robert Maxwell M.P., present at the meeting as representatives of the North Bucks Joint Consultative Committee were Buckingham Borough, Alderman Fleet; Bletchley Urban, Councillor J. Cassidy; Newport Pagnell Urban, Dr. A. Clay; Wolverton Urban, Councillor F. Atter; Buckingham Rural, Councillor Hodges; Wing Rural, Mr. Young, clerk to the Council; Winslow Rural, Councillor L. Melville, with - both as representatives of Newport Pagnell RDC - Ray Bellchambers as chairman and Mr. R. Dunbabin as secretary. Giving details of the programming for the new conurbation the Minister said that by March he hoped to issue the draft order, with the New Town Corporation appointed by the end of the year. After the final designation order the Master Plan for the development would then be prepared, and assuring the deputation that this preparation would be speeded up he reaffirmed that the proposed designated site, comprised of some 27,000 acres, would contain a town built not on a radial plan but one that would be a "complex of communities." Included in this large area would be land required for open spaces, and he had no reason to suppose that all farming should cease within the proposed extent. As for their grievance regarding compensation he said he was sympathetic to the question, into which the Minister of Agriculture was looking. Changes to the legislation would be required, and, even to the extent of giving up some of his own department's legislative time, he was prepared to support these to enable the amending legislation to be passed. Regarding interim development he confirmed that the Agency arrangements operating at present in the area should continue. They could even be extended, for pending the approval of the Master Plan it wasn't the intention of his Ministry to put a dead hand on the area. In fact to make advances available for house purchase he would consider issuing loan sanctions to local authorities, should it be found that by reason of the Designation Order the Building Societies were unwilling to fund accredited purchasers. This would be a matter for each local authority to deal with. Regarding this aspect Councillor J. Cassidy, chairman of Bletchley Council, commented; "I think the important point for us in Bletchley is this specific assurance that our own development can continue. Even the Minister recognises the problem of a development within a development, which is what it is. We are developing under one Act and the Development Corporation will be developing under another. The integration between the two will create problems." In other words Bletchley on one hand and the Development

Corporation on the other.

Writing in the month's edition of *The Wagon*, the inclusion of New Bradwell within the proposed new city was welcomed by the vicar, the Rev. R. Russell, who hailed the announcement as 'good news', since it would surely entail a great deal of demolition and rebuilding of the old and generally dilapidated railway houses. Also there would be a vast influx of people coming into the parish whereby the church 'will be responsible for helping to build a new community where the family-ness that they enjoy may be passed on and developed.'

Despite not including the village, albeit encroaching on the area, on Wednesday, February 9th at a meeting called by the parish council support for the opposition of Newport Pagnell RDC to the new city plan was agreed by Wavendon parishioners. This was by a vote of 31 to 4, and saying "Although I am not a tenant farmer myself, I can see that they will be the people hardest hit. They will be losing their livelihood." Local farmer Mr. F. Benson said they should stay out of the city if only from the tenant farmers' point of view. As for his comments Mr. R. Dunbabin, clerk to Newport Pagnell Rural Council, said they didn't know where the industry, housing or parks would be placed in the city. "We are asked to sign a blank cheque for something about which we know nothing." Then when asked whether the people of Wavendon could expect a new road being built through their village to the new city, he said that Bucks County Council would be improving the roads in North Bucks long before a city was built. Being the trend for roads to by-pass villages he said that villagers shouldn't be worried too much about an airport in the area, since Luton airport would probably be expanded to take the increased traffic.

On the following day a meeting to discuss the new city proposals was held at Bow Brickhill. Here the idea of new development was also rejected but only about 12 people had turned up. However on the same date there was a better attendance when in response to Richard Crossman's invitation to comment on the proposed development area Walton Parish met to formulate their reply In fact this was the second meeting, for regarding the first, held on January 26th, it had been felt by some parishioners that this was a somewhat 'scratch affair,' with allegations made that not all the village knew of the event. In fact certain members of the community considered that 'one inhabitant,' who was now abroad, had almost entirely taken over the meeting with the resolution that should a new town have to come then the interests of the existing residents should be looked after. With only one of the 30 parishioners voting against this was accepted, but since then it had become a cause for second thoughts in the parish. Thus proposed by Mr. R. Scanlon, and seconded by Mr. H. Waite, a second resolution in addition to the initial proposals was now the agenda, although before any discussion took place Mr. G. Hootton, the chairman, said he had received a letter from Councillor F. Hawkins, of Wavendon, protesting against this second gathering. Stating that he was unable to attend, he had written that the calling of this parish meeting wasn't in order, and since the necessary notice hadn't been given then any business conducted could not be legalised. However, Mr Scanlon, as the newly appointed secretary of the Parish Meeting, said that he'd posted the notices in accordance with the Local Government Act, and with it being agreed that the meeting should continue the parishioners were then asked to consider the following message to the Minister; "That the parishioners of Walton in the County of Buckinghamshire most strongly object to the choice of North Buckinghamshire as the proposed site for a new city. They request the Minister of Housing and Local Government to reconsider the choice of the area provisionally designated. They request the Newport Pagnell Rural District Council to resist any proposal whereby any part of the Rural District Council area is included in any area designated for a new city. In particular they request of the Minister that the parish of Walton, which is on the perimeter of the provisionally designated area, be wholly excluded from such area. They further request the Parliamentary Representative for the North Buckinghamshire Constituency, The Buckinghamshire County Council and Newport Pagnell Rural District Council to use their best endeavour at all times with the Minister and anybody appointed by the Minister to ensure that the parish is so excluded." This was carried by 10 votes to 4 (or 5) and Mr. Hootton, confirming that he had sent both the RDC and the Minister copies of the resolution from the previous meeting, said various people thought that hadn't quite conveyed the feeling of the meeting, and wasn't strong enough. Mr. Scanlon said he'd therefore drafted the new resolution after speaking to a number of parishioners who felt the previous one to be inadequate; "In drafting this it is borne in mind what the Member for North Bucks has said from time to time; what the Chairman of the County Council has said from time to time;

and what the Chairman of the Newport Pagnell Rural Council has said from time to time." Thus he felt this resolution really reflected the feeling of the previous meeting, but Mr. P. Monk said "Surely this contradicts the last resolution?" Another speaker pointed out that 29 had voted for the resolution and one against at the last meeting, to which Mr. Scanlon said "This is further to that resolution. We can add to it." Another voice called out to say that the parishioners were being made to look "a lot of idiots," and when Mr. Monk said they didn't want to be left just outside Mr. Scanlon replied that it was a matter of opinion whether to be just in or just out, warning that it should not be assumed that immediately the area was designated they would get compensation within 24 hours or even six months. They would have to put up with disturbance for many years, and there would be no compensation until the development corporation decided to develop Walton. That might be 20 years hence. Also they shouldn't overlook the possibility that business men in the 'city' would consider it desirable to live just outside, and be prepared to pay for it. Of the opinion that their inclusion was practically certain, Mr. Monk said it was on these grounds that they must fight, and saying that he didn't entirely disagree Mr. Scanlon said there would be no hope at all unless they adopted this form of resolution. The parishes in the area had to reject it as a whole and form a joint committee when it came to the public inquiry.

As the County Council representative, Mr. F. Menday said they should attempt to go all out for compensation on the assumption that "this city is already here or more or less here." He held that Mr. Scanlon's point of property being worth more 'just outside' was very debatable, and they shouldn't be led astray by the thought that any fortunes were going to be made. "It will be very unpleasant here for the next 20 years. As I see it lots of the small villages will be the last things to be taken. They will attempt to leave these as open spaces. I think we shall see, in the very near future, the Pooley plan will come very much back into its own. There will be a cluster of industry and a cluster of houses and they will come back to the villages for open spaces. I wouldn't be too worried in a place like Walton." In fact he thought those with the most concern were property owners who might want to move out of the area. Of the opinion that the area as a whole did not want the city, Mr. Scanlon said that now was the proper time to make this point, and if they objected there was just a faint hope they would not get it. He was quite sure that Walton would likely to be last, and if they were at the end of the line then compensation would also be at the end of the line. With the meeting coming to a close he then called for any more comments, but none were forthcoming.

It was now apparent that on Friday, March 11th the Minister of Housing, Richard Crossman, would visit North Bucks to discuss the proposed development with local authorities and ascertain their views. It seemed that only Bletchley and Wolverton, the two towns which were left out of the Pooley plan, were in favour, with Wavendon and Walton as the latest to join the opposition, all the other interested parties backing Newport Pagnell RDC's "No" to the plan. As for the question of compensation, the secretary for the Country Landowners' Association in the region, Major P. Duncombe, said they intended to press the Minister for adequate recompense for any owner occupier who became dispossessed through the building of a new town. As with the NFU his Association was urgently aware that better compensation was also needed for the tenant farmer, and it was hoped that in the near future a meeting could be arranged between Mr. Crossman and members of the CLA towards a formulation of constructive proposals. In fact as the probable outcome of high level talks held in Newport Pagnell between the representatives of the Council for the Preservation of Rural England, the Country Landowners' Association, the NFU and the National Union of Agricultural Workers, three recommendations concerning the proposed new city were put to the Minister in a letter which, jointly signed by all four bodies, stated:

1) That there should be no new town in North Bucks. Immediate consideration should, on the contrary, be given to the siting of new towns on common land and heath land.

2) That if expansion must come to North Bucks, it should be in the development of existing towns, such as the development plan proposed for Bletchley - which must retain their identity and independence - rather than by means of a new town.

3) That if the plan for a new town is not abandoned the acreage should, nevertheless, be reduced, and the density increased. As an example the North Bucks Study proposed that the railway should be the western boundary of the new town, and that all land west of the railway should be excluded from the development plan.

The letter also requested that the Minister should meet a deputation from the four bodies at the earliest possible date, and to delay making the draft designation order until after such a contact. However, should the draft designation order go through as presently outlined then the organisations would fight the scheme 'wholeheartedly.'

During the month 'new city meetings' were also held at Broughton and Milton Keynes, where respectively a unanimous "No" was sounded to the Minister's proposals. When more suitable sites were already available in other parts of the country both gatherings thought it folly to take good agricultural land, with the consequent dispossession of farmers. With Mr. R.W. Barrett as chairman the well attended meeting at Broughton took place by permission of Mr. and Mrs. Edmonds in the Old Rectory, whilst the sizeable meeting at Milton Keynes was held in the Social Centre. Here Geoffrey Dover acted as chairman and both meetings were addressed by Mr. R. Dunbabin, clerk to Newport Pagnell RDC.

In addition to the existing eight, another local authority now wished to be represented on the North Bucks Consultative Committee, set up by councils to vet the Government's proposals for the area, with especial regard to the proposed new city. This was the Leighton-Linslade Urban Council which had concerns about the possible effect of the city on their town. In consequence at a press conference one Wednesday in February the clerk, Robert Cranmer, in speaking for the members said "We are going to ask Beds. County Council for all that it knows of the plan and we want to send an observer to the meetings of all local authorities in North Bucks to keep our eyes on things." The chairman of the council, Joseph Pilson, added that "When we were Linslade, in Bucks, we were consulted about all these plans. But now we are in Bedfordshire and merged with Leighton Buzzard, we don't seem to know what is going on."

Writing in the February edition of the parish magazine, the Rev. Harry Hedley, the rector of Bletchley, penned that the new town announcement "means a tremendous challenge to the church of this district. ... We in this parish are well aware of the opportunities presented. We have already approached the Urban District Council with a request that land be set apart for the use of the church on the Abbeys Estate. This has been granted and in due course another man will be working in that area. The houses which are to be built at Water Eaton will necessitate a man working in that part of the parish. This is all very exciting but it does mean that we must have more people prepared to work for the church. We need more leaders in the various clubs, more cleaners, more visitors, more magazine distributors etc., etc." All this means more money he said, and so with this in mind during the autumn another Stewardship Campaign was to be held such that, "With your help we can put the church in the position to go forwards ministering to all those who are coming to live with us here in Bletchley."

On more secular matters, according to local estate agents the new town proposals hadn't made much difference to the local house property market, for, whilst not being so certain about the effect in some of the villages, they were practically unanimous in saying that over the area as a whole, including Bletchley, other factors were causing an upward trend in both demand and prices. One agent reported that even in Loughton, the approximate centre of the area, three properties had sold smartly 'at useful prices' in the last two months. As to why, Frank Mattinson, of Brown and Merry, thought the railway electrification was an encouragement for people to move here; "What is also important is that the proposed area is far larger than will ever be needed to accommodate the population envisaged, and therefore much of the land in the proposed area is unlikely to be developed at all and not all farmers need be dispossessed."

During the month, in a letter to Robert Maxwell M.P., the Minister of Housing, Richard Crossman, gave an assurance that the determination of the proposed new city would not be made without local opinion and interests being given full consideration. In his letter he said he was very glad to receive comments from the people who would be affected, and as required by the New Town's Act 1965 he was presently in consultation with local authorities. This assurance came as a result of his being informed by Mr. Maxwell of the anxiety of Messrs. C.E. Gurney and Sons regarding their farmland abutting the A422 Wolverton - Newport Pagnell road. As pointed out this included some of the finest feeding and arable land in England, and at a great financial outlay they had established a modern grain drying plant which now served several farms in the vicinity. However, even if Mr. Crossman included this land in a draft designation order Messrs. Gurney would still be able to lodge an objection and state their case before an independent inspector at a local inquiry. At such an inquiry an officer of the Ministry would be present to explain the reasons for any Ministerial proposals, and before making a final decision the Minister was constitutionally bound to consider the independent inspector's report. This he promised Mr. Maxwell he would arrange to be published.

Until more became known regarding plans for locating the centres of the intended new city, Wolverton UDC were now delaying the proposed building of flats in Cofferidge Close and Oxford Street, Stony Stratford, and Wood Street, New Bradwell. Outlining this Dr. David Hall, chairman of the Housing Committee, said that in the light of the proposed new town the council had previously decided to proceed with these developments. However, the Minister had now indicated that the new conurbation would have more than one centre. Therefore it was possible that one of these could be the Cofferidge Close area and so it would be somewhat premature to go ahead with the scheme, primarily should the new flats have to be demolished within only a few years. In fact a call to the Ministry by the clerk had confirmed these fears, with the council being given a definite "No" when asking if it should go ahead. As to how the council stood in law this was another matter, for the tenders of contractors had been accepted. Thus during the meeting the council agreed to arrange an interview with the Minister, so that a policy could be formulated with regard to their scheduled schemes to include the Calverton relief sewer, Stony Stratford relief sewer, sewage disposal works, Althorpe Crescent housing estate, East Wolverton development generally, and the Newport road site.

How best to archeologically excavate the 27,000 acres of the designated area, in the limited time available, was discussed on Friday, February 11th when the Bletchley and Wolverton historical societies met at the Cock Hotel, Stony Stratford. Also present were interested individuals and representatives of the North Bucks College of Education and Bletchley Grammar School, and in conclusion a committee to prepare plans for the surveying, recording, and photographing of all threatened buildings and sites in the designated area was formed under the chairmanship of Mr. A. Snaith, of Loughton.

On Wednesday, February 23rd at the meeting of Newport Pagnell RDC an attack on council procedure was made by 79 year old Wavendon Councillor Fred Hawkins, who complained that the Council's own meeting, which rejected the plan for a new town by 15 votes to eight, and in so doing was the only authority of the eight affected not to welcome the plan in principle, had broken Standing Orders. At the onset he said the ultimate proposal adopted by the Council's special meeting on February 3rd (namely to completely dismiss the Ministry of Housing proposal to build a new town in the area) was contrary to standing orders, since discussion on the subject had commenced at the Council table before any proposition had been put to the members. Further, he alleged that the main speaker that afternoon, Loughton representative Councillor A. Snaith, who opposed the development, had spoken for longer than the statutory allowance of eight minutes. "It was a strange meeting" he said. "There was certainly no order to it, with interruptions everywhere, and I feel that an attempt was made by a group with vested interests, namely farmers, to override previous discussion taken by the Council. I know when we accepted previous development plans they were presented by a different Government and the opposition now might well be because of this." So that a debate might ensue he then called for another meeting to take place, being heard later in the meeting to allege that the village meetings to discuss the city plans - which in most cases were violently opposed - was the work of a 'Tory Farming conspiracy.' Yet despite being opposed to his Council's decision not to welcome the proposals Councillor R. Bellchambers defended the legality of the special meeting, and apologised to Councillor Hawkins if the debate had seemed unruly. It was a meeting which had dealt with a controversial subject, and if there was any idea that it had not been conducted on proper lines then he was to blame. Basically the whole meeting was a discussion on recommendations put by the Planning Committee regarding the new town, and he agreed it had been "a little unusual." The past chairman of the Council, the Rev. H. Sparling, then said that from also having "strong misgivings" about the validity of the special meeting he supported Councillor Hawkins on some points, and - although he readily accepted Councillor Bellchamber's experience in Council matters - he, had he been chairman, would not have approved Mr. Snaith's resolution. Nor would he sign the minutes to that effect that morning. There were certainly people who came to the special meeting with the idea of 'stampeding' a proposal through but others, quite rightly in his opinion, came merely to pass comments. Yet regarding the matter of the six points forming the Planning Committee's recommendation he thought these should still be sent to the Minister. However it was obvious he alleged that some members of the Council came to the meeting and voted without even knowing what these six points were.

Councillor Snaith then hit back at his critics, and stating that he strongly objected to the allegations by Councillor Hawkins, that the meeting and its ultimate result were out of order, said that having consulted with the Clerk before the meeting he gained the impression that everything was in order, since the meeting basically discussed only one topic. Alleging there was still a misconception that nothing could prevent the town, he quoted from the Minister's letter asking for comments, and pointed out one sentence which clearly stated that in the light of these the Minister would decide whether to go ahead with the draft designation. The operative word was therefore 'whether.' "Up till now he has taken no statutory step to start the development," at which Councillor Bellchambers explained that such a step had been taken merely by asking for comments which, he pointed out, the Minister had to do by law. As for Councillor Hawkins, continuing his protest that the special meeting was out of order he asked for Standing Orders to be suspended, such that the Council could vote as to whether to send the six points to the Minister. With this seconded by the Rev. Sparling the motion was then put to the Council, albeit to be subsequently defeated by 8 votes to 7. By this time, interrupting several speakers Councillor Hawkins claimed the rejection of the Minister's proposals to build the new town was purely a Conservative instigation but Little Brickhill representative Councillor E. Holdom, a local farmer, said he was surprised to hear Councillor Hawkins raising a question on the breaking of Standing Orders; "If anyone in this Council persistently breaks Standing Orders, it is Councillor Hawkins himself. To infer that there is any political connection with the Council's actions is completely wrong."

On Thursday, February 24th County Councillor T. Bradshaw, who farmed at Hardmead, said at the meeting of Bucks County Council that "Opposition to the new city is very grave and is increasing every day. Newport Pagnell Rural District Council has flatly rejected the plan and it is a very bad proposal as it takes so much good land which cannot be replaced in the future when food gets short. It is my firm conviction that all these new towns should be built upon a poorer class of land which is unsuitable for producing food. Surely we have got a duty to future generations to preserve good land ..." He therefore opposed the new city proposals welcomed by the County Council, which, the members were told, was pressing for monetary help to ease the project's financial burden on the ratepayers of Bucks. It was also seeking a grant for the widening and strengthening of the roads around the new city area, with County Councillor Stanley Comben, the Planning Committee chairman, saying "We hope to have similar satisfaction as we had when the M1 was built."

With all the uncertainty regarding the new town it seemed that farmers facing the threat of dispossession could find opportunities abroad, for at the annual dinner of the Newport Pagnell branch of the NFU, held at Bedford, it was hinted that they could possibly take up farming in Portugal. Styling themselves as 'international land agents' a firm in Grantham had established contacts in Portugal where, with the expectation that the settlers would teach the Portuguese modern farming methods, the authorities would make land available and welcome any English farmers. Some form of financial arrangement might be made, with the only stipulations being that the language should be quickly attained and, because of the nature of the land, the farmer should sink his own well. In fact mostly from northern counties a party of about 20 farmers had looked closely at the type of farming being carried on, particularly the growing of eucalyptus trees and rice fields, but having been with the group Geoffrey Dover, a farmer of Milton Keynes village, said on his return that the ground was very rocky.

Including informal talks with the eight authorities affected by the proposed new town, the Minister of Housing, Richard Crossman, planned to spend seven and a half hours in North Bucks on Friday, March 11th, and at the meeting of Bletchley Council on Tuesday, March 1st Councillor J. Cassidy, the chairman, told members that the Minister had accepted his suggestion that a luncheon should be arranged at Wilton Hall. The Minister had also asked that facilities for a press conference and television interview should be provided, and Councillor Cassidy had recommended that following a luncheon in the Wilton Hall annexe this could be staged in the main hall. The draft programme for the visit would be 10am to 11am with Newport Pagnell RDC and UDC, 11.30am to 12.30pm with Bletchley UDC, 1pm luncheon, 2pm to 2.30pm press conference, 3pm to 3.45pm Wolverton UDC, 4pm to 4.30pm Buckingham BC, Buckingham RDC and Winslow RDC, and 4.45pm to 5.30pm Bucks CC. If it could be arranged, also with the 'North Bucks Association,' which, following a preliminary meeting earlier in the month, had been formed on Sunday, February 27th at the Stoke Hammond home of David Kessler, the chairman. From being against the national interest their aim was to oppose 'in every way possible way' the building of a new city in North Bucks, in co-ordination with all the other groups and people who were against the proposals. The President was the former North Bucks M.P. Sir Frank Markham, who said that in his opinion the proposals were a threat to not only the villages but also to Bletchley. Indeed, should a Gallup Poll be taken as to whether people wanted the new city he thought the majority would say "Don't know." As for the remainder there would be more against than for. Following the formation of the Association a statement read;

> "The North Bucks Association has been formed to oppose in every way possible the proposed designation of a new city in the area as being not in the national interest. The association, which is non-political, has appointed a committee and the following officers: President Sir Frank Markham, Leighton Buzzard: Chairman Mr. David S. Kessler, Stoke Hammond: secretary, Mr. Arthur Snaith, Manor Cottage, Loughton, Bletchley: treasurer, Mr. M.R. Scanlon, Walton. The association has taken steps to collaborate with other bodies in opposition to the Minister's proposal and it is hoped that a delegation will have an opportunity of expressing its views to the Minister in the near future. In the meantime the secretary would welcome hearing from others who are in sympathy with the aims of the association."

In a special statement issued on Monday, February 28th Mr. Snaith, a Newport Pagnell Rural District Councillor, had reiterated that the formation of the Association was an attempt to co-ordinate opposition to the Government's new city plan which, until now, had only been sporadic. Saying that steps in this direction had already been taken he hoped that a deputation might meet the Minister of Housing at an early date to express their views. Pointing out that the Association was non political, he nevertheless agreed that on the surface it might appear to be guided by political motives since two of its senior officers were staunch supporters of parties in opposition to the Government. In fact one of these, Sir Frank Markham, said the Association was greatly in favour 'of the normal and reasonable expansion' of the existing local towns, but the new town proposal involved taking not 22,000 but well over 40,000 acres of good farming land. Moreover its proposed position 'athwart' the main London and Birmingham communications was very much contrary to the national interest, not only from the problems of traffic but because every firm in the area automatically used London docks. Thus a city in this area would only add to the Capital's congestion. His hostility stemmed from the very conception of a new city, and "What triggered opposition was the publication of the further Ministry document which envisaged not only a city of a quarter of a million people, but said that this should not be regarded as finite since it could extend to Buckingham, Bedford, Leighton and so on." In view of so vast a change from the original review he felt bound to bring public attention to the implications. For example, did people realise the potential traffic bottlenecks caused by having a city of a quarter of a million in this area? The industries alone would entail an extra 50,000 vehicles a day going over the Fenny Stratford crossroads. Then there were the problems of water and sewage; "The Beds County Council, of which I am only an ordinary member except for my membership of the Finance Committee, is saying that it cannot approve the scheme until satisfactory arrangements for sewage have been made. For if the sewage of a city of this size went into the Great Ouse it would increase the volume of fluid by two and a half times - and this in the slowest running river in England and quite apart from the question of purification. From all this one cannot escape the conclusion that from the national point of view this is a very ill-thought out scheme." "I think it would be real wisdom for the towns concerned themselves to give this thing more study. It does seem that Wolverton and Bletchley have gone into it without considering all the implications. If a new centre, with new shopping development and so forth, grows up between Wolverton and Shenley, then Bletchley begins to die. We have seen it happen so often in other areas where there has been new development near an older town. Nor, as far as the villages are concerned, has the Ministry given any hint that any effort will be made to preserve and safeguard sites or amenities. We have written to the Minister asking him to receive a deputation when he comes to the district on March 11th, or if that is not possible, then to have a speedy interview with him in London. We shall seek to collaborate with all other opponents of the scheme, the NFU, the historical societies, the local preservation societies and so forth and are hoping to have many active members."

In contrast to those opposing the new city, at Stoke Hammond on Wednesday, March 2nd a parish meeting agreed to tell the Housing Minister that they welcomed the proposals, with the proviso that careful regard should be taken concerning the appropriation of the necessary land. The village also called for adequate and fair compensation to landowners, tenant farmers and farm workers, with Bletchley councillor C. Head saying "None of us could tell you what lies over the hill. There is no doubt over the last five years the civil servants in Whitehall have made up their minds that the excess population should be housed in North Buckinghamshire. This sets enormous problems. There are big arguments at the moment on the water situation. Some people hold entirely different views to the Water Board." Mr. David Kessler said they'd been asked to give their opinions and therefore they would be wrong if they didn't express their views on the matter. They should consider it carefully at local level and "My own view is that we should show ourselves in harmony with the NFU who have protested because it is going to take up valuable farming land. There are other areas of the country where the new city could be planted. I suggest this is not a good scheme either from the view of the country or the locality. I hope we shall disapprove the scheme." Mr. J. Davis said "It seems to be that no matter where the new city is to be finally, somebody will groan and groan." As for County Councillor Gadsden, he considered that the farmers must have full compensation - "I have done no other work in my life but farming." Regarding housing he said "I am certain in my own mind that broken marriages are caused by people not starting married life in homes of their own. ... I think we have to be very careful in thinking about opposing the new town for we know it is essential these homes shall be provided and that somewhere shall be found for them to be built. ... I do hope that we are going to support this new town and that we are at least not going to oppose it from this Parish Meeting. We have to look at it a little wider than our own area and what it is going to do to our little village."

In a talk to Wolverton and District Archaeological Society, on Thursday, March 3rd at the Cock Hotel, Stony Stratford, Mr. C. Gowing urged "I hope your Society will do extensive field work to find sites in the new city area." He was the curator at the Bucks County Museum, Aylesbury, and regarding the development of the proposed new city said "This area had not been worked on in the same way as the area to the north of it. It was hoped that any important sites which were found within the designated area might then be included in 'green belts' rather than for building purposes."

Parading a variety of placards stating 'Hands off our land,' on Friday, March 11th some forty North Bucks farmers gave the Minister, Richard Crossman, a lively reception when half way during his tour of the draft designated area he arrived for lunch at Wilton Hall, Bletchley. Simultaneously at Bletchley Council Offices six members of the NFU Steering Committee were waiting to present him with the official farming objection to the plan, and when he didn't arrive the Chairman of the Committee, Mr. W. Snook of Bletchley, said the farmers felt they'd been slighted. Speaking at a press conference at 2pm Mr. Crossman said the new city proposals had been well received by Bletchley and Wolverton, and he had the impression that opposition did not 'overweight' support. "We want not only to build good houses - we want also to build good relations with the local people," and he hoped there would be a final designation order for the new city and also a public inquiry by July, with a New Town Corporation to be formed by the autumn. In answer to a questioner he said the city wouldn't have a centre, for with a population of 150,000 a single centre would unbalance the whole scheme. Instead there would be a number of self contained centres with their own shopping areas. However, there would be an administrative unity for the whole area, and by including Wolverton and Bletchley this multi centred development would be ensured. A multi centre city was indeed planned and from his own experience most of the land would probably be bought by negotiation, and not by compulsory purchase. As for the 27,000 acres in the last report, whilst little would be available for farming, excepting on the perimeter, much would be used for parklands and open spaces. Explaining that the purpose of his visit was for local authorities in the draft area to meet him - having within the time allowed made their formal objections and observations on the proposals - he believed this was the first time a Minister had done so. There were two reasons for this (1) the area designated was a much bigger area than usual and (2) because the whole scale of the proposed town was much bigger. "My conviction is that in the past with first generation new towns more trouble had been taken about getting the buildings and architecture right than in getting the relationships with local communities right. We want both good buildings and good relations with local people." Whilst as such there would be no green belt around the area he said there would be plenty of room for open space within the 27,000 acres. Also there could be the expansion of areas within 10 miles of the designation, and for that reason he would be meeting with Winslow and the other parties concerned. Yet careful planning would be employed to prevent any urban sprawl in the area outside the designated site. Asked if in view of objections there was any question of dropping the whole scheme he said "No. My impression is that the objections do not overweigh the support I have found." As for "What about the objection from Mr. Maxwell?" he said he hadn't registered an objection. Regarding the time to be taken for a master plan he said that although the usual period was about 18 months they had to do this in a year. The area would be one administrative unit but with several centres. During the session he was pressed at length on the amount of land to be taken and its value, to which he countered that according to the Ministry of Agriculture's grading none of the land in the area was "top grade." Indeed he thought it true to say that the land came under "second class" or below, and when having to plan for a new town in Bucks this was the best area because of the small percentage of quite good land, with most of the extent not being top grade. However this prompted a call of "Rubbish," which in response to his enquiry came from the Conservative candidate Mrs. Elaine Kellett. "Oh, it's a party intervention," he remarked, to which, apologising for the interruption she retorted, "It's a housewife's intervention, who wants food to eat in the years to come." On the matter of a water supply Mr. Crossman said he'd been assured on this matter by his engineers. Water disposal was a greater problem than water collection but although it was a serious problem it could be overcome. As to why the new city had not been planned further away, say at Denham, he said they had to deal with the fact that by 1981 there would be no room in London for some one million people. They had to move them out and could do this either in a planned movement, as was proposed, or else build in the green belt area. Also it would complete the circuit of such new towns around London. When asked if he was merely providing a town for commuters he said he thought only a small percentage of the newcomers would travel to London everyday, for experience had shown that after the settling down of such towns as Basildon and Harlow, which were much closer to London, only 15% of the population were commuters.

In regard of the comments made during the Press Conference by the Minister, Mr. Snook said "Of course at that stage he had not met our steering committee or I am sure he would have had a different impression. That is one reason we were sorry that we did not meet him in the morning as had been previously arranged. One would have thought that the views of 150 farmers who might lose their land and their livelihood would be the first the Minister would wish to hear." In fact regarding the scheduled meeting with the Steering Committee it seemed there had been misinformation, for it was intended for the evening instead. The morning had been inadvertently stated in a letter received by Mr. Snook from Robert Maxwell, who when later made aware of the issue explained it was a misunderstanding due to an administrative error at his office; "There was nothing more to it than that." The farmers were therefore not informed, and regarding the confusion the Minister said during the evening, when he attended a joint meeting at Buckingham with representatives of the NFU, the Council for the Preservation of Rural England, and the National Union of Agricultural Workers, "I did not know about the other meeting." Afterwards a meeting took place, of which Mr. Snook said "I told the Minister that the members of the deputation felt hurt at having waited for him and then did not turn up and he explained that he did not know about the arrangements. We reaffirmed to the Minister that we were still not convinced that this area was the best one for building a new city."

Speaking at Wolverton on Saturday, March 12th Mrs. Elaine Kellett, the Conservative Candidate for the Buckingham Division, said "The new city is of very great importance to everyone in North Bucks, and everyone is entitled to know what is going on. You would have thought therefore that when the Minister responsible came here he might at least have held a public meeting, so that the people whose whole future will be affected could question him about it. But not a bit of it, he was as scared of facing the people of North Bucks as Wilson is of facing Mr. Heath. Instead he met local authorities and others and held a Press Conference all behind closed doors, and at the Press Conference we found out just why he dare not risk a full Public Meeting. He hadn't a clue what he was talking about once he got off his prepared brief." She said one of her main objections to the city was the nearness to London, by which it could well develop into a commuter city; "I could hardly believe my ears when I heard his answer when asked about this. He said it would not become a commuter city because it is eighty miles from London. There was a stunned silence as everyone digested the fact that the man responsible for deciding on this vital matter was making up his mind on totally incorrect facts. He also confirmed my fears by saying - I took his words down - 'The Board of Trade will try to persuade industry not to come here, but to go to Durham and places like that.' This is exactly what I've been saying all along." She thought the city as presently envisaged would be a thoroughly bad thing, whilst regarding Robert Mellish, Joint Parliamentary Secretary to the Ministry of Housing, in reference to his recent statement that, "If a man is not a Londoner he will be accepted (for housing) only if his employer has failed to get a Londoner through the Ministry of Labour," she said, "What a miserable prospect for our housing queues."

During the month the local planning authorities in South East England were asked by the Ministry of Housing and Local Government to comment on revised estimates of population changes up to the year 1981. This was part of the review of the South East Study which, published in March 1964, anticipated an increase in population of 1½ million between 1961 and 1981, implying much faster growth in the South East. However a recent report to the Standing Conference on London Regional Planning now drew attention to three significant points:

1) The Ministry still expects a population increase of about 1½ millions in the south east between 1961 and 1981, but the national growth now forecast is more than one million higher than that on which the original study was based. The implication is that the population in the south east as a whole is not expected to increase much faster than in the rest of the country.

2) A reduced programme of new towns and town expansion schemes is now proposed and thus more of the population increase will need to be accommodated by the normal processes of local authority and private development.

3) The Ministry now envisages less growth in the Metropolitan Region up to 40 miles from Charing Cross than was suggested in the original study, and correspondingly more growth in areas further from London. In particular expansion schemes proposed in the original study for towns nearer to London such as Chelmsford, Reading and Southend are not being pursued.

As an alternative to the Ministry's proposals, on Monday, March 21st Robert Maxwell, the local Labour candidate, publicly revealed his scheme for 'twin towns' based on Wolverton and Bletchley. The occasion at which he addressed both verbal and written questions was an election meeting at Wilton Hall, Bletchley, but of the proposals Sir Frank Markham said "They are completely old hat. The idea of twin towns have been put forward many times before, both by Wolverton and Bletchley, but what Mr. Maxwell has not gone into is the fundamental question of water supply for the development, and the disposal of storm water and sewage effluent." Continuing, he pointed out that these questions had been raised by Mr. Lawson, of Passenham, at the meeting between the Minister and the North Bucks Association, which now planned to prepare a case for presentation at the summer Public Inquiry. Mr. Maxwell's scheme would also be put to the forthcoming inquiry and with emphasis that 'twin cities' would take up far less farming land than a single vast new city, with several centres, would also be forwarded to the Minister. Additionally, Mr. Maxwell claimed his scheme would not cause as much controversy as the Minister's proposals, from being welcomed by those farmers and people living in the villages to be affected. Strongly supporting the immediate expansion of the Wolverton Urban District Council area and also Bletchley - 'where the people seemed unanimous in their desire for the town's rapid expansion' - Mr. Maxwell said "There is no reason why Bletchley's expansion should not be accelerated on a massive scale which would bring much large scale industry into this town like the motor industry." These would be firms able to provide the London rates of pay and he alleged that from wanting to see their towns modernised, shopping facilities improved, and better opportunities for work and recreation, the same aspiration applied to the majority of people in the Wolverton-Stony Stratford-New Bradwell area. The claimed advantages of the twin city plan would be to allow Bletchley and Wolverton Urban District Councils to, albeit in consultation with the County Council, Central Government, and/or Greater London Council, draw up their new town maps and their development master plan right away, with the scheme not only helping to re-house 120,000 Londoners but also providing for a natural increase. The areas of land would only require some 8,600 acres - about 5,000 acres at Bletchley and 3,600 for Wolverton - as compared to the 27,000 acres envisaged by Mr. Crossman. Such a scheme, Mr. Maxwell maintained, would still allow Bletchley to expand to a population of 100,000, with that of Wolverton, Stony Stratford and New Bradwell increasing to 75,000. Thereby all those villages and parishes which had raised objections could be left out or, should they desire, be included later. Addressing an audience of some 200 he said he visualised a cultural, recreational and sports centre situated between the twin towns near Little Woolstone and Woughton on the Green. As well as from the M1 and A5 easy access for transport would be a feature, and he also viewed a monorail service as being practical to connect Wolverton and Bletchley via the recreation and sports centre. It would also take in the two existing railway stations of Bletchley and Wolverton.

Asked for her views on the twin cities plan Mrs. Elaine Kellett said she basically agreed that in contrast to a single new 'super city' the growth of Bletchley and Wolverton on their own was a better way of developing North Bucks. However, she wondered how the electorate would view Mr. Maxwell's ambition, since this was the third time that he'd changed his mind. When the designated area was first proposed by Mr. Crossman he had welcomed the idea. Then later he told a meeting of farmers that he would fight it "tooth and nail." Now he had produced his own version! Yet even if the new town was realised she held concerns over a recent statement by Mr. Crossman, whereby the Board of Trade would not allow industry to come to the area. Instead it would be directed to the north east, and she was also shocked to discover Mr. Crossman's admittance that he knew nothing about Bletchley Council's own plan, nor the County Council plan for the town's expansion. In fact figures released during the week showed the role North Bucks would have to play in accommodating the population explosion was not as drastic as first thought, and she felt this intimated that the vast new city was now unnecessary. When asked for his comments John Cornwall, the Liberal candidate, said the suggestion of twin towns made nonsense of an earlier statement by Mr. Maxwell that the new city question should be kept outside politics. In fact so similar was Mr. Maxwell's suggestion to his own that he wondered if Mr. Maxwell had been reading some of his speeches.

With the intention to discover and record all that could be archaeologically found in the district, during mid March at the North Bucks College of Education, Bletchley, the first meeting took place of the newly formed North Bucks Historical Committee. This was composed of members of the Bletchley and Wolverton historical societies and others of like mind, and the hope was expressed that farmers would raise no objection to responsibly conducted archaeological surveys in the proposed area of development. Whilst the actual area had yet to be been designated it was the committee's opinion that the field work should begin as early as possible, before any obliteration caused by the construction work. Should evidence of archaeological sites be found then dependent on the goodwill of the farmers the actual excavations could begin next year. Agreement was reached that the Bletchley society should be responsible for Bletchley, Fenny Stratford, Milton Keynes, Newton Longville, Shenley, Simpson, Tattenhoe, Walton, Water Eaton and Woughton, with the Wolverton society responsible for Loughton, the Woolstones and the towns and villages to their north. The Bletchley Camera Club had offered to help with the necessary photographic survey of the area, and with it being realised that the project would involve an appreciable cost the means of raising funds were discussed. For immediate expenses both societies had made donations from their own funds, and the committee had also received an anonymous donation of £1. As the curator of the County Museum, as well as being the Ministry of Works correspondent, Mr. C. Gowing duly agreed to join the committee which also included Mr. A. Snaith, chairman, Mr. G.K. Tull and Col. I.B. Addis, vice chairmen, Mrs. L. Skinner, secretary, and Messrs. Litchfield, treasurer, F.T. Allen, R.J. Ayers, R.F. Bailey, E.C. Cockerill, C. Gowing, R.W. Griffiths, B.A. Kettle, D.C. Mynard, H. Pengelley, Stickland and T.M. Walters.

Comprised of Sir Frank Markham, David Kessler, of Stoke Hammond, Edgar Daniels, chairman of Loughton Parish Council, Derek Lawson, of Passenham, Mr. R. Scanlon, of Walton, and accompanied by Miss B. Trevana, a planning consultant, on Tuesday, March 22nd a delegation from the newly formed North Bucks Association met for nearly an hour with the Minister for Housing and Local Government, Richard Crossman, who regarding the new city development said that nothing had yet been "cut and dried." With the potential of traffic problems it was stressed that the area was too near to London and Birmingham, and emphasis was also placed on the problems of drainage into the Ouse Valley. Commenting afterwards Sir Frank Markham said "The Minister gave us a very, very good and extended hearing." "He now realises the volume of local objections from the three Parliamentary candidates and many local authorities, including the Beds. County Council." Further, Sir Frank said that "The Minister very much welcomed the points which we put forward, and took particular interest in the point that Buckinghamshire, in its strategic position between Birmingham and London, would create all kinds of traffic, commuter and other transport problems." Seemingly the Minister considered the idea of one vast city in the area to be a "misleading concept," and in fact claimed not to be responsible for the views contained in a recent report on the construction of what had been referred to as the 'New City.' This he thought was a misleading concept, for he was more inclined towards a multi centred aggregation. Also it was revealed in the meeting that plans were now well in hand for a Public Inquiry in July, to be conducted by a completely impartial inspector.

In anticipation of this Inquiry, despite no issue of a draft designation order having as yet been made the NFU had begun to prepare the agricultural case, and in a press statement issued after a meeting of the Union's steering committee, held on Tuesday, March 29th, it was stated that in the view of the North Bucks farmers the Minister couldn't possibly have accurate knowledge of an area of well over 21,000 acres. They were therefore determined that the full facts should be brought to his attention through the public inquiry, with the statement further including that "Every farmer within and on the fringe of the proposed designated area will be visited in the next few weeks, and his farm boundary traced and referenced on a Master Plan. A comprehensive record of his farming methods and personal circumstances will be taken. At the same time witnesses are being approached who will study the new town proposal from the standpoint of their specialised knowledge. The final case will then begin to emerge. The Steering Committee of the North Bucks NFU, have consistently stated that farmers are by no means antagonistic to the need for more houses in the country. They are concerned to see, however, that the problem of housing should not be considered in isolation from the still more fundamental need to feed the nation." Perhaps the farmers therefore welcomed the news on April 1st that Robert Maxwell had been returned as M.P. for Buckingham by a majority of 2,254, with the Liberal candidate, John Cornwell, losing his deposit.

In other contemporary matters the opinion that Newton Longville should be excluded from the new town area was expressed at the annual parish meeting by the chairman, Mr. R. Davies. He said that two weeks ago representatives of Winslow RDC had met the Minister, and whilst there had been no official notice he felt certain that the village would not be included.

At the annual meeting of the NFU, held in London on Tuesday, April 5th, Mr. W. Snook affirmed that until improved compensation payments were approved by the Government those farmers in North Bucks whose land was threatened by the development of a new town would refuse to give up their land. The present legal basis for a dispossessed farmer's compensation was a minimum of one year's rent and a maximum of two years, of which he said "These terms are mean, inhuman and unrealistic." As a member of the committee representing some 200 potentially affected farmers he knew this problem at first hand, saying "This threat is a veritable nightmare. The farmers involved were likely to lose their homes and their livelihoods. Many will also lose the chance of ever farming again in their lifetime. ... Tenants in North Bucks are determined to make a stand by refusing to release any land, until fresh legislation is on the statute book." Successful in this intent he therefore proposed a resolution calling on the NFU to hold discussions with the Government towards passing new legislation, by which dispossessed tenant farmers would be granted not less than ten years' rent, or five years' profits, when their land was compulsorily acquired. Then after the meeting a press statement was issued, worded as per the statement at the steering committee's meeting on March 29th.

At the meeting on Wednesday, April 6th of the Newport Pagnell Rural Council, Councillor Arthur Snaith said that Richard Crossman was 'surprised and concerned' at the stopping of development in villages within the proposed area. He added that during his recent visit to Mr. Crossman, the Minister had expressed his opinion that development should carry on, saying he sympathised with landowners and others who would be caused hardship through the discontinuation. Thus Mr. Snaith now hoped that information as to why development was not proceeding would be made available by the council. In response Ray Bellchambers, chairman of the council, explained that all building plans had to go to the Minister for ratification. Therefore, since it seemed to be a case of the right hand not knowing what the left hand was doing, the council agreed that the matter should be taken up with the County Council. In other business, for assisting those country lovers who didn't want to live in the midst of a new town the planning committee suggested that the council should acquire land in villages outside the proposed area. With plots sold to those wishing to relocate this could then be laid out in small estates, and in consequence the council decided that the housing committee should look into this possibility in their forthcoming sites review.

With the public inquiry into the designated area to be probably heard in July, objectors were now advised to give written notice of their reasons before May 16th to the Minister, who, whilst expressing sympathy with those not in favour of urban development, said he was convinced of a case for the proposals. In his opinion the site would prove attractive to industrial, commercial and office development, with the potential for 'good, sound, rapid, prosperous and self generating growth.' 'Most of the land proposed for designation is at present used for agriculture. In making this proposal the Government have weighed the needs which the new town must help meet and the advantage of the site against the effect on agriculture and the quality of the land. They do not think a site could be found in this area less damaging to agricultural interests. It is the Minister's intention to secure building that will take place at economical densities, and that the growth of the new town is planned with full regard to the need to conserve good agricultural land.'

Of an opposite view, at a meeting held on the night of Tuesday, April 12th, the Steering Committee of the Bletchley and Newport Pagnell branches of the NFU (composed of Messrs. W.G. Snook, chairman, G. Cowley, R. Bullock, W.E. Gurney, V.E. Phillips, T.G. Williams, and as secretary and organiser Mr. R.P. Furnival, the NFU Group Secretary for North Bucks) gave their formal backing to Robert Maxwell's proposals for 'twin towns,' and expressed the hope that he would continue to press his ideas at the highest possible level. Indeed it was agreed that his suggestions were very similar to their own proposals, put to the Minister by a deputation some 12 months ago, for the NFU saw the Maxwell plan as the ideal compromise between the plans prepared for the Minister and an outright rejection of any massive development in the area. Nevertheless, in anticipation of the draft designation the committee had drawn up their plan of campaign for the coming Public Inquiry, and as a leading soil scientist Mr. B. Furneaux would advise on the weaknesses and strong points in the Minister of Housing and Local Governments New Town proposal. These would then be incorporated into the farmers' case, to be presented at the Public Inquiry by Mr. N. Wallace, Barrister at law, from NFU headquarters. Already in progress were discussions with experts in the realms of water supply, drainage and planning, for these were aspects which the NFU felt had not previously been considered. Also land use in general, and with the designated area having been divided into six parts, each member of the steering committee was tasked to undertake a survey of one of these divisions. In fact a complete survey of one area had already taken place, with preliminary work commenced on another two.

Then on April 14th the draft order was issued, to an immediate reaction that the designated area hardly altered from his original proposals, despite the heavy criticism these had received from the farming community, the North Bucks Association, headed by ex M.P. Sir Frank Markham, and all the villages and hamlets in the area who had conducted their own parish meetings. Newton Longville was the only reprieve from the original plan of 27,000 acres which, now reduced to 25,200 acres, also excluded all the gravel working at Great Linford. Contained in a statement issued with the draft order the Minister said that over the course of 20 years an incoming population of 150,000 would be accommodated by the new town, with a long term growth of 250,000. As for the town's primary purpose this was to provide housing and employment for people presently living in London, and so to ease the overcrowding in the Capital. Both of a high standard of design and layout the aim was to provide a balance between industrial and residential development, with the provision of appropriate social and commercial facilities. Also issued with the statement and draft order was an accompanying seven page memorandum in which many points that had 'puzzled' local inhabitants were clarified. These included the controversial topics of the part agriculture would play in conjunction with the development, and the issues of water supply and drainage. Regarding the latter it was now stated that the water supply for the new city would be eventually derived from the Thames Catchment area, where new reservoirs were to be built near Aylesbury. Agreements entered by the Bucks Water Board and the Great Ouse Water Authority had already ensured provision for the increasing population of Bletchley, but since these would end in 1975 it was envisaged that new agreements would be entered into, as well as deriving supplies from the Thames area. In fact it was the Ministry's anticipation that the Thames area would supply the new development with about 30 million gallons a day, with it also being realised that the discharge of effluent into the River Ouse would need to be of a very pure quality. Also that this discharge would help to maintain an adequate river flow in dry weather. However, the River Authority had drawn the Minister's attention to a number of issues affecting land drainage. Therefore consultations with the Authority would begin at the commencement of the development, regarding the prospect of which a North Bucks branch of the Council for the Preservation of Rural England had been formed during the third week of April. This aimed 'to protect and preserve pleasant scenes not only in the country but also in towns and villages. Also to watch and express opinions on important development proposals, to safeguard historic buildings and woods and trees and to act as a link between the public and the Local Authorities, where planning matters raise questions of principle.' 'If people care enough about the towns, villages and countryside of North Bucks to join and support the branch, much may be achieved. If not, unwelcome decisions may be forced upon us from above.' The branch would cover the Bletchley, Newport Pagnell and Wolverton Urban Districts and the Newport Pagnell Rural District, with Mrs. S.C.F. Allen of Lathbury Park as chairman, and as treasurer Arthur Snaith, of Manor Cottage, Loughton. The secretary would be Mrs. Margaret Astley, of Newport Pagnell, who reported that the launch of the branch was being well received locally. Nevertheless despite 1,000 leaflets having been optimistically printed it was difficult to presently provide any numbers of membership, since people had been afforded little time to return the membership forms.

On Friday, April 22nd Winslow Rural Council decided to accept the draft order, for the Ministry had now complied with the Council's request for part of Newton Longville to be excluded from the designated area. Therefore it was felt they could no longer object to the proposals although together with their letter confirming no further objections the Council would also include a note deploring the use of valuable farming land. Should any further objections be made then these, said Councillor C.D. Kitchener, must be made through the local committees set up to appeal against the new town. As for an application for support from the Leighton and District Preservation Society, this the Council decided to ignore, with Councillor Miss E.M. Johnson saying she couldn't see how a new town in North Bucks had anything to do with people living in Bedfordshire. Also the Councillors doubted the authenticity of the Preservation Society's claim that the Ministry of Housing and Local Government had asked it to prepare a report on the new town.

April 22nd was also the date of a luncheon given to the Press by the leaders of the County NFU. Here local editors, agricultural correspondents and representatives of the farming press were informed by Stanley Moss, chairman of the County Branch, that "Last year we were talking about this wretched new city, and this must still remain a major part of our thinking at the present time. As far as we are concerned we are wholly opposed to the proposal as it stands at present. We are not opposed to housing people, we are for it. We realise some farming land has to go, but this very nebulous large expanse of land designated now is far larger than is necessary. We don't like this modern thinking which looks to the United States and South America for inspiration in town planning - where size is no object. We feel that the planners should be getting down to a sense of town planning of our own, based on this very small island, in that they should be thinking of development upwards and not on a linear basis. From the point of view of the townspeople concerned, my own opinion is that this plan will absolutely ruin Bletchley and Wolverton and will turn these two potential development towns into little suburbs of a new city." Describing the plan as an attempt to marry two independent civic communities by force, he said when asked how the farmers would portray their case at the public inquiry that an NFU headquarters counsel was presently preparing their argument. This would be presented by their representative and "I think he will tackle it from the point of view of meeting and discussing the situation with other bodies who are opposing the plan, and that he will endeavour not to duplicate the arguments by stating something that other objectors may be covering." As chairman of the Steering Committee Mr. W. Snook said that either by the NFU 'or some other body' the town planning aspect would be covered at the inquiry; "We have secured the services of a scientist and a water expert to put the best possible case at the public inquiry, and we are in close contact with other opposing bodies." "With regard to objections, anyone can object as long as they put in their objections before May 16th, and this applies also to individual farmers."

Indeed, having been told that any objections to the proposed development should be put in before May 16th, a meeting of some

100 representatives of 12 parishes threatened by the development took place at Loughton village hall on Tuesday, April 26th. Here the chairman of Loughton Parish Council, Edgar Daniels, pointed out that Loughton and Shenley had 2,400 acres right in the centre of the project, and regarding the recent conference which the leaders of the North Bucks Association leaders had with Mr. Crossman he said it was the first time the Minister had heard the real objections of the villages. In fact consequent to being told about schools and building projects being stalled the Minister had sent a personal letter saying he was raising the matters with the Ministries concerned. Mr. Daniels continued that Mr. Crossman indicated at the meeting that if their objections were strong enough then, just as Newbury was now 'out,' this plan could also be out. The North Bucks Association was hoping to raise over £1,000 for its fight against the plan at the public inquiry, and as the president Sir Frank Markham, the former M.P. for Buckingham, described as "horrible" the possibility that many beautiful villages in the area would be bulldozed. "I am convinced it would be a national disaster to build the new town here," he said, pointing out the problems of increased traffic, sewage disposal, and also the extensive flooding which sharp rainfalls and the slow moving River Ouse would create in the Passenham and Newport Pagnell areas. Even without the vast number of industrial vehicles bringing goods from the ports the A5 and M1 would be congested by household traffic, and he advocated building the new town on land further away from London, suggesting Norfolk as the location, or perhaps in the Southampton area on poor farming land, and near the ports. If the Association lost the battle then he said their second intent would be to get the Minister to amend the plan to exclude areas of historical or scenic interest; "I am convinced a new city in this area would be an ultimate disaster for England. I am convinced a gradual expansion of Bletchley and Wolverton and the villages is the most desirable thing for this area." As for Mr. A. Snaith, secretary, he said the wording of the New Towns Act was such that the Minister could make a designation order if he was satisfied, following consultation with the local authorities involved, that it was expedient and in the national interest. Requesting that the Minister should now reconsider his decision a resolution was duly passed by the meeting worded "This meeting of representatives of parish councils and parish meetings in the proposed new town area, whilst welcoming

the reasonable development of existing towns and villages, supports the North Bucks Association in asking the Government to reconsider its proposals as outlined in the Order of March 31, for a vast new town in the Bletchley Wolverton area."

By now it was clear that when the Public Inquiry opened in July there would be a two pronged attack on the new town proposals. The North Bucks Association would concentrate primarily on planning objections, with the waste of valuable land as the main theme of the NFU. Indeed the support being gained from all quarters had produced an increased confidence that the case for opposition must influence the thinking of the Minister, an opinion bolstered by the independent experts in the fields of land use, agriculture and planning, who had been tasked by the NFU to impartially consider the development from different angles. Already they had unanimously reached a preliminary verdict that it could not be justified in such a large area with a low density of population, and, as pointed out by the NFU Steering Committee, this agreement was given further credence from their reports having been produced independently. In fact a further area of the agricultural survey into the new town was now complete, with member farmers pledging to support a fighting fund established to pay for the cost of presenting the case. Donations from members of the public sympathising with the agricultural case were welcomed, with the treasurer being Mr. R. Furnival of Newport Pagnell, secretary of the North Bucks branches of the NFU.

Yet there would be no opposition from Newport Pagnell UDC for on Tuesday, May 3rd Norman Hollis, chairman of the Housing and Development Committee, successfully moved the resolution "that no objection be made to the Minister's proposals." This followed the council having been told by the clerk, Mr. F.A. Hall, that the Minister had taken note of its observations that the initial boundary of the new town would envelop the M1 service area, so depriving the town of a large piece of rateable land. Of a net rateable value amounting to £800pa some 388 acres had consequently been 'handed back' but although welcoming the project Councillor C. Evans said he would be happier had the Minister drawn his proposed boundary to the city away from the few houses close to the M1 bridge on the Wolverton side.

Then the following day, now that the draft designation order had been published a special meeting was called to clarify the standing of Newport Pagnell RDC on the question of major development. This upheld an earlier decision to object to the new city plans, and the next step for the Council was to prepare a case for presentation at the Public Inquiry. As chairman, Councillor Ray Bellchambers said the first stage was the resolution and the next to consider whether they wanted to formally object, by which they would have to set out the grounds for objection. It was then decided that the official neutral observer should be the clerk to the Council, Mr. R. Dunbabin, who in answer to a question said that since they had objected they would presumably appear to explain their objections. The chairman then said an appearance could be made by one of the officers or their solicitor, it did not necessarily have to be a councillor, for Mr. Crossman had said that inquiries had developed into legal battles between counsel. That was not the purpose of inquiries and he would rather people appeared to put their own point of view and their own problems. Councillor Baxter said that from a purely neutral point of view it should be the appearance of the clerk, who saying it was not intended to be a legal battle in any way said he would obviously want to be there, and probably call people to explain the matter further. Stating "I would be very willing to co-operate with the clerk," Mr. Snaith in opening the debate said "I feel that the proposals are not expedient in the national interest, that it is a gross waste of agricultural land, and that this value will be shown by the NFU at the Public Inquiry." Continuing, he listed many of the arguments already forwarded over the past months by the farmers and various public bodies, and dwelt for some length on the problems of communications, pointing out, consequent to having checked some figures, that since because of the electrified railway line Bletchley and Wolverton were now "only 40 minutes from London" more commuters than ever were travelling to the capital. This would make the new town a commuter town "for sure", and with the new city's population mainly coming from the capital it would soon be a "London-looking" town. In fact he believed that employers in the area were already having to prioritise jobs to the people moving in from London. In conclusion he said "We regard North Bucks with far too much affection to see it spoiled and we should resist this development with all our worth." On a point made by Councillor Snaith, at this juncture Councillor F. Watkiss, of Woburn Sands, said that every affected parish in the Rural District had been against the proposed development. However, as the main opposition to Councillor Snaith's views 79 year old Walton councillor Mr. F. Hawkins, who from having recently been ill was permitted to sit while making his comments, said "I am not satisfied that there is growing objection to the scheme." In fact he believed any meetings called by Mr. Snaith "and his friends" were bound to be reactionary, and if anyone at these meetings did voice an approval to the city question "then Councillor Snaith would be very surprised." Saying that such meetings therefore had no significance he offered that the only way to gauge the real public feeling was to hold a referendum. Also he thought certain actions taken in the area were being purely done to embarrass the Government - "It is only a matter of embarrassing the Government to have these objections at this time." - and in conclusion he accused "Councillor Snaith and his friends" - a scarcely disguised reference to ex-Conservative M.P. Sir Frank Markham - of making "exaggerated statements." The idea of razing Loughton and other places to the ground was false, and he ended by saying "The idea of a concrete place like the front at Blackpool where there is not a tree in sight is totally wrong. There will probably be as many open spaces in proportion as there are in Bletchley now, and I know that in cities which I know well, like Nottingham and Leicester, the amount of agricultural land left is greater than that which we have in our existing small towns here."

Yet having himself been 'attacked' by Councillor Hawkins, Alderman Walter Beesley, of Hanslope, supported Councillor Snaith. Whilst he welcomed the South East Study, 'with its hints of development in the area,' the changing face of North Bucks had now turned him against the planned large scale development. They had been told that the new development was to house an increased population within the area and so it was now an enormous difference to be told it was simply to house London overspill. Also he stressed the problems of water and sewage, reminding the members that after rainfall the amount of 'run-off' from houses, shops and factories was six times greater than from the natural drainage of agricultural land. How could the Ouse, the slowest flowing river in the country, possibly cope? Councillor G. Williams said he'd be very happy if Councillor Snaith could include in his resolution that if the Minister insisted on building the new town then the line ought to be along the A50, and not right up to the M1. Of the other speakers Councillor R.O. Sharpe, of Moulsoe, who being against the development of the city wished to see the existing villages and hamlets built up instead, urged the committee to "look after itself." Over the last 20 years it had been badly neglected with the allocation of houses still inadequate. In their rural district and parishes there was room for an enormous amount of infilling in places which wouldn't take any good agricultural land. They needed to build up the rural district and increase the villages, for if they didn't do something then some of them would die out. There were very strong arguments against the new city and he believed a new city could be built elsewhere on ground which was not so valuable. "I think they want to look to some other place." They had people "walking around in hard hats" but mostly they decided on the wrong places, and had done so he thought in this case. As for Councillor J. Baxter, the Council's vice chairman, he backed the minority view in favour of the development, saying "We seem agreeable to expanding the existing towns and villages, but even if we do this we shall still have the water and sewerage problem. It is merely more spread out. We are wrong to object, for if it does not come I can see Bradwell joining with Wolverton, and Bletchley joining with Loughton and we shall have an unplanned sprawl." In conclusion, and saying "Let us resist it for all we are worth. I hope the council will lodge its objection to these proposals and make arrangements to present these objections at the forthcoming inquiry." Councillor Snaith then saw the passing of his following resolution by a vote of 14 to 4:

1) That this Council objects to the draft North Bucks new town order as being not expedient in the national interest.

2) That the designated boundary on the east side be moved from the M1 to the west, the new boundary being the A50 Woburn Sands road. (This was prompted by Councillor G. Williams of Broughton.)

3) This was a list of the Council's reasons for objecting such as the loss of agricultural land, water, sewage and other major problems.

During May the impact that the development of a new town would have on local traders was forecast by Mr. R. Blane, managing secretary of the Bletchley Co-operative Society. He was also the newly elected chairman of Bletchley Chamber of Trade, and saying it was all too easy to find the multiples pushing the small traders 'right out of the picture' he urged all the members to do their best to improve the lot of traders. Then in referring to the likelihood of a New Town Corporation he hoped there might be a small chance that they could find representation on it.

On the grounds that it took too little land, objection to the new town draft order was now to be made by Bletchley Council, which said that the town's river line boundary did not give sufficient depth to allow for what it had in mind for the Fenny Stratford end of the town. Instead the council wanted the boundary to be the Bow Brickhill road and Galley Lane, for thereby 463 acres would be added to the 25,200 already proposed.

With an attendance of some 50 people from Loughton, Shenley Church End and Shenley Brook End, on Tuesday, May 17th at a meeting at the Loughton Memorial Hall a Residents' Association for the Shenleys and Loughton was proposed by Mr. J. Davis. This was seconded by Mrs. K. Higgs with a committee then elected comprised of chairman Mrs. Greenwood, vice chairman Mr. Bodley, secretary Mrs. A. Frankham. Shenley Brook End representatives Mr. Tolton and Mr. Groom. Shenley Church End, Mr. A. Bass and Mrs. Higgs. Loughton, Mrs. A. Snaith, Mr. A. Greenwood, and Dr. Lack. Mr. W.S. Johnson agreed to act as treasurer. Supporting all the other objecting parties the intention was to fight the proposals for the new city, and in presiding one of the prime movers Mrs. J.M. Greenwood, of The Wheatsheaf Stores, Loughton, said in explaining the origins of the meeting that it was felt more weight would be lent to the fight by the direct opposition of the residents themselves. Other speakers included Mr. D. Bodley, for the long standing residents, and Mr. W.M. Ridgewell, for the newer people, and with a form of objection signed by all those present it was decided that the following two days should be spent obtaining more signatures, since from previous inquiries about 100 people had expressed their support. An objection on the grounds of "the disruption of happy community life" would then be lodged at the Ministry of Housing and Local Government on the morning of May 18th by one of the members, Mr. D. Gill, who worked in London. By the meeting the hope was expressed that other affected villages would follow suit, with the Residents' Association striving to protect the interests of individuals.

Also during the month Mrs. O. Bodley as one of the members proposed that Shenley Women's Institute should send a protest against the new town to the Minister of Housing. This was duly agreed by all the members present and objections to the New Town Order had now also been sent by John Cornwall, the Liberal candidate at the General

Election. Thereby he followed up his election promise to oppose the plan, with the beginning of his letter worded; "My objections are based on the apparent lack of research, foresight and planning in the proposal. I submit that the Minister proposes to achieve by planning the kind of ribbon development that arose without control in the 1930's, but on a larger scale. Infilling along the motorway and the improved railway is a dubious substitute for far sighted national planning. The Ministry should state clearly whether the new town is intended to function as an independent centre or as a suburban satellite of London. The thirty seven minute rail service to Euston makes the new town area more suburban than many existing suburbs much closer to London. Please tell me which industries cannot be located further from London. The proposed town cannot be an effective provincial centre without the restoration of local communications." He intended to appear and object at the public inquiry, which the Ministry of Housing and Local Government announced during the third week of May would be held on Monday, July 4th at Wilton Hall, Bletchley. This was anticipated to last several weeks although speaking at Bletchley at the annual meeting of the Divisional Labour Party the North Bucks M.P., Robert Maxwell, said that 10 days had been allotted. However he would ask for an extension of time if necessary.

Of the some 80 objectors the principle amongst them would be the North Bucks Association, headed by former Conservative M.P. Sir Frank Markham, the NFU, and Newport Pagnell RDC, with all the views to be presented to the presiding Inspector, Mr. Geoffrey Chapman Godber, CBE, LLB. The clerk since 1944 of Salop County Council, he was now aged 53 and before going to Shropshire had been deputy clerk of the peace Northamptonshire from 1938 to 1944, a member of the Committee of Inquiry into Inland Waterways 1956-58, and also a member of the Central Advisory Water Committee in 1961. His brothers included Sir George Godber, chief Medical Officer of Health, Ministry of Health, Ministry of Education and Home Office, and Joseph Godber M.P. for Grantham. He had held ministerial posts in the last Conservative Government. As for Mr. R.T. Godber, a son of Joseph, and therefore a nephew of George, he provided a local and topical aspect by residing at Warren Farm, Little Horwood. At the meeting Mr. Maxwell said the Government's decision to locate a "mammoth new town" in the division would bring about a testing time for the people of North Bucks. Uncertainty was now over with it being futile to try and persuade the Government to build it elsewhere. "Let us be quite clear on this. It is already decided that the new city will be right here." Thus the public inquiry would not deal with this question although they could press for changes they knew to be vital to the needs of the existing local communities. The new town would be built very rapidly, and claiming that the present proposal was excessive for a town of between 100,000 and 150,000 he said they could press for a considerable reduction in the amount of land to be taken. Also that the New Town Corporation should include at least four local people "who wouldn't allow themselves to be bulldozed aside." Urging everyone concerned to direct their energies "in unity" he pointed out that the construction of the new town would begin in 1967, and in reply to "What about the brick men?" he said, regarding Mrs. Kellett's comment that the new town would be made of concrete, that some concrete would be used as also industrialised methods, but he would "like a farthing for every brick used."

Whilst a Development Corporation had yet to be appointed, a new Special Town Development Committee with executive powers was being set up by Bletchley Council. Presiding over this would be Councillor J. Cassidy, who at the annual meeting on May 24th declined the nomination as chairman, despite two speeches strongly urging him to continue for a third year. The vice chairman, Councillor Frank Evans, would now fulfil the role instead. Meanwhile on the same date due to an apparent 'stop go policy' affecting proposals to develop Cofferidge Close, Stony Stratford, Wolverton UDC decided that to ultimately obtain a firm yes or no to the building plans the clerk should the next morning phone for an appointment with the Minister of Housing, Richard Crossman. In the past half hearted approval had been received from Whitehall but the position was then reversed when the North Bucks new town proposals raised doubts as to whether it would be correct to proceed. Thus towards the close of a lengthy debate Dr. David Hall, chairman of the Housing Committee, proposed that positive steps should now be taken, saying in his summing that "They are not all a lot of nanny goats in Whitehall. Somebody up there knows how this city will be formed and I would take the risk of sending our plans to the Ministry in the hope that we find the right department and get a definite answer." As for the new city, "I would refute arguments that by bringing families here from London you are killing the area. Bringing in families and building more houses is not killing an area, it is opening it up; and if a development corporation comes in - as it surely will - then certainly their first consideration will be to build more houses." In fact Wolverton UDC had decided to make no formal objection to the Minister's proposals, and prior to the passing of the decision in clarifying the position vice chairman Councillor Frank Atter had asked the members if they all fully understood the question, for "I know some people are lobbying for the development of Wolverton and Bletchley alone … and it must be made clear what we are agreeing to. It is for a multi-centred city as announced by the Minister when he came here."

On the question of the proposals, despite his previous comments that the new city was a foregone conclusion Robert Maxwell, Buckingham M.P., was still trying to persuade the Housing Minister, Richard Crossman, that a 'twin-city' would be a better option than one large conurbation in North Bucks. Regarding the proposed development, when prompted by a constituent's concern in April he had also taken up with the Minister the difficulty that some people might face in selling their properties, receiving a reply worded " The Newport Pagnell Rural District Council tell me that while they are ready as a housing authority to consider buying houses within the suggested area in cases of hardship, they do not feel able to do so in the present case because, at the price asked, they would be unable to re-let the property at an economic rent. They are, however - and tell me they have so informed your constituent's agents - ready to consider making an advance on mortgage to a prospective purchaser. I could not press the Council to go further than this. They can only act as a housing authority and there is naturally no authority to buy for New Town purposes unless and until a development corporation is set up. Sales of property have slowed for a variety of reasons in many areas. The best I can do is to see that any uncertainty created by the new town proposal is ended as quickly as possible. The Public Inquiry will be in July and I have refused requests to defer it till September - and I expect to announce a decision in the early autumn." Then on May 18th in response to having been sent a list of properties he wrote in a further communication to Mr. Maxwell; "In looking at the list we must bear in mind that many factors other than the New Town proposal may have been affecting the local property market. I know that a number of local estate agents have been quoted in the sense that that the New Town proposals have had little effect. I do not of course suggest that there are not cases of genuine difficulty. This list reinforces my feeling that I have been right to refuse requests to defer the public inquiry until September. The remedy for any uncertainty caused by the new town proposal is to come to a decision as quickly as possible, and this I expect to do in the early autumn. Unless and until a Development Corporation is appointed, there is no authority that can buy for new town purposes though, as you know, the local authorities can consider buying houses which would be useful to them as housing authorities."

Despite much of the extent being in the Rural District area, on Wednesday, May 25th the report at the meeting of Newport Pagnell RDC that Bletchley UDC wanted more land for expansion raised hardly a comment. The intended acreage lay between Fenny Stratford and the Brickhills but the members were reminded by Councillor R. Bellchambers that "Land cannot be added to the draft order for the new town unless all parties are in agreement." Since this acreage would be required for a more uniform expansion of the town, Bletchley would ask the Minister at the public inquiry to add the amount to the draft order, such that (Bletchley UDC claimed) the town could expand more rapidly to 70,000. However, objection to the proposals was raised by Councillor E. Holdom, who farmed at Little Brickhill. He said that with some parts producing up to four tons of barley the land was some of the best in the country, whilst in an obvious allusion to the remark by the Bletchley UDC chairman, Councillor Jim Cassidy, that "anyone objecting to a new city wants his head examined," Councillor F. Watkiss, of Woburn Sands, retorted "if we agree to these proposals we should want our heads examined." Then towards the end of the meeting the clerk to the council, Mr. R. Dunbabin, reported on the bungalows at Shenley. These had been at the contract stage but progress came to a halt when the new city proposals were announced. However a communication from the Ministry now stated their construction to not be "likely to be prejudicial" in the building of the new town, which many took as an indication of the Minister's intention not to deal harshly with many of the existing villages, which might even remain virtually unaffected.

"If prompt payment of subscriptions is anything to go by, then the farmers of North Bucks are solidly behind their Union Steering Committee in the preparation for the agricultural case against the new

148

town." Such was the initial wording on Thursday, May 26th of a press statement issued by the Steering Committee of the North Bucks NFU, which revealed that within days of members being circularised for funds the money had begun to pour in. "The costs of the case will be very heavy and considerably more funds will be necessary if the committee is to meet its commitments, but if prescriptions continue at the present rate, the committee is certain it will be able to put up the best possible case at the public inquiry." Indeed they welcomed the choice of Inspector, Mr. Godber, for "Those interested in farming believe he is especially suitable in view of his knowledge of agriculture and urban development, albeit on a much smaller scale than is envisaged in North Bucks." As the NFU secretary, Ray Furnival said after a recent meeting that "This initial response is most encouraging. Some NFU members have given well in excess of what they were asked." The public were also affording the NFU much support, from a realisation that there could well be a burden on the rates, a great loss of good agricultural land, and the concern that the present communities might lose their separate identities; "They see that for a country which produces only half its food from the land, to waste productive land is a dangerously short-sighted policy, and they believe that extensive waste would occur in the multi-centric, low density town which is envisaged." A complete schedule had now been produced by which all farms within the proposed boundary would be visited by a 'research team' by June 10th. Reports by the experts briefed by the committee were all expected by the following week, and after then a number of meetings would be held to decide the final direction of the case. It was also expected that additional evidence on behalf of the NFU would be given by individual farmers, many of whom from having submitted their own private objections would be called to give evidence.

Consequent to a letter received from the Ministry of Housing, which regarded the forthcoming public inquiry at Bletchley into the new town proposals, a matter of concern was discussed at the meeting of Stoke Hammond parish council on Tuesday, June 7th. This deplored Bletchley Council's proposed extension of the new town area - namely some 193 acres of Great Brickhill between the River Ouzel and the road north of Galley Lane Farm and Galley Lane Spinney - for thereby the edge of the new town would be brought into close proximity with the unspoilt Brickhill woods. Since no part of the parish was involved it seemed that no objection could be made but nevertheless after a full discussion it was decided to write to the clerk of Wing Rural Council, in which was included the parish of Great Brickhill, stating the views of the Stoke Hammond members. Subsequently on Tuesday, June 14th from being in sympathy with these concerns Wing Rural Council decided to add its support to the objections of the parish councils at Great Brickhill and Stoke Hammond. However, Mr. K.F. Young, the clerk, told the members that it was fairly safe to assume that the additional area was only to provide a Green Belt around Bletchley, and it ought not be supposed that the land would be developed. The reason for Bletchley's proposal was "to enable the development in the Bletchley area to be more broadly based and to secure a better form of layout and utilise what is already in existence" but Councillor I. Gadsden, of Stoke Hammond, questioned the clerk's interpretation, since Bletchley had explicitly stated their need for the land such that a shopping centre could be brought nearer the centre of the town; "I think we should keep an open space for the benefit of the public at large." Newport Pagnell RDC was objecting, and he suggested that Wing RDC should do the same. The clerk then reported that both Great Brickhill and Stoke Hammond were voicing strong objections, and in consequence the council decided to afford them support.

Having been held on Thursday, June 9th, at a meeting of the Bletchley branch of the NFU angry farmers decided to ask Robert Maxwell, M.P. for North Bucks, by what authority he had recently said that the building of the new town was a foregone conclusion. Other remarks by someone else, that those against expansion needed to "have their heads examined," had also caused a furore, and the chairman of the union's steering committee, Mr. W. Snook, pointed out that consequent to the members being circularised 10 days ago they had received nearly £500 in contributions. These he thought showed the feelings they had on the matter, and "It also shows that they are willing to keep in line with their previous arrangements that they would support us in the public inquiry." He said their barrister was visiting all the farms in the area to determine the real position of each, and specifically to discover the hardship that farmers would face; "There is just the Shenley area to be covered this week. ... The barrister tells me he hopes to get the whole area covered with every individual farmer visited by the end of the week. The soil scientist, I understand, will be making a start with his survey next week. You can see that the committee - and I may say this with the greatest sincerity -- the whole of the members, plus the secretary, have worked darned hard in the past six months and very much so in the last two months." The committee held regular meetings about every other week and maintained contact with the barrister almost daily. As for the other points he wished to raise, one was the remark that anyone against expansion would need to have their heads examined. On reading this many farmers were greatly annoyed, and "All I would say is that farmers are indeed alive to the situation. They are indeed alive to the population bulge which is needing additional housing."

Of the other organisations opposing the new city proposals, the Buckinghamshire Branch of the Country Landowners' Association would be represented at the Public Inquiry by Mr. Michael Gregory LLB, Barrister at Law. He hailed from CLA Head Office in London, and the main theme of the objection would be the extravagant use of agricultural land in the designated area, and the low proposed density of population. Indeed the CLA had a number of members who were likely to be affected by the New Town, with the majority being owner occupiers who had invested considerable capital in their farming enterprises.

As some measure of reassurance, prior to the Public Inquiry on July 4th the Minister said in a lengthy statement on Wednesday, June 22nd that he fully realised the character of the villages in the designated area were bound to change. However, he would ensure that the Development Corporation "sensitively integrates" buildings and groups of buildings into the development, and thereby not destroy them. Also that the parish churches of Loughton and Old Bradwell would be preserved, as with many of the buildings of historical interest which had been referred to him by the Wolverton and District Archaeological Society. Regarding the preservation of the rural landscape in the Ouzel Valley, Calverton Weald and Whaddon Chase, he said if these were included in a designated area then the scenic value need not be wholly lost. As for the question of farming within the boundaries of the new city; "It is also intended that the development will avoid the permanent creation of large agricultural enclaves which it would be uneconomic to farm." Regarding suggestions of changing the boundaries of the draft order he pointed out that Bletchley UDC had asked for the addition of 463 acres to the south of Bletchley. Yet this could only be granted if all the local authorities involved were in agreement, and since objections to this proposal had already been received the inference seemed that permission would not be allowed. In general the lengthy statement expressed confidence that the various criticisms and doubts, such as water supply and sewerage, could be met, whilst on the matter of compensation for tenant farmers the Government was urgently seeking a remedy, and that a Development Corporation would have power to make discretionary allowances for loss through disturbance. Of the criticism that such large scale development should not take place on productive agricultural land; "The Government have weighed the housing needs of London, which the new town must help to meet, and the advantages of the site against the effect on agriculture and the quality of the land; they do not think a site could be found in this area less damaging to agricultural interests." Nor did the Minister think the needs could be simply met by the expansion of existing places, or that North Bucks should be excluded from the area of search for such sites. "The present proposal is not a unique solution for these needs. No single development could be. Proposals for major developments are also being investigated in many areas around London and all these developments taken together will still not suffice to meet these needs."

As for the second main criticism, that from being too near London it would develop into a commuter town, thus in conjunction with Bedford and Northampton leading to a continuous conurbation from London to the Midlands, the statement read "The aim would be to create a balanced community with industry, shopping, public services, recreation and other amenities to the high standard to be looked for in a town of the importance envisaged." The provision of employment in step with the growth of the town should ensure a community not dependent on commuting to London. The main problem would be to co-ordinate proposals for a new town in North Buckinghamshire with the nearer towns, particularly Northampton and Bedford, whose total population would have needs to be viewed as a whole. The growth of these towns and its effect on the adjacent country would require special co-ordination, and given this there was no reason why these developments should create problems similar to those in existing conurbations. He said it was important to ensure from the outset that the new town would be capable of expanding in the long term to accommodate, including the existing population, a population of a quarter of a million, at an overall density of 9.9 persons per acre. "In forming his judgement of the size of area here required, the Minister has had in mind that the development would be on a much larger scale than anything hitherto undertaken in this country, and will present novel needs requiring new principles of structure and design. It is also necessary to provide for the integration within the new town of the existing towns of Bletchley, Wolverton and Stony Stratford. The intention is to secure that building will take place at economical densities and that the growth of the new town is planned with full regard to the need to conserve good agricultural land. It is also intended that the development will avoid the permanent creation of large agricultural enclaves which it would be uneconomic to farm."

As for a reduction in the area, Newport Pagnell Rural District Council and the meeting of Broughton parish both proposed to exclude the land east of the A50. Excluding the land east of the Grand Union Canal was the suggestion of the North Bucks Branch of the Council for the Preservation of Rural England, whilst Whaddon Parish Council, the Winslow Branch of the Council for the Preservation of Rural England, and local residents wished to omit the land west of the A5.

As for someone in favour of the new development, Dr. A. Clay, a Newport Pagnell rural councillor and a past chairman, said that industry attracted to the new town would help them and the country far more than farming. As a member of a panel answering questions on the town he was speaking at a two hour formative meeting organised by the Woburn Sands and District Preservation and Protection Society which, attended by some 50 persons, was held on Wednesday, June 22nd at Fulbrook Secondary School, Woburn Sands. His fellow panel members were Ray Bellchambers, chairman of Newport Pagnell Rural Council, John Cornwall, former Liberal Parliamentary candidate, and Mr. W.G. Snook, chairman of the NFU's Steering Committee, and in introducing the chairman, Ted Enever, of Bow Brickhill, Mr. J. Macario, vice chairman of the Society, said the Preservation Committee was trying to formulate some kind of policy about the new town. They had invited members to send in questions with the first of these being "What are the opinions of the speakers concerning the application by Bletchley Council for the extension of the town's boundary across the canal and Ousel towards the Brickhills, which would appear to be the first step towards eating into what could be used as "green belt" land?" Stating that his were personal views, and not those held by all the members of the Rural Council, Mr. Bellchambers said that since the originally proposed area was sufficiently large the application was unnecessary, and he would oppose it. Dr. Clay said that in his opinion the boundary had been agreed, and since Bletchley as a community would cease to exist when the new city came it was up to the Ministry to decide how to incorporate the town and also Wolverton into the new development. Mr. Cornwall said that while he opposed Bletchley's suggestion it was certainly not an established fact that the new town was coming, for he had just received a letter from the Ministry stating that no final decision would be taken until after the public inquiry, beginning on Monday. People would not be brought to the new city until the jobs were there. In another question the panel was asked that if the new town was of the high planning and architectural standard as wished by the Minister, could they expect anything to be done in the way of redeveloping the 'shambles' that was now Bletchley Road. Agreeing that Bletchley Road was a horror to pass through Dr. Clay said that despite his ignorance of planning he realised as he looked at Bletchley Road that if town councils tried to devise plans then they made a chaos of it. Being in agreement Mr. Bellchambers said nobody would be proud of Bletchley Road. This was the reason for him saying that if a new town was built for 20,000 it could not be increased to 70,000 without bulldozing right through the centre and starting afresh. Bletchley had been developed on a shoe string, and whilst in basic agreement Mr. Snook thought it only fair to point out that Bletchley had housed more overspill people than anywhere else in North Bucks, and had to do it piecemeal. Also during the meeting he questioned whether the new town would really be in the national interest, and referred to the application by Bletchley Council for the addition of more land. Yet Mr. Bellchambers in pointing out that all the other involved authorities had to agree said "Newport Pagnell Rural Council has objected and intend sticking to its decision." Also he said that Newport Pagnell also wanted to expand but were kept back as the sewerage question was too critical. The idea behind the meeting had been to start the formulation of a policy by which the 450 plus members of the Society could press as a body of opinion should 'town' problems arise in future years. However, in summing up the general mood Mr. R. Jones, a Woburn Sands grocer, said "The more I hear, the more confused I become and if everyone was honest, most feel the same." He then said that when the original map was first published with Woburn Sands "just out of it" the villagers were more or less told to mind their own business about the town. Now if he was asked to make his mind up it would be difficult. Also confused was John Macario, of Aspley Guise, for whilst the panel had made some good points he wondered if the present local authorities would have any say in what happened if the town was built. In reply Mr. Bellchambers told the audience that "If the existing local authorities play their cards properly, their views will be considered by the eventual Development Corporation set up. We must not take a dog in the manger attitude or they will do what they want." His Council was opposed to the town but his own opinion was that 27,000 acres taken out in one lump was to be preferred than the expansion of numerous small villages into large suburbs. On the actual building of the town Dr. Clay said "We are not going to starve, not going to be crushed by shops and houses and there is no reason why farming should not go on. The conception of the new town is that people can live in places within a mile or so this beautiful countryside and not in slum areas. We are called upon to make sacrifices and the loss of a cottage or two would be worth it." Hastening to agree, Mr. Bellchambers added that the town couldn't possibly be built at speed unless it was started in a country area on virgin soil. It would otherwise be a slow process to start at Bletchley and work outwards. However Mr. Snook countered that the loss of land would be more than "a fleabite." There were 17¾ million acres in which to build without touching peoples' homes in the North Bucks areas, and "If for any reason, farmers have to return to till poor land some years ahead, this move will now be regretted." As to making sure that the town's architectural standard would be of a suitable excellence, the panel agreed that it must be free of 'chaos,' with Mr. Bellchambers adding "As councillors we want to have a say in the planning if possible, so it will be successful. We know the geography of the district." In summarising, Dr. Clay said "I see this as a first attempt to bring people from a dark satanic age … this is not only one town, there are twelve more to come." As for Mr. Bellchambers; "It is an opportunity to house by 1980, 250,000 people in a good environment and see that people living in the area are the least disturbed. This in itself is enough to make me pro-city." From Mr. Snook, "I cannot agree. We should be able to have our new town, but leave the good fertile land for the future." After the meeting an officer of the Society commented that the members were probably none the wiser about forming any opinions about the town. However, the object was to find out what people thought, 'if they did think,' so that if necessary a body of opinion could help tackle 'town' problems of the future.

Regarding the site of the proposed new city, during the month an objection had been lodged with the Minister of Housing and Local Government by Bedfordshire Water Board, at a recent meeting of which it had been unanimously decided that being represented by Harold Manham Q.C. they should be one of the Authorities participating at the public inquiry. "This is a particularly urgent matter for Bedford" said Mr. T. Sawyer chairman of the Board, with Mr. E. Marples, chairman of the Works Committee, stating the same in presenting his report. Their concern regarded the substantial increase of effluent to be discharged into the Ouse upstream of their water intake at Bedford, whereby greater difficulties would be incurred in the treatment of water at the Bedford water works. Thus in his report Mr. Marples included that since the quantity and quality of the additional effluent would cause a reduction in the amount of water taken from the river then, involving the Board in additional expense, there would have to be an increase in the amount of supplies taken from the Great Ouse Water Authority.

As the principle objectors to the proposed North Bucks new town, the local branches of the NFU and the National Union of Agricultural Workers were to present a joint case at the Public Inquiry, scheduled to open at Wilton Hall, Bletchley, on Monday, July 4th. As secretary of the local branch of the NFU, Mr. R. Furnival said "It is indicative of the anxiety felt by those who work on the land at the sterilisation of agriculture which is likely to occur, not only within the new town boundary, but also beyond." The costs for presenting their case had been cleared in advance and Mr. Furnival said "This combined with their (the Inquiry team) confidence in the strength of the agricultural case, should make a formidable objection." In presenting the farmers' case Mr. Furnival and Mr. K. Van Heegan would be assisting Neville Wallace, Barrister-at-Law, and with the evidence to called of the experts instructed by the NFU, and also from local witnesses, Mr. Furnival stated that local farmers had been stiffened in their opposition by the remarks of the local M.P., Robert Maxwell, that the Inquiry was a foregone conclusion. As another of the 80 objectors the North Bucks Association (which had been specifically formed to fight the New Town Plan) issued a statement during the week claiming that the dice was loaded against the objectors, since the Minister had announced that none of his representatives could be cross examined. The Association also attacked the Minister's document (to be issued on his behalf at the inquiry) claiming that it gave no information whatsoever regarding those physical and economic planning principles which he intended to follow in the development of the New Town. 'It leaves objectors "to beat the air" so far as his intentions are concerned.' Indeed, the Association had sent him a formal complaint on this point.

At a Wednesday meeting of Newport Pagnell RDC, the members were told by Councillor E. Holdom that he held grave concerns for the council's housing programme. "The Ministry only seems to be concerned with the great conurbations," he claimed as chairman of the Housing Committee, and answering a question said it was quite possible that it might be at least a year before the council was able to build at all. With regard to the matter the council then agreed a unanimous approach to the M.P., Robert Maxwell, and to send a deputation to the Minister. Also on the subject of local building projects, at a meeting of Wolverton UDC in speaking of the re-development of Stony Stratford's centre Councillor Miss Aileen Button said "It must not be deferred any more, we must get on with the job." Yet the council had received a letter from the Ministry of Housing and Local Government stating that the development of this enclosure as a municipal housing site should be deferred for the time being. Also the letter stated a belief that by deferring the development of the town centre, including Cofferidge Close, there would be an opportunity for the re-planning of Stony Stratford. Supposedly in view of the New Town this would be 'of value' but Miss Button said they must get on with the job, "and if the Minister does not like it he will have to lump it."

Presided over by Mr. F. Watkins, a 'lively' meeting of the Newport Pagnell and District Parish Councils Association took place at Newport Pagnell on Monday, June 27th. This was held in the Rural District Council Chamber, where in five minute periods a panel consisting of two supporters of the New Town and two opponents against answered various questions. Saying the Prime Minister had recently congratulated the farming community upon a 6% increase in productivity, as against a 1% increase in engineering, Mr. V. Phillips, a member of the county executive of the NFU, held that development should be on non viable land, as for example the Yorkshire moors. It was ridiculous to think of housing the nation upon land which must be kept to produce the country's food. However, of the other speakers Mr. R. Bellchambers, chairman of the RDC, said that in order to draw the best brains and the best building techniques the development must be concentrated in one area. Not only was land required but also facilities and services, which couldn't be found on Dartmoor or the Yorkshire moors. Also with the need for the work to be undertaken quickly there must be a crash programme to provide gas, water, electricity and all other services, and this could best be done with large scale development. In contrast Mr. A. Snaith, of Loughton, thought they should infill, expand and develop existing towns, for the large cities were a great social problem. A new town in North Bucks would mean the longest possible line of communication to the sea, and there were also the substantial problems of water, drainage and sewage. The country produced only 50% of its own food and he said the nation could not afford to lose more land, since in the event of a nuclear attack home grown produce would become vital. Additionally, with the village school as an integral part he wanted to preserve village life and the flora and fauna.

Replying as to whether the New Town would mean the end of Parish Councils, and the end of footpaths, Mr. Bellchambers said the present form of local government would probably continue, at least until the new development was of a sufficient size to warrant a County Borough status. As for footpaths, on a recent visit to Stevenage he had noted their preservation and use as pedestrian ways in urban areas. Mr. Baxter wondered why farmers hadn't opposed extensive gravel workings, to which Mr. Phillips said that in general these had been ultimately restored to an agricultural use. From Emberton, Mr. A. Stuff thought that industry should be concentrated as far as possible around the coast, to cut the line of communications and to help exports. Mr. Phillips agreed this to be an excellent idea but whilst Mr. Baxter thought it couldn't be done Mr. Snaith said there should be more development near the ports, at which Mr. Bellchambers pointed out that the development of ports was already underway. Mr. Phillips then gave figures showing the relative wheat output per acre in Britain, Australia, Canada and Denmark, which indicated Britain being well ahead in farming practice. As for the policy of 'supporting smaller places,' this was a concept favoured by Mr. J. Daniels although Mr. Baxter felt such a practice would mean the eventual uniting of Hanslope, Castlethorpe, Haversham, Wolverton and Bletchley in one ugly urban sprawl. On the matter as to whether the new town would be for Londoners 'or our own descendants,' Mr. Snaith said it appeared to be almost entirely for Londoners. The Minister, said Mr. Phillips, had spoken of 'decanting' London, and he therefore supposed the 'sediment' would come to Buckinghamshire. However, Mr. Bellchambers said he understood that when the process of decanting took place the sediment was left behind. That the speakers appeared to assume the New Town was coming was the opinion of Mr. A. Cony, of Lavendon, and therefore was the enquiry just a mere formality. Regarding this the panel members said the Inspector would hear evidence and then report to the Minister. Thus no one could yet say whether the town was confirmed. Also during the meeting Mr. W.C. Daniels, of Old Bradwell, raised questions about transport, with the panel members agreeing that the town would need its own integrated system.

The 'marathon' public inquiry into the proposed new city began on Monday, July 4th with over 200 people crowding into Wilton Hall, Bletchley, to hear the proceedings conducted before Mr. G.C. Godber, the independent inspector in charge of the event. Amongst the objectors were the local authorities, the NFU, the National Union of Agricultural Workers, the Country Landowners' Association, local farmers, two brick companies, the North Bucks Association, and the Council for the Preservation of Rural England, and in opening the proceedings Mr. A. Sylvester-Evans, a Housing Ministry spokesman, read a long statement from the Housing Ministry. This expressed the main criticisms of the draft order as being focussed on the choice of the site, the extent of the area proposed for designation, questions of water supply and drainage, and the impact of urban development on an area of rural character. With the inclusion of Bletchley, Wolverton and Stony Stratford the total area covered by the draft order was 25,200 acres, and in determining the size of this requirement the Minister had been mindful of the development being on "a much larger scale than anything hitherto undertaken in this country." This would present novel necessities needing new principles of structure and design but as for a water supply Mr. R.S. Cox, appearing for Bucks Water Board, said there would be no insuperable problems, although the question of adequate supplies up to and after 1975 would depend on the speed of decisions and development. Replying to a later question Mr. Sylvester-Evans said the Ministry was not committed on the question of reservoirs, for there was the possibility of using an alternative method. As for compensation for the agricultural workers it was his opinion that farm workers who lost their jobs were covered by the Redundancy Payments Act. Speaking for the Country Landowners' Association, Mr. M. Gregory suggested that the proposal to take 25,200 acres was considered "grossly extravagant" but after providing figures of acreage Mr. Sylvester-Evans replied "I think you will find it is not as wildly unreasonable as it seems." Following further questions he said it was wrong to say the plan "came out of the blue," just as it was wrong to assume that the Minister had just taken a line on a map and said "There will be a new city there, it will be for 250,000." A great deal of work had gone into the proposals, with much having already been done by Bucks County Council. The problem of London housing had to be solved, for there was a need to accommodate a million Londoners between now and 1981. As stated by its Deputy Clerk, Mr. R. Hamilton, the Minister's proposal was (subject to certain qualifications) supported by Bucks County Council, and evidence was next given on behalf of Newport Pagnell Rural Council, of which the clerk, Mr. R. Dunbabin, said in his summing up that his Council objected to the location of the new town as not being in the national interest. When alternative sites could be found on marginal land in other places it would be a wasteful use of good agricultural acres. Also the new town would not relieve but add to the congestion in the South East, and cause considerable social upheaval.

On Wednesday, July 6th at the continuing public inquiry Neville Wallace appeared on behalf of the North Buckinghamshire Steering Committee of the NFU, the Buckinghamshire branch of the National Union of Agricultural Workers, and the individual members of the two unions who would be affected by the proposed new town. Within the proposed site he said a small percentage of farming land had already been earmarked for development and would, with the consent of the farmers concerned, be lost to agriculture irrespective of the new town. Presently of the 20,150 acres of agricultural land in the designated area approximately 10,400 were owner occupied and approximately 9,800 acres tenanted, with both of these represented by the NFU. For 18 months the members of the steering committee had forwarded constructive proposals to the Minister regarding how, with a minimal effect on agriculture, the London overspill could be re-housed, "And the fact that the costs of this case have been more than covered shows the degree of support which the Steering Committee has been given by farmers generally." Continuing, he said "The same concern at these new town proposals is felt by farm workers as it is by the farmers. To the best of our knowledge this is the first time that the National Farmers' Union and the National Union of Agricultural Workers have co-operated in presenting a joint case at a public inquiry - certainly this is true of this part of the country and probably it is true of the nation at large. The fact that these two principal sectors of the agricultural industry, who often appear on opposite sides of the table, have joined forces is proof, not only of the unity of the agricultural case, but also the strength of opinion and sincerity of all concerned in the industry in believing the designation order before us to be disastrous." After reference to other new towns he then pointed out that "The huge size of this project is something that the minds of most of us cannot comprehend and therefore makes it all the more difficult to oppose." His submission he said fell under four main aspects. Firstly the information on which the Ministry relied was often, as far as agriculture was concerned, either inaccurate or incomplete, with the result that its deductions were not valid. Secondly, the concept of a new town in the light of modern national needs and national agriculture was "out-dated and obsolete." Therefore it should be discarded, especially when that concept was taken to the lengths which characterised the present proposal. Thirdly the development, which they admit must come to the area, should involve less disruption of agriculture in its size and effect. Fourthly, farmers and farm workers should not be expected to make a greater sacrifice in the interests of development than was required by other sections of the industry - and that if they had to be sacrificed then compensation should be realistic and business like. "It was with the deepest concern and regret that we learnt that the Ministry was proposing that no witnesses should appear on their behalf at this inquiry." He then reminded that last December at a public inquiry into the locating of an airport the Aviation Ministry had provided a number of expert witnesses, with the proposed acreage being much less than that for the new town. "Had we been able to hear evidence from an agricultural expert, the task facing this inquiry and ourselves as objectors, of assessing the importance of the agricultural argument would have been so much easier The sterilisation of such an enormous area to agriculture will have repercussions far beyond any that have followed existing new towns, and we must ask this inquiry to remember that the only new towns established sufficiently long ago to enable results to be assessed involve a far lesser acreage than 10,000." They had read much about the advantage of the site for the housing needs of London but little on the effect on agriculture and the land. The Government seemed to consider the quality of the land to be poor, or at best mediocre, and if this was their opinion then he hoped the evidence to be put forward would prove the area to be above average and first class. Also they would be calling witnesses to highlight the colossal problems faced by those who farmed adjacent to new housing estates, the depression it caused, and the difficulty found in re-adapting to rural conditions by the people who were re-housed. The long term effects were impossible to gauge or assess, and members of the NFU and NUAW were "justly incensed" that the Ministerial statements had so lightly treated the effect on agriculture. Should the Minister be suggesting that farming could continue indefinitely within the new town boundary then he had changed his opinion from when he visited North Bucks. However, "I do not wish to deal further with the Ministry statements at this stage, except to remark that we consider the agricultural argument to have been dealt with very shoddily." "The second plank of our case is that the concept of a new town in the light of modern national needs and national agriculture is outdated and obsolete and that it should be discarded - especially when that concept is taken to the lengths which characterise this present proposal." "My clients have never set out to be agricultural Canutes, to imagine that they can hold back the tides of overspill development." Nor, he said, did they oppose all forms of development in that area of North Bucks, but what they were saying was clear in the submitted notice of objection. Thus the grounds of the union's objections were that the proposed density was too low on proper principles of land use, and that the loss of productive agricultural land was excessive and an irreparable blow to British agriculture. The nation could not afford to lose this food source, and the total effect of the projected development would prejudice agriculture for a much extended radius of several miles. Also the grounds included that a London overspill population was unlikely to appreciate a rural environment, or to be able to adapt itself to such conditions. Additionally, that the hardship caused to owners, tenants and workers engaged in agriculture would be extreme.

From his profession as a soil surveyor and consultant, Basil Furneaux said that whilst it was appreciated some measure of development must be inevitable in most districts, it seemed unfortunate that much development took place not on vacant but on agricultural land. Many farmers had invested a great deal of capital, and "Many of these men will be dispossessed before they have seen a return upon their money." "It is quite clear, that if any major development is to be undertaken in the designated area it will be entirely against the interests of the nation as a whole as well as those of the farming industry if it be in any but the most compact form that can be properly achieved. All along the northern margin of the designated area was a strip of good farming land on the alluvial soils and the river gravels of the River Ouse and on the adjacent limestones as well. Much of this is first class farming land. While some of it is excellent pasture it is liable to flooding. The last is unsuitable for development." In further stating his case he said that as much as possible of the adjoining gravel and limestone land should be preserved, including a stretch where it swung round to the south of Stony Stratford from Calverton and Lower Weald. "While this does not imply that this land is land that should be retained it must be emphasised that the boulder clay land that comprises the bulk of the designated area is farming land with great potentialities of productivity under modern conditions. Not one inch of it must be lightly taken out of farming or future generations will come to revile the crass stupidity of this age when Britain did not value her land." As for his opinion of the 'Twin City Idea' he said "It would place agriculture in the position of a nut in the crackers. It would be right between two urban developments. There would be two urban fringes to be dealt with. I would have thought it would be most destructive to farming." As the NFU Organiser for Bedfordshire and Buckinghamshire, Keith Van Hegan said the basic objection was that the whole plan emanated from the South East Study, and it was his opinion, and that of others, that it should never have been published in isolation. There should instead be a national study and national recommendation on the transferring of industry. George Field, an owner occupier of Bradwell Abbey Farm, near Wolverton, said he was almost in the centre of the new town area, and with arable farming being his main interest it had taken him about five years to make it into an arable unit. Already he had been affected by the new town, for several plans had been shelved due to the uncertainty. Summing up Mr.

Wallace then said that the land in question was good quality farm land which should not be used for the project; "This land, we submit, in this designated area is the back bone of Britain's agricultural resources. It should be for the Government to show that no land of poorer quality was available for use for development. Our opinion is there is up to 17½ million acres of poor land, although I agree we have not submitted any formal evidence on that point." Therefore his conclusion was that the whole of the new town proposal for North Bucks should be scrapped altogether.

Outlining the case for Bletchley Council, which was seeking additional land, Mr. A. Ormerod said the Council had always supported the idea of expansion in the area, whilst of his comments Councillor J. Cassidy, chairman of Bletchley's Special Town Development Committee, said "Without doubt now, and for many years to come, Bletchley will be the heart and indeed the only largely built up and developed community within the area of the proposed new town." Now that the Minister had decided not to accept the County Council's plan for a virgin city in the north of the county but to instead integrate existing towns, and in particular Bletchley and Wolverton, he would strongly contend that the case to be put forward on behalf of Bletchley district should be stressed not from a parochial point of view but from that of the success or otherwise of the new town as a whole. As stated by the Minister in the Draft Order, the main point of the new town was to provide housing and employment for people now living in London, and Mr. Cassidy reminded that "The Bletchley Urban Council have been doing just this under the Town Development Act since 1951 and the population has risen from ten to 23,000 and it is continuing to rise." The proposals of his Council would ensure the ability of the built up area of Bletchley to expand slightly towards the Brickhills, to thereby shape a balanced and well laid out community. "Because it is a growing but existing community, Bletchley has acted as a sponge which can absorb new people and bring them to a full enjoyment and appreciation of their new locality fairly quickly and consequently the social problems are nowhere near as serious as those in a new town and the percentage of drift away is very small compared with some of the new towns."

As Engineer and Surveyor and Development Officer of Bletchley Council, Mr. J. Smithie, said the Council claimed special experience in the field of town development, since they'd been involved in the work for longer than any other local authority in the country. Therefore "It is not perhaps unreasonable that, having already accommodated so such of London's overspill that Bletchley should be given special recognition within the area of the proposed new town." However, in suggesting an increase of 563 acres to the designated area Bletchley Council were fully conscious of the need to preserve the amenities of the Brickhills. Stating that he was representing all Parish Councils and Parish Meetings within the designated area, Mr. A. Owen in appearing on behalf of the North Bucks Association said "I am told I represent some 3,000 individuals." From the meeting of a delegation of the Association with the Minister earlier in the year they understood he had an open mind on the new town, but now with the issue of the draft designation Mr. Owen said "I must tell you there is a great deal of disquiet and anxiety amongst the objectors to this affect - that the decision has already been made." "It does not help matters and the fears are not dispelled when you get a local Member of Parliament, the member for this constituency who happens to be a member of the party which is the Government, recently making a categorical statement in the Press - and, as far as I know, never denied by him - that the Government had already taken a decision to set up the new city in this area." In fact the Minister had given his 'open mind' assurance after this publication, but the Inspector countered "I would not be wasting my time here. I have other things to do. The frolics of individual irresponsible politicians mean nothing to me." Mr. Owen then continued "As you know, the suggestion for a new town at Bletchley was put forward in the South East Study. This Study was concerned amongst other things with the probability of an increase in the population of South East England by approximately three and a half million. The South East Study had said it must all be subject to very careful detailed examination. No one at that stage could say whether the suggestion for a new town would survive detailed examination. Before deciding on a site for the scheme there would obviously have to be detailed examination. It was vital. Where is it?" In fact the previous day he had asked Mr. Sylvester-Evans this question, to be told that the detailed examination had been undertaken by his staff, and the only published matter was in the Memorandum. This was where the real uneasiness and disquiet of the objections arose, said Mr. Owen. "We have a feeling there is a political undertone in this way. It is common knowledge that the Minister has been attacked many times for failing to keep up with the number of houses promised, either here or there." Of course everybody wanted new houses but the proposals must not be put in the context of just obtaining another housing figure. There was a strong case for opening up and developing stretches of the British Isles which were under populated and under used, and the case he was forwarding consisted of two parts; "The proposals for a new city of a quarter of a million people at Bletchley are fundamentally wrong and cannot be justified. ... When a new city was to be built, careful consideration had to be given in relation to other centres of population," which he mentioned as being Birmingham and London.

As one of the experts called by the North Bucks Association, being a Chartered Town Planner and Senior Lecturer in Town Planning at the University of London, as well as President of the Town Planning Institute, Lewis Bingham Keeble said a plan he'd produced was an attempt to supply the preliminary work for producing an outline regional scheme. He thought the essential thing, which had never been revealed in any official reports, was to research the amount of land in south east England which, having regard to the forecast of a very large population, could be regarded as suitable for development. The impossibility of doing this at an early stage in any great detail became obvious and he therefore decided that the only practical undertaking was to make a blanket assessment of the total land available for development, on the assumption of 20 persons to the acre as an overall density for developed land. Following further explanations he then said that in his opinion there was no possible doubt that the estimated land needs of south east England could be easily met without creating a new city of a quarter of a million at Bletchley. Having conducted associated research, a lady town planner confirmed this view, saying "As a result of the quite wide investigations that I have undertaken in connection with the Bletchley inquiry, there is no doubt in my mind that it is an ill conceived project and should not be proceeded with."

On behalf of two Loughton residents - Mr. McCorquodale and James Marchant, a Bletchley solicitor - it was submitted by Charles Kelly that there was no need for "a new town here at all." If there had to be a new town then it should not be placed in this very pleasant area but somewhere else. As to why the area had been chosen in preference to any other he submitted that Mr. Sylvester-Evans had produced no evidence, and said "We have merely been told that the Minister in his

166

wisdom has decided that North Bucks should fall under the axe." In giving his evidence Mr. Marchant said that country life was something he would not wish to give up. No other style would be acceptable and if the draft designation was made into an order "It had occurred to him that he might emigrate." Villagers had been quite unanimous in opposing any scheme of the kind envisaged for a city, and "The feelings of the inhabitants is that anything of this kind would be deplorable."

Elsewhere, speaking at the meeting of Newport Pagnell UDC, Dr. A. Clay in referring to the town's new sewage system said that with the prospect of a New City it would be wrong to spend much money on a sewage scheme. "This expenditure will only last a few years and until central sewers can be used, if and when a New City comes. I think you will see no town can afford such an expenditure. The public will realise that it is not the Council's lack of a sewage scheme, but we must wait for a New City sewage scheme. We must have faith on future projects of the town."

On Thursday, July 7th the fourth day of the Public Inquiry opened with evidence given by Edgar Daniels, chairman of Loughton Parish Council. Reaffirming the objections to the proposals as being a waste of agricultural land, an increase in the congestion of the south east, and the costs to solve the problems of water supply, drainage and sewage, he said "But most important from the villagers' viewpoint it would change the face and character of the area, destroy its rural charm and alter the way of life of the inhabitants who have chosen to live in a rural area. This could mean that that many people who have chosen retirement in a really rural village will now be faced with the problem of whether or not to move to another area if this giant colossus eventually descends upon our village." Mrs. J. Greenwood, appearing on behalf of the Residents' Association of Loughton and the Shenleys, and also on behalf of herself and her husband, said she'd met only one or two isolated cases where there was not wholehearted objection to the new town, and to laughter remarked "I think one or two ladies wanted their husbands to give up agricultural work and thought it was the only way to do it." She said even the younger people were against the proposals, adding that the aim of the Government should be to attract people to other parts of the country, where industry was badly needed. Regarding her own objection she explained that she and her husband had a store which offered a full service, and if a shopping centre was established in close proximity they could be in a serious position. If a new town was to come then Robert Guy Alexander, the honorary secretary of the Bucks branch of the Council for the Preservation of Rural England, said that the Government must be guided by the principles stated in the recent White Paper *Leisure in the Countryside*. In part this stated that the Government should be concerned not only with the development of the national economy but also with the location of employment and population, such that new towns could be located in areas where it was pleasant to live. He had been requested by his committee to urge that regarding North Bucks the first priority in all planning should be the economical use of land. As chairman of the branch Patricia Allen said that in terms of living and acute shortage of labour they thought the proposed vast urban development would merely add to the problems "of this over populated south eastern part of the country." "We consider that it would be a grave loss to the nation if all this were to vanish as most of it inevitably will if such vast urban development takes place."

Appearing for the Radcliffe Trust, Michael Mann said the estate, being the second largest in the designated area, comprised 1,782 acres; "I think we are beaten by a short head by the Merchant Venturers of Bristol." There were six farms and three parcels of allotments, and their objection centred on the designated area being extravagant in extent, 'and in particular that the inclusion of their land was a contravention of established and beneficial planning principles.' Presently a green belt was provided by the estate which they asked should be retained. However, not necessarily for all time, since 'when genuinely and properly needed' they would be willing to sell parts to the Development Corporation. The trustees, he said, were concerned at the position of the tenants. Over many years it had been the policy of the Estate to accept a tenant's son as his successor, by which "This policy has, of course, removed the uncertainty which is one of the main worries of an agricultural tenant, the security of succession in the family." Thus on the general grounds of his previous reference he asked for the estate to be excluded.

Speaking on behalf of Miss Stella Uthwatt of Great Linford, and also Great Linford Parish Council, Mr. A. Shaw said that if the town was realised then the number of acres in relation to the people to be accommodated would be "astronomical." Therefore he claimed there was no need to include the village in the area simply to retain control, and it should be excluded from the designation. For the Calverton

Resident's Association, Mr. Wallace said all the residents supported the objection "Because Calverton is the genuine article. It is no pseudo village predominantly inhabited by the executive class escaping from the mad rush of city life. ... The church and the manor have been in Calverton from Domesday and perhaps even before. This village is a veritable jewel of historic and scenic interest and to take it for development would be sheer administrative Philistinism." As chairman of Whaddon Parish Council, for his particular aspect Mr. W.T. Taylor said the objections were based on the unanimous views of a meeting representative of the whole parish. The Ministry had classed the land as being of negative value but they disagreed and viewed the proposals as "sheer madness." The tax payers would strongly object, and in his own parish they would have fast, heavy traffic passing through one of their largest built up areas. From Home Farm, Hardmead, Mr. T.J. Bradshaw, a member of Bucks County Council and chairman of the North Bucks district committee of the Buckinghamshire Agricultural Executive Committee, said he was certain that the land in the proposal was "of tremendous food producing potential." The country could not afford to lose the agriculture found in the designated area, and "I object to the proposed North Bucks new town on the grounds that it would be a gross waste of agricultural land and that sufficient consideration has not been given to the requirements of food for the coming generations."

John Cornwall, former Liberal Parliamentary candidate for North Bucks, based his objections not so much on technicalities but more on human grounds and the fundamentals involved; "I don't question the Minister's judgement on the information that he was given when he made the draft designation order, but I do question that he was adequately advised on some basic information." Also he was not convinced that the Minister had been fully informed about the tendency of ribbon development on a massive scale, which the proposal would imply; "I feel we have something here very useful for recreation and the general health and well being of the country which it would be a bad thing to sacrifice provided, of course, that a sensible alternative can be found." (Having fought the North Bucks constituency for the Liberals at the March General Election, when the party polled 4,914 votes and he forfeited his deposit, in September his re-adoption as prospective Parliamentary candidate would be announced.)

Of the individual objectors Mr. W.J. Jones, of Furtho Manor, had concerns regarding Manor Farm, Woolstone, the purchase of which was to accommodate his family members. Presently his 30 year old son was the occupant but "Now he is to be thrown out against his will." In reply Mr. Sylvester-Evans said that if the proposals for the new town area went through then the Minister would set up a Development Corporation. This would approach landowners to negotiate a price but if this was refused a Compulsory Purchase Order could be sought. However, the Corporations were instructed to be as sympathetic as possible regarding extra discretionary payments. These were possible under the present law, and he added that the NFU and Country Landowners' Association were currently holding discussions with the Government about altering the law regarding compensation for tenant farmers. In fact as a member of the Country Landowners' Association, George Pitcher, of Seeleys Farm, Beaconsfield, was one of the 80 objectors to the proposed New Town, and told the Public Inquiry that since all his land was near to built up areas the production of food was greatly prejudiced by trespassing, vandalism, stealing and mischief making. Giving many examples of the problems and instances he said "In my opinion, judging from my own experience, farming adjacent to a new town of 250,000 people would be extremely difficult and probably uneconomic, unless the farm land was protected by physical barriers adequate to prevent or discourage trespassing by the inhabitants of the town."

Saying that in his opinion the building of the new town would cause considerable damage to the farm, Mr. A.J. Cony of Lavendon Mill, Olney, appeared on behalf of his mother, and expressed concern that heavy rain would cause flooding if the town was built. Also that since they had fishing rights he felt the value would be considerably reduced from sewage effluent entering the river. In conclusion the hearing was then adjourned until Monday, when an evening session would be held for those objectors unable to attend during the day. Thus on Monday, July 11th, following evidence given by Eric Burton, Estates Manager of the London Brick Company, during the morning session the possibility of another public inquiry - this time into a 'master plan' for the scheme - was referred to by Mr. A. Sylvester-Evans, the Housing Ministry's representative, who said "It would be the Minister's intention and, I am sure, the Development Corporation's, to give every publicity to the Master Plan and, if necessary, to hold a public inquiry into it." Then after the Inspector had expressed thanks for all the arrangements that had been made, including the use of Wilton Hall, Mr. A. Ormerod, who appeared for Bletchley Council, said they were grateful for his kind remarks, and on behalf of the counsel who had appeared at the inquiry thanked him for being in the "hot seat." Also for the way the inquiry had been conducted. Whilst various reasons had been expounded to exclude parts of the area from the new town no one, said Mr. Ormerod, had suggested the exclusion of Bletchley, the success of which under the Town Development Act had been such that all the organisations, including the NFU and the Country Landowners' Association, had to a greater or lesser extent agreed that the town was doing a good job, 'and that in itself it ought to develop.' Apart from Newport Pagnell no other authority except Bletchley Council had seen fit to appear before the Inspector. Indeed, they hoped their attendance had demonstrated throughout the inquiry their determination to develop 'along the right lines.' Also he thought that during the inquiry everyone seemed to agree that North Bucks did not have a 'Divine right' to be totally excluded from trying to solve 'this acute problem of London.' On behalf of the NFU, Mr. W. Snook then thanked Mr. Sylvester-Evans and also the Inspector, who expressing thanks on both their behalf for the appreciative comments said he would submit his report to the Housing Minister. This if possible would be prior to August, and there were smiles when having asked if any more objectors wished to be heard he said "I have only five lines left in my note book, but I have another note book."

One of the main concerns regarding the proposed new town was the question of a water supply but published during the fourth week of July the annual report for 1965-66 of the Bucks Water Board stated their readiness to meet the expected growth within the next few years. Provisional agreement had already been reached with the Great Ouse Authority for a bulk supply from that Authority's reservoir at Ampthill, and a geological survey of two potential reservoir sites, one near Waddesdon and one near Whitchurch, had now been commenced.

In early August, at a meeting of Bletchley Council tribute to the way that Mr. A.W. Ormerod had conducted their case at the recent New Town Inquiry was paid by Councillor J. Cassidy, who, as chairman of the Special Development Committee, said it was significant that of all the objections nobody had objected to the development of the town. Yet despite the prospects of development the production of bricks at the Bletchley works of Flettons would cease on September 30th, with the firm claiming this to be in view both of the present financial situation and the belief that for some time there would be a continuing decline in demand. Earlier in the year the night shift had been stopped with about 40 men laid off, and now over a period of time a further 70 were to be laid off, with 31 employees having already been given a month's notice. Nevertheless the works was to be kept in order, with a view to restarting whenever possible. Comprised of two large kilns of two chimneys each, at Water Eaton the firm had been operating since 1945, and in recent times all the clay had been brought to the works by road from the firm's pit at Loughton. However there was also a small reserve at Water Eaton.

At their monthly meeting on Tuesday, September 6th, Mr. F. Hall, clerk to Newport Pagnell UDC, said that the North Bucks Branch of NALGO would shortly be entertaining Robert Mellish, Under Secretary at the Ministry of Housing and Local Government. Including the site of the proposed new city, during the afternoon he would visit various parts of North Bucks and then be a guest in the evening at a dinner at Bletchley. As for the new Housing Minister, there was now a strong rumour that Anthony Greenwood would make a positive reference to the exact site of the new town on Friday, October 21st, when he was due to open the new £1m Bucks County Council office block at Aylesbury. Dependant on the weather, for an hour he would also view the county from the air and no doubt take an especial interest in the North Bucks area for, in a private interview with Robert Maxwell, he said that despite the country's economic situation there would be no delay in plans for the proposed new city in his constituency.

Perhaps stating the obvious, at the meeting of the North Bucks Licensed Victuallers' Association on Tuesday, October 25th the chairman, Frank Bowman, said if there was to be a quarter million population somewhere in the Bletchley, Wolverton, Stony Stratford area there was obviously going to be a lot of new pubs. However he hoped there would be sites for 'free houses' in the new city area, for this would make for more proper competition within the licensed trade; "I think we should start now, and say we do hope the authorities just don't allow these sites in them to brewers ad-lib. I do hope they will allow free enterprise and leave room for free houses too, and make for proper competition."

In the first week of November it was stated by a spokesman for the Housing Ministry in London that no date had yet been fixed for an announcement regarding the new town, with it being unlikely that any announcement would be made in Parliament. Yet despite no official decision Bucks County Council seemed to view the city as being inevitable, for it was stated in its memorandum of evidence to the Royal Commission on Local Government; "In the north there are large agricultural areas with three or four small and medium sized towns. It is in this area that a new town of 150,000 inhabitants, probably growing to 250,000, is to be built to take overspill from London and later from the south of the county." "As an illustration of the balance which is to be found in such a varied county may be mentioned the fact that the County Council not merely accepted, but themselves suggested, the new town in the north as an alternative to further widespread development in the south where pressures on the fine countryside are already great." Yet understandably the farmers were still pressing for information and Mr. R.P. Furnival, the NFU Group Secretary, said that having written to Mr. A. Sylvester-Evans (who had spoken for the Housing Minister at the recent public inquiry into the new city proposals) he was hoping to have a reply on the updated situation at their annual dinner. This was held on the evening of Wednesday, November 16th with the view of Stanley Moss, the NFU's county chairman, being that the Government had "sat upon" the new city report for so long. This was endorsed by Robert Maxwell, who said promises both private and public had been made to him that a decision on how much of the 27,000 acres of North Bucks would actually be taken for the new city would be announced by October. In fact as recently as the previous Friday he had re-raised the question, only to again be told both publicly and privately that a statement would be made by the middle of this month. However, "I am sorry to tell you now, that promise is not going to be lived up to." Indeed he didn't think much of "the learned gentleman" who held the inquiry but "he does not think much of me either." As for the initial reason for the delay, Mr. Maxwell thought this was due to Mr. Crossman, who had been the Minister of Housing at the time of the inquiry, having now been made Leader of the House. Thus with the appointment of a new Housing Minister the Civil Service had procrastinated, arguing that it was unfair for a new Minister to decide too hastily upon such a weighty matter - especially one involving thousands of people, and millions of pounds of public expenditure. Mr. Maxwell accepted there might be four weeks delay, but those four weeks were up next week and he had now been told that a statement could not be made even then. At this a voice called out "shame," to which he agreed, saying he didn't intend to just accept it. Being stalled by such uncertainty was not only unfair to people but also harmful, and he thought it obvious that the government had differences of opinion as to whether to reduce the quantity of land to a minimum, or to proceed with the original acreage.

Speaking of the gross injustice of farmers' compensation he said that when he first took up the fight everyone discouraged him. Yet now agreement was virtually assured. The Government accepted there should be a change in this basis, and not only the hundred or so farmers involved in the new city would benefit but also all the tenant farmers in the country. As for the new date for an announcement regarding the new city he hoped to be able to report this to the branch during the next week, saying "I shall press that this must happen in November ..." In fact earlier in the meeting Stanley Moss had asked "Why this delay in issuing the verdict on the new town? Why should people have this threat hanging over their heads for this length of time? It is an ongoing disgrace. Progress has been sterilised, applications for improvement grants frozen. Why the delay? Was the hearing premature? What is the reason for this loss, worry and trouble people have been put to? Is there some hanky panky going on behind the scenes? The inquiry was held. It was of a judicial nature and justice demands that there should be a judicial verdict. Nothing should be going on behind the scenes."

Once destined to be the heart of 'Pooleyville,' it was appropriate that during the month Loughton was the village to host the first open meeting of the North Bucks Historical Committee. This had been founded earlier in the year to co-ordinate the recording of the proposed New City area, and being organised by the committee the object of the occasion was to meet the residents of the affected villages. The venue was the Memorial Hall, where as the chairman Arthur Snaith in welcoming a large audience explained that the Wolverton and Bletchley Archaeological Societies had decided to combine to record all they presently saw in the towns and villages of North Bucks. The co-operation of people in the villages was welcomed, whilst of the projects in progress a survey of the flora and fauna of the area was being undertaken by Mr. Higgs, of Loughton, with a collection of slides taken from old photographs also underway. A brief introduction to the archaeology and history of Loughton was next given by Charles Green, of Wolverton, who together with Mr. E. Cockerill, also of Wolverton, had not only prepared a display of pottery unearthed in the locality but had also drawn maps to indicate local finds and field names of Loughton in 1769. Before any building took place he asked people to monitor any disturbance, and said that when the new city came they'd probably discover more about the area than they knew at present. Possibly the most interesting part of Loughton was at Seckloe, and following his talk a slide show of past views of Loughton took place, plus a display of old photographs lent by residents of the village.

On Thursday, December 8th during his scheduled visit to the area Robert Mellish, Parliamentary Secretary to the Housing Ministry, said he made no apology for having nothing definite to say about a decision regarding the new town. There had been many objections to the proposals at the public inquiry, and so it was only right that the Minister should give full consideration to them all. When it was announced so too would that concerning compensation for tenant farmers. Firstly at a ceremony to open Mellish Court his itinerary began at Bletchley, where attending a lunch given by Bletchley Council at Wilton Hall he included in his speech that "You may ask why there has been so much delay, but I would ask you to consider the magnitude of what the Government is on the verge of doing - the building of a city to house 250,000 people. There has been great argument about this idea, and a public inquiry, with many objections. The Inspector's report has been in front of the Minister for some time. He has taken great care and trouble, and I think rightly, to consider each and every one of the objections." Concluding he then said "Assuming the designation is finally decreed and the Minister signs the order, and assuming the Minister of Agriculture makes his statement about tenant farmers, I would hope that you will have in this area - I think you have them already - people who are forward looking and will plan for the generations yet to come." During the afternoon he undertook a scheduled tour of North Bucks but due to the urgency of the Rhodesia debate in the House of Commons his planned engagement as chief speaker at the annual dinner of the North Bucks branch of NALGO, also held at Wilton Hall, had to be cancelled. Instead his place was taken by Councillor F.W. Cornford, chairman of Wolverton Urban Council, who speaking on the assumption that there was going to be a new town told the Nalgo officers - and his "amateur colleagues" - that it would be largely up to them as to the kind of place they would have in North Bucks; "We don't want, in North Bucks, another Basildon or Crawley. Let's learn from the experience of others, but don't let us repeat their failures." "Your members will be involved in it from the word 'go.' It depends entirely on the way the thing is initially set out as to the way it will end up in 20 to 25 years' time." "If they just let the designers come in and lay it out and allowed them to get on with it, they would end up with something similar to other new towns." "Don't let them do that to ours." "Why should a row of eight houses all look the same?" "I charge you all. Let's see what we can do to make something of this new town that is unique. The site and conception are unique. Nowhere else is the idea of separate townships. I would say please let's do all we can to really make the thing something outstanding." Once the houses were up he said they had to get people to move into them, and if they just shoved people in then there would be no community. If they had to wait until the children grew up together to get a personality stamp on the place the town would be old before a community was established. Apart from Bletchley he felt the area was fairly insular, for people had neither moved in nor out very much. Therefore the "amateur" side of the council had a tremendous job to do; "If we do not pull responsibly together, then nothing will be achieved. The development people will say 'we can't allow this to go on,' and will do it their way … We members will accept the challenge with the exception of myself. I will take the compensation for loss of office and retire." (Laughter.) "But I'm sure the younger members are looking forward to the opportunity of serving the community in North Bucks and will do all they can to make sure the new town is a credit to North Bucks and to the children that follow after us."

As for a credit to the village of Loughton, the appeal by Messrs. Bass & Goodway against the County Council's refusal to allow planning permission for two houses, to be built on land at Leys Road, had been turned down by the Minister of Housing. The case had been heard on October 7th with Mr. J. Cater, the Inspector, reporting that even if the development of the site didn't prejudice the satisfactory layout of the proposed town's geographical centre, then development in isolation for one or two houses on this 'awkward shaped plot' would result in a wasteful and unsatisfactory use of the half acre of land. However, for the appellants Andrew Marchant argued that one or two houses surely couldn't upset the proposals, since the whole area was affected by the "new town blight."

Yet it seemed the blight was still some way off, for when asked about the possibility of an announcement regarding the new town a Ministry of Housing spokesman said "there is nothing we can say yet, I am afraid." "We would expect it to be announced in the House, but it could be just circulated to the Press instead." Also there was no news forthcoming about the question of tenant farmers' compensation, with a spokesman for the Ministry of Agriculture saying "We have no news yet of any announcement. It would have to come either as a statement in the House or as a Parliamentary question. The House rises tomorrow and nothing like that is scheduled." However, during the month at the Bucks County NFU executive meeting the London delegate, Mr. T.R. Blackmore, reported "I have said several times that the Minister is about to make an announcement. I can now say that the Minister is on the point of making a statement. The terms have been agreed, and it is now only a matter of days before he will make the announcement. I am not at liberty to give you details. I can say that the profit element has been discounted … "

Thus it was with continuing uncertainty that the year came to an end. Not least an uncertainty regarding any development in New Bradwell, since the Ministry of Housing and Local Government had withheld any action in case their decision hampered plans for the New Town. In fact Wolverton Urban District had forwarded an application to develop certain land for residential purposes but although this was not rejected their plans were to be delayed, with the Ministry stating a reluctance to approve anything which, pending the Minister's decision on the proposed new town, went beyond immediate need. "We are anxious to avoid taking any action at this stage which might hamper any development corporation which the Minister might appoint in the task of preparing a master plan for the new town. It is hoped that your Council will accept the necessity for this course of action even though it may lead to some difficulties in the interim period."

1967

THE BIRTH OF MILTON KEYNES

After the Christmas recess Parliament would reassemble on January 17th, which was also the approximate date that the decision on the proposed new town would be announced. Simultaneously the NFU expected to hear the decision regarding compensation for tenant farmers, with Mr. W. Snook, chairman of the NFU steering committee, saying, "We have been told by our headquarters to expect an announcement in the middle of January and the 17th has been suggested to us as the most likely date. They have given us the information following the resolution which was recently being tabled by the local branch which pressed for an early decision on the question of compensation. If it is delayed any longer than that we shall have to take some action regarding loss of profits resulting from the delay." Yet an Agricultural Ministry spokesman said, "On December 14 our Minister said in the House he regretted that he was not yet in a position to make a statement on this matter of compensation - and that is still the position." Indeed the uncertainty seemed echoed by the comment of a Housing Ministry spokesman that, "I am almost sure nothing will come about the new town this week."

Then on January 12th came a statement from the Ministry of Housing and Local Government announcing that Anthony Greenwood as the Minister had decided to make an order under the New Towns Act designating nearly 22,000 acres of land in North Bucks as the site for a large new town:

'This includes the existing towns of Bletchley, Wolverton and Stony

Stratford. He has decided to call the New Town "Milton Keynes" - this is the name of a small village within the area…'

Over the next 20 years the 'New Town' was designated to accommodate some 150,000 Londoners, with the existing population and future growth likely to provide a total population of about 250,000 by the end of the century. In fact this was all part of a Government programme to provide 1 million Londoners with homes outside the Capital by 1981, and in his letter the Minister included 'A large and complex urban area on this scale must have a structure providing opportunities for growth at the pace required and capacity to adapt to new needs as they are recognised. It must avoid dependence on a single centre which is at the root of so many of the problems of existing towns. This is not simply a matter of "new ideas" but of planning the development of a large city which will work efficiently in the conditions of the remainder of this century and well into the next … it is vitally important that the site should be defined with sufficient latitude to allow existing towns of Bletchley, Wolverton and Stony Stratford to be incorporated within the new development: and in a manner which preserves rather than obliterates their strong and independent sense of local community.' As for the advice from the Inspector subsequent to the Public Inquiry, namely for about 5,100 acres of land on the east, and 1,600 acres on the west, to be excluded, the Minister said in his communication that 'if all this land were excluded the population could be accommodated only as in a rigid and constricted urban structure which might well recreate the problem of existing towns.'

Also in his statement he said the Government was seeking an urgent remedy regarding the problem of compensation to those tenant farmers whose land would be taken for development. Regarding this he hoped a public statement would be made shortly, and also shortly he would be making the order designating the site of the proposed New Town, with the consequent appointment of a development corporation. This would be tasked with the responsibility for the town's construction, and he would ask that it took into account the various matters raised both at the public inquiry and in the written representations which had been drawn to his attention by the Inspector.

In consultation with the local authorities and the other bodies concerned the corporation's initial task would be to prepare a master plan for the approval of the Minister, who, regarding the worries raised by the objectors, had not been persuaded that the land was in general of a sufficiently high quality to preclude the building of a new town on the scale proposed. Nor that the provision for storm water drainage, sewerage and sewage disposal presented 'problems of such magnitude as to make it unreasonable or uneconomical to carry out the development.' In fact in broad terms the Inspector had considered the site to be acceptable, although he was 'entirely in sympathy with the objection put forward in so many different quarters that more land has been asked for than is necessary to accommodate the target population under good conditions.' Indeed, 'the proposal contemplates too low a density of development and an excessive disruption of agriculture; the area to be designated can and should be substantially reduced.....' He had therefore recommended excluding some 1,636 acres on the western side of the designated area at Calverton, and all the land - a total of some 5,102 acres - on the eastern side between the motorway and the Grand Union Canal and the River Ouzel. Further, he advised the need for special care in the safeguarding of Stony Stratford and the surrounding fertile land, and 'If my recommendations are adopted the result will be a designated area of about 18,600 acres, appreciably bigger than Leicester with its population of 267,000. This is sufficient to accommodate 279,000 people at 15 to the acre - not at all a high density - or 223,200 at 12 to the acre.'

In fact his comments were heeded, for with Mr. Greenwood removing Broughton and Calverton from the original designation the area was now basically the same as the draft area, except for the exclusion of some 2,900 acres on the west, to include Calverton, and some 400 acres on the east, which cut out Broughton. As for the name of the new town this would be that of the village of Milton Keynes (population 159) with the development to be the largest New Town under the New Town Acts, taking in nearly 22,000 acres of land, and with an expected population by the end of the century of around 250,000.

From ending the many months of uncertainty the decision was welcomed by Councillor R. Bellchambers, chairman of Newport Pagnell RDC, who said that since the Minister had agreed to the particular request of the council to exclude some 400 acres in the east "it is exactly what I expected ... The decision to call the town Milton Keynes is gratifying, it will retain forever the link with this rural area." "I personally welcome the challenge. In my opinion this New Town is one of the Government's answers to the play 'Cathy Come Home.' Everybody who saw the play should think seriously before taking any action likely to delay the New Town." As for his comments, John Cornwall, the Liberal prospective parliamentary candidate, remarked, "The choice of the name 'Milton Keynes' is interesting and should 'catch on.' There are opportunities for humorists in the foreseeable situation." When about to fly to Bangkok during a round the world business trip, Robert Maxwell, the Labour M.P. for the Buckingham Division, received the news whilst changing planes at Calcutta airport, and telephoning his reaction said in a brief message; "I am glad that the uncertainty has at last been ended by the Minister's announcement about the new city. I am delighted by the choice of the name Milton Keynes." He was pleased the Ministry had reduced the acreage by a little, although by not as much as he'd asked.

Despite the announcement local farmers were continuing their stand against the new town. Also their fight for realistic compensation for any loss of land, and at the Union's AGM, which would open in London on Monday, January 23rd, a resolution from the Bucks branch of the NFU would be forwarded via Mr. W. Snook, chairman of the NFU Steering Committee, stating; 'This branch is concerned at the lack of decision of the Government of fixing adequate compensation for farmers dispossessed in the acquisition of land. It urges headquarters to continue the fight for legislation which will make it mandatory for compensation in the terms of a minimum of 10 years rent or five years profits, to be made to all tenant farmers who lose their land for development purposes, so enabling a grave injustice to be rectified at the earliest possible moment.' The committee considered full justification had been done to the hard work put into the case and since new duties now arose - to include the need to establish a permanent liaison with the new town development corporation, whenever this was appointed, the negotiation of compensation for the members on a united scale, and, if necessary, to appear at the public inquiry into the master plan - their need was still ongoing. However in the meantime an early general meeting would be called of the NFU members in the area, with the committee urging them not to sign any documents relating to the new town before this had taken place.

Apart from the farmers' objections, local air pollution was also a worrying concern, for during the past 10 months members of the

Woburn Sands and District Preservation and Protection Society had been operating an air pollution sampling station. Adjacent to the south east corner of the new town this was located on the Woburn Sands ridge, and the results proved of such concern that in the last week of January a letter outlining the facts to Anthony Greenwood would be sent worded; 'Certain definite trends have been noted in relation to the concentration of air pollutants which appear to originate from one or other of the brick making areas according to observed wind direction. In particular high concentrations of sulphur occur sufficiently frequently to be regarded as serious health hazard to the future inhabitants of the new town. We urgently request you to take note of this matter since we are quite sure that you will agree that it would be wrong to endow a city worthy of the 21st century with a polluted atmosphere characteristic of the industrial revolution of the 19th century. We assure you of our help and co-operation in seeking a solution to this problem.' In fact on the evening of January 19th at a special meeting members of the Society's executive committee emphasised the seriousness of the findings, not least since 1966 had been a year of low brick production. Thus apart from the Minister, copies of the letter would be sent to local M.P.s and the clerks to the local authorities.

From being excluded from the designated area there had been initial relief at Broughton but as more details emerged it became apparent that the village would be bisected, since the boundary ran from the M1 flyover along the Milton Keynes side of the A50 to the Milton Keynes turn, along this road to the small humped back bridge some 200 yards from the A50 junction, and then across the fields towards Wavendon and Bow Brickhill. The main part of the village street, which before the construction of the bypass had endured heavy traffic, would therefore once again become a much used route and following this revelation Gerald Williams of Brooklands Farm, who represented the village on Newport Pagnell RDC, said "I think it is worse being on the fringe than if we were in the town. With houses so close everyone will bring their cats and dogs onto our land for a walk and use our land as a rubbish dump." "These farmers are going to lose all that they have built up for themselves and their sons, during the last thirty years and more." "It would not have been so bad if the Minister had accepted the whole of the Inspector's proposals. But I think credit should be given to the steering committee of our NFU, and I don't think there has been another public inquiry where the inspector was so much on the side of the objectors, in this case the farmers." For 13 years he had farmed his 280 acres at Broughton whilst another farmer, Ronald Adams, of Broughton Manor, whose extent lay on the fringe of the new town, had lived there all his life. Potentially he would lose 27 of the 285 acres he had farmed since 1927, and being strongly opposed to the idea said "They did not take a lot of notice of us at the inquiry, but we must wait and see what compensation farmers will receive before we can say if farmers are having a fair deal." As for the opinion of one of the oldest of the village residents, Mr. R. Barrett, of The Nook, he said "I don't like towns and as for this one, it is taking some of the best agricultural land in the country." At one time he had lived in London and had never liked towns since.

The question of compensation for dispossessed farmers was again 'hammered home' at the NFU conference in London on Tuesday, January 24th by Mr. W. Snook who, protesting that the terms were still awaited, despite Government promises that an announcement was to have been made some time ago, said "We in Bucks will release no land until we have this compensation on the statute book. My fellow farmers have stated that they will go to jail first." Then at the Coronation Hall, Water Eaton, on the evening of Friday, January 27th a meeting behind locked doors took place at which, by his position as chairman of the Steering Committee, he reported to his fellow farmers on the work performed by the committee members in fighting the NFU case at the public inquiry last July. He thanked all the members for their co-operation and especially Bucks NFU County HQ, National Headquarters and the committee members for their help and guidance at the frequent committee meetings. Approval of the way the NFU case had been handled was duly expressed by the meeting which also approved a detailed financial statement. As the barrister who had presented the NFU case at the public inquiry, Neville Wallace then outlined the tasks which the new steering committee should tackle. The most important was to establish immediate contact with the development corporation and its staff, thereby to advise on agricultural matters and reach a close liaison regarding the phasing of development and the question of dispossession and compensation. He stressed that unity must be preserved amongst the members, and said to achieve the greatest effect they must all act as one. As an outcome of the meeting a resolution was passed to be forwarded to NFU headquarters stating that all compensation paid to tenant farmers should be free of tax; that the new compensation should be firm for a minimum period of five years, with provision then made for upward revision to account for the fall in the value of money and the rise in the cost of living; that the new town authority should give an early indication of its master plan and the phasing of development; the compensation to be paid to any owner or occupier at once if he finds another farm before the time arrives for the acquisition of his present farm; that compensation be paid direct to the tenant by the acquiring authority. In other business four new members were elected to the steering committee, these being Mr. G. C. Field, of Bradwell Abbey, Mr. G. Dover, of Milton Keynes, and Mr. J. Cook of Sherington (all of whom had farm land within the designated area) and Mr. M. Fountaine, of North Crawley, who farmed land near Woughton on the Green. Since they were now outside the designated area Mr. G. Cowley and Mr. V. E. Phillips resigned from the committee, which now comprised Messrs. W.G. Snook, R. Bullock, J. Cook, G. Dover, M. Fountaine, G. C. Field, W.E. Gurney, T. G. R. Williams, and R. P. Furnival, secretary.

Regarding the proposed new development, fears that Bletchley's 'deep freeze' would continue were expressed at a Tuesday meeting of Bletchley Council, with the apprehension having arisen from a suspicion that the new town announcement would be used as an excuse for doing nothing. Indeed, regarding a request by the council for details of the improvement proposals for the High Street and Aylesbury Street junctions the members were informed that the reply from the Divisional Road Engineer stated 'I regret that I am unable to supply this information you require at present. As you will be aware, Bletchley is affected by the proposed new town. Until the Master Plan for the area has been prepared it would be imprudent to proceed with any costly highway schemes in the area as the overall highway pattern could be materially altered when the Plan is produced.' This was "just futile" said Councillor W. Caldwell. For seven years they had been waiting for something to be done, and now it was going to be left until the pattern for the new town or city had been drawn up. However, Councillor J. Cassidy said it was tempting to rush in and say "let's march up Whitehall," but what else could they expect? The Minister of Housing had designated North Bucks as the area for the largest new town of all time, and the Ministry of Transport couldn't know what was going to happen to the A5.

As for the continuing uncertainty faced by the farmers, on Thursday, February 9th B.B.C. television cameras were at Shenley to film scenes for a programme concerning the plight of those who were to lose land for the new town. One of those interviewed by Mr. J. Cherrington was Mr. J. Bonham, a Shenley farmer, and with the B.B.C. unit scheduled to visit Geoffrey Dover's farm at Milton Keynes on February 10th the programme was expected to be transmitted early in March, for national coverage. Meanwhile protest meetings were still being held in the affected villages, and of these on Thursday, February 9th at a gathering of the Loughton and Shenleys' Residents Association James Marchant, a Bletchley solicitor who lived at Loughton, issued a rallying call saying "Battle must now be joined in earnest. The Inquiry was no more than an expensive exercise. You can't call it a fight when your opponent is also the referee. The Inspector himself said the basic decision was outside his scope. I accordingly appeal to everyone who is not content just to hold his hand out for compensation to get in touch with me as soon as possible." However on finding no support when he urged that the matter should be taken to the courts he told the meeting "I am surprised by the defeatism which seems to have descended on everybody. We all knew what the Minister's decision was going to be. Mr. Godber (the Inspector) said it in so many words. So far as I am concerned, the position isn't changed. I don't regard the situation as hopeless." Yet someone with new town experience was Cyril Richardson, a chartered surveyor and estate agent from Stevenage, who addressing the packed audience said that 20 years ago they had fought the new town coming to Stevenage. Not only was the matter taken to court but also the House of Lords, to which Mr. Marchant said "They lost but that isn't to say we would lose. We are concerned with a very much bigger proposal and a more controversial one." "I for one have not given up. I hope to carry the fight a good deal further. I think the whole idea is quite monstrous. This was very well demonstrated in the Association's objection at the inquiry. It summed up the case against the city and I still think it is unanswerable. It has been foisted on us by Whitehall, it's certainly not in the national interest. I would call on anyone in the area, of the same mind, to come forward." Only one person of sufficient means would be needed to take the fight on, with time being the major problem. Any proceedings would need to begin by the end of the month but despite no support forthcoming from the meeting the Association's chairman, Mrs. Joan Greenwood, who had sported their case at the inquiry, commented "I must express admiration for Mr. Marchant's fighting spirit. Emotionally I would say yes, 'I'm with you.' But my brain tells me there is no chance. It is too big a thing." "I am afraid the days of barricading ourselves in our homes has gone." As for Mr. Richardson, his advice to shopkeepers was "Modernise your shops right away. Get ready for it, because you are going to make an awful lot of money."

Hopefully those tenant farmers facing dispossession by the new town would also soon receive more money, for as revealed by the Minister of Agriculture, Fred Peart, they would now receive an effective minimum of five years' rent as compensation, in some circumstances possibly six, as compared with the one to two years' rent at present. He was answering a question on compensation put to the House on Tuesday, February 21st by Robert Maxwell, and said "The Government intends to introduce as soon as possible legislation to provide for special additional compensation payments, at the rate of four years' rent, to be made to a tenant farmer who is displaced to development, forestry or other non agricultural purpose, whether he is displaced by a private landlord or a public authority." However, local farmers had pressed the Government to base compensation on ten years' rent, and so when commenting on the announcement the secretary to the Newport Pagnell and Bletchley branches of the NFU Ray Furnival, said; "We are naturally disappointed about the terms but it marks a big improvement - some 400% - on the present payment. However we now want this settled as quickly as possible. Although the Government says it intends to take these steps, we want to know when." As for the reaction of the chairman of the NFU Steering Committee, Mr. Snook; "I welcome the proposed fresh legislation and I believe this to be a step in the right direction. I am disappointed that we were not allowed the full terms and we shall always seek to rectify the grave injustice done to tenant farmers."

During the first two weeks of March a team of research workers from the Department of Agricultural Economics at Reading University would be visiting farmers and farm workers in the designated area. In terms of the potential land, buildings and other fixed equipment to be removed from agricultural production, and of the associated land force that would be displaced from their current employments, the intention was to compile a comprehensive account of the farm businesses of the threatened area, with the study designed to provide data for the calculation of the immediate costs of development in terms of displaced resources. Also as a 'backcloth' against which to interpret and measure changes within the region, as farmers and their capital and farm workers migrated to be reabsorbed elsewhere in this, and probably other, economies.

With the new city now imminent, during the month at their Wednesday meeting members of Bucks County Council were informed that since they were the Planning Authority any case deemed likely to have an important effect on the New Town development was to be referred to the Housing Minister. Five points were to be duly borne in mind:

1) It was not the Minister's wish that all development should be stopped.

2) Avoid any development that might prejudice the possibility of integration of existing towns into the structure of the new town. Avoid development that would prejudice the improvement of roads or their junctions.

3) Limited in-filling within existing villages may be reasonable, but should be avoided if it might make more difficult the task of integrating the villages into the new development.

4) Development in open country is likely to be premature, pending preparation of the master plan.

5) When the Development Corporation is established the Minister will direct the planning authority to consult it on applications for planning permission within the designated area.

Regarding the last of these, aged 54, and educated at Eton and Exeter College, Oxford, Lord Campbell of Eskan had now been appointed part time chairman of the 'Milton Keynes Development Corporation,' following the announcement of which he said in a statement "The Chairmanship of the Milton Keynes Development Corporation will now demand my deep involvement in a new kind of creative organisation and in the social and economic problems of my own country. I can't imagine any job which more combines social, economic, aesthetic and administrative above all human considerations. I only hope I shall prove equal to the demands." The announcement came on Tuesday, March 21ˢᵗ when in a reply to a question by Robert Maxwell, MP for North Bucks, Anthony Greenwood, as the Minister of Housing and Local Government, said he was glad to reveal that Lord Campbell had accepted his invitation to be part time chairman. He hoped to announce the other members of the corporation soon, with four representing local authorities and another representing the Greater London Council. Devoting up to half his time in his new role Lord Campbell would undertake the position for three years, being subject to renewal on April 1ˢᵗ of each year. As for his previous experience, to then become President he would be retiring from June 1ˢᵗ as Chairman and a Director of Booker Brothers and McConnell, which in a statement said that having largely created the group in its present form Lord Campbell, after 20 years as chief executive, had now decided to relinquish the responsibility of management. However his services would be retained by the Board to particularly advise on Commonwealth and international sugar affairs, as well as other matters relating to business in developing countries. In other pursuits he was chairman of the company publishing the New Statesman, and on becoming a peer in the previous year had accepted the Labour Whip in the House of Lords. With a family by his first marriage of two sons and two daughters his home was at Crocker End House, Nettlebed, Oxford, from where regarding his new position he said the Master Plan would be produced as soon as possible 'but not so fast as to make a bad job of it.' As for his previous role, speaking in London he said "Of course, giving up the chairmanship of Bookers is a wrench after running the company for over 20 years. But that is a long time for one man to run one company and vice versa. I reached my decision after long and careful thought, to close consultation with my immediate colleagues and friends, and came to the final conclusion with their complete understanding and support." However, "As Chairman of the Commonwealth Sugar Exporters Group I shall still have my hands full of sugar."

In the near future, having visited other new towns he intended to pay a return visit, by which to critically study their planning and environment, and so "profit by their good points and learn from their mistakes." Also he would study the potential effects of air pollution in the new city, for on occasion 500 micrograms of sulphur dioxide per cubic metre had been recorded at Woburn Sands. According to a medical authority on town planning 50 micrograms was the maximum, and, saying that he had been interested in solving both air and water pollution problems long before being appointed chairman of the Development Corporation, Lord Campbell said the Board would take the question very seriously "and if necessary we shall go to the U.S.A. for help where a lot of work in this field has gone on." In the wake of Lord Campbell's appointment Bletchley Council had sent a letter of congratulation, the reply to which stated, "I particularly appreciate the courtesy of your Council embodied in your welcoming and heartening letter of March 22nd. As soon as I can get to work - when other members of the Board of the Milton Keynes Development Corporation are appointed - I shall make a point, if I may, of arranging to come and see you and talk and seek your advice. I have a great deal to learn. My one hope is that with the Board, I may be able to serve the people who now live and will live in the area."

At its first annual meeting at Milton Keynes, on Saturday, April 8th the Lord Lieutenant of Buckinghamshire, Brigadier Sir Henry Floyd, county president of the Council for the Preservation of Rural England, praised the officers for their initiative in establishing the North Bucks Branch of the Council. He said the new city was bound to come for "You obviously cannot be like Canute and expect the waves to turn back." Therefore such organisations would be urgently needed when it was built. When that time arrived the members should concentrate their efforts on constructive criticism of the master plan, and make a special point of rallying support for the preservation of the 'delightful villages' in the new city area. Yet he cautioned that no doubt there would be a danger that many of the new town's executives would seek homes outside the boundaries of the new city, leading to the potential consequence of urbanising many of the towns and villages. Urging members to advise about which buildings and sites to preserve he stressed the importance and need for this to be done 'in good time,' for although many people would like to preserve rural England, "many, many people who should be taking an interest don't bother. My personal view is that you should take great care of the villages in North Bucks outside the perimeter of the great city." Remarking that he had driven up that day through some lovely villages he noted they were still quite small, and these he said should be retained as such; "People, when they become executives and get on in business want to live outside the boundaries of the city where they work. There is the danger that these villages will themselves become urbanised unless you do all you can to prevent it." For the advice that he could give to the people of North Bucks he had consulted Mr. Pooley, the Bucks County Architect, and Mr. R. Millard, Clerk to Bucks County Council, by whose guidance the North Bucks branch of the organisation could 'arm itself with facts' about the villages and towns in the area. Thus this information would then be ready for presentation to the Development Corporation the chairman of which, in the words of Mr. R. G. Alexander, county secretary of the branch, was a man "with two feet on the ground, and very sensitive to the preservation of all that is good in this country; I hope he will find that in the CPRE he has ready allies." Mr. Alexander also hoped that the members would list details of special country village aspects and buildings, for in due course these could then be submitted to the Corporation. He next reminded the members that in objecting to the excessive amount of land taken for the new city the CPRE had made its position clear both at the public inquiry and in written objections to the Minister. Presented by the North Bucks Historical Association the meeting then closed with a show of slides which, as part of a record of the new city area, were now being carefully collected by the society. These were viewed with great interest, and formed a topic of interesting discussion during a tea which followed.

With echoes of 'Pooleyville', Mr. Gwilym Roberts, the M.P. for South Beds., had now suggested a possible hover train from London to the new city. Consequent to his study of this development in other countries he thus wanted to know what progress had been made in this country, and Anthony Wedgwood Benn, as the Minister of Technology, was to reply to his questions in the House of Commons. Travel to the new town could be envisaged as a system of high speed hover trains linking Bletchley, other neighbouring towns and London, and 'The possibility of undertaking a shopping trip at an everyday speed of anything up to 500 miles an hour, with only a cushion of air separating the passengers in a hovertrain from the miles of concrete runway below has reached the stage of being something more than a Jules Verne dream. It has reached the stage where we may soon learn what the present Minister of Technology has in mind for future Milton Keynes commuters.'

On the afternoon of Wednesday, April 12th Bletchley Council held a special meeting "to consider the further confidential communication received from the Minister of Housing and Local Government in connection with the appointment of the Milton Keynes New Town

Development Corporation." Councillor F. Evans, chairman, said he thought it appropriate for the special meeting to be called, "so that we can in fact resolve our attitude towards the Minister's suggestions for names of the Development Corporation." He said when they received the confidential letter concerning the chairman of the Corporation there was so little time that only an informal meeting could be arranged, but this as events had proved was sufficient. "These names may provoke some comment from members," he added. "I thought it best to hold this special meeting of the council so that we could send our views." Pointing out that the Minister's information was confidential he assumed that while the names of those eventually appointed would obviously no longer be confidential, any others would remain confidential in perpetuity. He then called for a formal resolution to exclude the public and Press, and with this agreed the 'one member of the public and the Press' left - some two minutes after the meeting had opened.

Then in the Commons on April 21ˢᵗ Robert Maxwell, as the M.P. for Buckingham, was to ask the Minister what progress had been made regarding the other appointments to the 'Milton Keynes New Town Development Corporation.' As per local rumours, these were expected to be Mrs. Margaret Durbridge, Newport Pagnell's County Councillor, Ray Bellchambers, chairman of the Newport Pagnell RDC, Jim Cassidy, chairman of Bletchley UDC, and Major Ralph Verney, of Claydon House, the recently resigned chairman of the County Council's Finance Committee. However, if this proved correct it would mean the lack of any representative from Wolverton UDC, which had made a strong plea to the Minister for inclusion. Thus when the names were confidentially made known, with regard to this apparent snub on Tuesday, April 18ᵗʰ the council after a private meeting asked Robert Maxwell to lead a deputation to the Ministry, where they duly saw Robert Mellish, a parliamentary private secretary to the Minister. Then on April 21ˢᵗ Mr. Maxwell received a letter from the Minister worded; "Mr. Robert Mellish has reported the points made by the deputation from Wolverton UDC which you brought on Tuesday. I have considered them very carefully. In the result I have decided to proceed with the appointments I have proposed and I shall be announcing them today. I should particularly like you, and the Council, to know that it implies no criticism of them that I have not accepted their suggestion for an appointment to the Board. The local people I have appointed are in no sense representatives of particular so called authorities and I hope you will understand that I could not undertake to make up a Corporation of 'representatives.' I very much welcome the support which the Council have given to the new town proposal. It is important to the success of the town. There will of course be many matters of common concern to the Corporation and the Council and I shall expect the Corporation to establish an effective working liaison with the authorities in the area. It is in this way that the interests of Wolverton can best be taken into account and their contribution to the development of the town made most useful. I am sure that Lord Campbell will want to arrange an early meeting with the Council to discuss this."

In fact the Development Corporation chairman was scheduled to visit North Bucks on Thursday, April 27th but only for a social visit to Lathbury Park at about 4pm, to draw competition prizes at a church function. As for other forms of drawing, members of Bletchley Arts Club had now resolved to paint pictures of the new city 'as it impresses them individually.' As stated in his letter to Robert Maxwell, and in reply to his written question, on the afternoon of Friday, April 21st the Minister publicly appointed to the Board of the 'Milton Keynes New Town Development Corporation' Mrs. Margaret Durbridge of Newport Pagnell, Ray Bellchambers of Old Bradwell, Major R.B. Verney of Claydon House, and also Jim Cassidy of Bletchley, who, in reply to congratulations, said he found nothing incompatible with being a member both of the Corporation and also Bletchley Council. This had been in the forefront of North Bucks development for a long while, and with reference to the forthcoming elections he said "There is no doubt in my mind if the people of Bletchley want me to continue to serve on the Council I shall do so." Also appointed was Mr. Alexander Meikle. Married with three sons, after an education at Shawlands Academy, Glasgow University, he qualified as a chartered accountant, and in 1964 was awarded the CBE. Prior to his new appointment he had been general manager of the Woolwich Equitable Building Society, of which he was a director since 1958. As deputy to the Board's chairman Mr. Walter Ismay, B.Sc. Eng., M.I.C.E., would be known as the Managing Director, at a salary of £10,000 a year. A bachelor, his home was near Tadcaster, Yorks., but he now intended to live in the area, of which his only acquaintance had been two half days in North Bucks spent motoring, walking and "generally having a good look round." Born in Liverpool he had grown up in Southampton and apart from employment at various times in London, Birmingham, and Leeds, had also worked for a year in America. Eventually becoming technical director, responsible for the co-ordination of major capital expenditure projects, from 1948 to 1958 he held an appointment in the Metals Division of I.C.I., whilst as for his new appointment this, having resigned his position as director and chief engineer of Yorkshire Imperial Metals Ltd., and deputy chairman of Yorkshire Imperial Plastics Ltd., would begin in early May.

Of the newly appointed Board members, Mrs. Durbridge, of Mill House, Newport Pagnell, was the wife of a solicitor and had a family of four children; three girls, one of whom was married, and a son who was a doctor in America. Serving on the County Planning and Finance Committee, she was a former chairman of the Mental Health sub committee and had recently been returned unopposed to Bucks County Council, to which she was first elected six years ago. She was vice chairman of Newport Pagnell Magistrates, and of her new appointment said; "It is, of course, a gigantic opportunity, a gigantic challenge. I've always felt that if a new town was needed in this area, which I felt it was, that it was very much better that it should be planned in detail from the start. I feel convinced that we will be able to co-operate with local district councils and the County Council, because it is vital to the district that the town should increase the amenities of the area. It is also vital that the area surrounding the new town keeps its character and remains rural. I would hate it to become a vast urban sprawl." Unsuccessful at his recent attempt to gain a County Council seat, Ray Bellchambers had been a member of Newport Pagnell RDC for 20 years and was now its retiring chairman. Employed as a foreman in the stores at Wolverton Works he was a life long Socialist, and said of the forthcoming development, "Whilst a substantial part of the rural land in the designated area will disappear, every effort will be made to preserve those points which are worth preserving. As the process goes on we must make sure that every effort to integrate the old with the new is made, to make it acceptable to both sides. The job is entirely different to running a rural area for one must think in terms of a completely urban district. The social problems which are likely to occur are the most difficult. Technical answers can be found for problems such as drainage, etc., but it is not always easy to find answers to social problems. I look forward to the challenge, it is the sort of thing I like to do." Saying he was rather proud to be a member of the Corporation, he hoped to represent the area to the best of his ability "and to make sure that the rural angle in this procedure had a fair crack of the whip." Of the other appointees, Major Ralph Verney lived at Claydon House and was the eldest son of Sir Harry Verney. Having served in the Bucks Yeomanry during the war he was elected to the County Council in 1951, and serving as an alderman for the past six years had resigned the chairmanship of the County Finance Committee at the Budget meeting in February, after 12 years in the position. A former President of the Country Landowners' Association he had spoken the previous year on the Conservation of Bucks at a meeting of the county branch of the Council for the Preservation of Rural England. For their work each Board member would receive £500 a year, whilst at a salary of £1,000 pa, two deputy chairmen had still to be appointed.

At their monthly meeting on Tuesday, April 25th it was still the opinion of Wolverton UDC that they been snubbed by the Minister regarding appointments to the Corporation Board. They had recently suggested that Councillors F. Atter and D. Morgan should be considered, but with this unheeded, a letter addressed to Sir Matthew Stevenson, the permanent secretary at the Ministry of Housing, complaining that the Board in its present composition was 'faulty and overloaded,' read; "Your letter of the 20th April has been noted by the Council, but only with disapproval as far as concerns the local appointment on the Development Corporation. The Council do not feel they can accept the explanation of the Minister that the local people are in no sense 'representative.' In the light of their local knowledge, they can place no other interpretation on the appointments than that they are 'representative'; and more particularly so, as long as Wolverton is excluded. They are of the opinion that the Minister should have redressed the faulty, overloaded, local appointments; and that the composition of the Corporation, by its very inclusions and exclusions, is literally 'representative,' as respects partisanship and territorial recognition. The Council can see no excuse for making appointments from local authorities who have not given unqualified support for the proposed new town, and none from this Urban District which has given such unqualified support. The Council contends that it is impossible to justify either the appointments, or the exclusion, on the grounds of relative merit and ability. Speaking on the basis of its local knowledge, the Council believes it to be essential in the general interest and in the interests of the Urban District, for a place to be given to its nominee. Unless and until this is done, the Council wishes the Minister to understand that its protest, most strongly and unanimously felt and made, will be maintained." Nevertheless the councillors stressed their continuing commitment towards giving every co-operation to the Board, 'and to receive any co-operation that the Board may desire to give them.' In outlining the Council's position the chairman of the Finance Committee, Miss Aileen Button, explained that the committee had three meetings concerning the Milton Keynes New Town. Another would be held on May 17th and later the committee would report to the full council with a comprehensive account. Of the recent events, she explained that having received a letter from the Minister containing the proposed names for the Board, the Committee, since no Wolverton councillor was named, decided to send Councillors Causer, Cornford, Cosford and Love to see the Minister. Extreme disappointment was expressed by the committee when this deputation was ignored, with the chairman, Councillor F. Cornford, telling the members that the Minister must be sent the strongest representation, stating that if the interests of the district were to be safeguarded they must have someone from the area on the Board. Indeed it was difficult to reconcile the word 'representative' when the chosen four were from four different areas. However he was quick to add "Co-operation must be our key-note." Regarding his comments, Councillor Dr. D. Hall said "This is a poor community and anything we have asked higher level for in the past has been turned down. I do not think we will get help from the county representatives now and we shall be stuck once again." Endorsing Dr. Hall's remarks Dr. J. Love said that "Wolverton town is the dog's body. This Board is to be a non-representative body but it is all representative. I do not know what experience these four people have in this field, but our own Mr. Atter is something of an expertee (sic) in this way." Also the Council objected to the contents of the appointments letter being published by the Press before they received the information, and this would be made known in their letter to the Minister.

Winslow Rural Council also had a grievance, for despite a Government invitation to give confidential views on the six men proposed as members of the Corporation it was revealed these appointments had been made without any reference to their advice. As the chairman Councillor L. Melville said at a meeting on Friday, April 29th "Our remarks on the matter could never have been considered as the Milton Keynes Corporation was announced by the Ministry of Housing and Local Government the day after we rang them up." "I think it is a complete nonsense when you are asked for advice by a certain date and you find the Minister publishes his decision the very day after that date. This clearly means he could not have given any consideration to our views." Two days previously, at the meeting of Newport Pagnell Rural Council it was reported that the issue of selling houses in the designated area had been discussed by the General Purposes, Finance, Rating and Establishment Committee, consequent to an owner of a property having enquired if the council would buy the premises. Due to the new town he was having difficulty in selling. It had been on the market for some time but a decision not to purchase was made, for as the committee stated "Whilst desiring to help those who have difficulty in selling their houses the Council cannot accept the responsibility of buying all houses at the asking price, as losses would be borne by the ratepayers."

Now becoming more acquainted with the area, Lord Campbell had been asked to write the foreword to a handbook to be produced by the North Bucks Sports Advisory Council. This had been unanimously decided at a meeting of the Council at the Buckingham Rural Council offices on Friday, May 12th. Affiliation was not necessary for clubs wishing to be entered into the book. Those interested were asked to write to 5, Whaddon Way, Bletchley. Lord Campbell seemed well qualified, as he listed his recreations in Who's Who as 'reading, hitting balls.' He was a member of the MCC and the All England Lawn Tennis Club.

Despite a continuing conviction that the Government's decision to build a new city in North Bucks was a mistake, the North Bucks Association nevertheless welcomed the Minister's appointment of Lord Campbell, believing that under his 'enlightened chairmanship' the area would have the best chance of developing into a city worthy of North Bucks traditions. That was also the opinion at a recent meeting of the Association held to report on the go ahead for the city's construction. The outcome of the public inquiry had been disappointing but as reported by the treasurer, Mr. R. Scanlon, the cost of £849 5s for the Association to present its case had been money well justified, as indeed had been the very existence of the Association. Indeed it was noted that the Planning Correspondent of the national newspaper the Guardian had observed that "only the North Bucks Association went into the attack with any realistic alternative to the official scheme." Whilst the designated area was now beyond doubt the Association agreed that it should still remain in being, not least to help protect the amenities of North Bucks in any way they deemed necessary, and to co-operate with other organisations of a similar aim whenever the need should arise. As the secretary, Arthur Snaith said "But it is now up to everyone to play their part in making it a happy community, a viable one. … I don't think that anyone can have been really surprised by the announcement. But what they may now be concerned about is the kind of plan the development corporation draw up, and the phasing of it. We ought to be watchful that something of the present individuality of the villages is conserved." This he thought should be done by starting the centre of the town on presently virgin soil, so that "the present characteristics of the villages likely to be swallowed up may well be preserved for ten years, 20, or even longer." Regarding the Inspector's report he said "The Minister had already made up his mind in principle, and although the enquiry was not unnecessary of a waste of time it would have taken some evidence to override it, other than that which we were able to produce. The situation was therefore somewhat loaded against us, but I still feel that our arguments were valid. Now that the decision has been made we must all try to integrate these people into the community."

Concerns regarding the new city's confirmation were also expressed by Leighton Buzzard Angling Club at their annual meeting, where in a report to 200 members Fred Groom, the secretary, said there was a very real threat that much of the Ouzel "from Water Eaton to the M1 at Broughton Bridge" would be taken over by the New Town developers. Since there was a possibility of losing their fishing rights, in seeking an alternative the club had therefore approached Bletchley UDC with regard to obtaining water on the Great Ouse and River Thame. The only sure way of obtaining water was to go into the open market, but that was very costly.

Following the alleged snub by the Minister, at the meeting of Wolverton UDC on Tuesday, May 23rd Councillor F. Atter told the members, "We have had one slap in the face from the Government and we do not look with any great pleasure on another slap in the face from the County Council." This regarded news that no local councillors had been appointed to serve on the County Planning Committee for the next three years but, with the idea having emanated from Robert Mellish, the Council had decided to form a small 'new town liaison committee' composed of Councillors Hall, Atter, Cornford, Cosford and Lister.

The residents of Milton Keynes village may or may not have been happy with the designated area, or that their name had been taken for its title, but some residents had even more reason for complaint when in early June the pop group 'Unit Six' began one night practice sessions in the Community Centre. Permission to rehearse every Tuesday from 7.30pm to 10pm had been given by the Centre's Management Committee some months before, but certain residents had since complained about the noise. In response the committee secretary, Mrs. Rene Smith, said "I think a lot of people can only hear the sound of the music when the wind is blowing in a certain direction. After we received certain complaints I was detailed to go and speak to the boys who promised to be as quiet as possible. But recently we have received more complaints, from two elderly gentlemen who say that the noise has rattled crockery in their homes and that they will take the matter up with the Rural Council." However the committee had heard nothing more from the first complainants and "When I visited the centre on Tuesday to listen for any noise I could not hear any sound at all from outside the building. That is why I believe that any noise heard is only caused by the wind direction." "I am sure the committee feels that pop music one night a week in a hall, which is as much for the youth of the community as any, is not asking too much." Before considering further action the committee would await any response from the Rural Council.

It was now announced that the first meeting of Milton Keynes Development Corporation would take place on Thursday, June 15th with a certainty that amongst the first items on the agenda would be the need to acquire a permanent headquarters. Indeed Mr. Ismay had said as much in April on his appointment as the full time Managing Director, whilst Jim Cassidy, as one of the Board members, remarked "it is possible that a proposition to purchase property will be put before the Board next week." Meanwhile the Corporation's Chairman had his mind on other tasks, for at midday on Monday, June 12th a small piece of turf was dug by Lord Campbell to mark the beginning of work on the Lakes Estate at Water Eaton, Bletchley, which, at a cost of £7 million, was being developed by Bletchley Council in association with Greater London Council to provide over 2,000 houses for Londoners. Before inviting him to dig the turf Councillor R. Fisher, Chairman of Bletchley Council, told him "We are rather looking to the fact that this could be the commencement of your new town, sir, because it is in the designated area and will be completed before your corporation is four years old." Watched by local authority representatives and those of the contractors Lord Campbell said, "I'm not going to make a speech. I don't know nearly enough about the development of Milton Keynes. I only know how to pronounce it." Performing the duty with a silver spade Lord Campbell said the Corporation "must have fruitful, effective and regular meetings and consultations with all the local and county authorities in the area including very much the Bletchley UDC ... The new city must not be imposed by the corporation on people. It should be planned by the corporation with the people and for the people who are going to live in it." "After all, our prime purpose is to build, not plan, homes and amenities for people and it is for this reason I am particularly happy and privileged to be invited to dig this first turf." As for the two remaining appointments to his Board these, being as expected from the London area, and each to be paid £500 pa, were now announced by Anthony Greenwood as Councillor H.W. Cutler, O.B.E., and Lady Serota, B.Sc.. (Econ.), J.P. As deputy leader of the Greater London Council, and chairman of its housing committee, Councillor Cutler had been a member of the Middlesex County Council for 10 years, two of these being as leader, and also for 14 years of the Harrow Borough Council, indeed being mayor of Harrow in 1959/60. As for Lady Serota, from 1964 to 1967, during which period she had been vice chairman of the Inner London Education Authority, she had been Chief Whip of the Greater London Council and from 1954 to 1965 a member of the LCC. Presently she was a member of the Seebohm Committee on the Social Services, and additionally a member of national advisory bodies concerned with children and young people.

As scheduled, on the afternoon of Thursday, June 15th the inaugural meeting took place of the nine strong Milton Keynes Development Corporation, headed by Lord Campbell of Eskan and with the inclusion of Mr. I. Mawson, chief administrative officer, Redditch, who was assisting the Board at this early stage. The Community Centre at Milton Keynes village provided the venue, and as expected one of the first decisions was that from being within the designated area Wavendon Tower should become the permanent headquarters. Also it was decided to invite the County Council plus the five local authorities having land in the designated area to join a liaison committee meeting at least quarterly. This would be under the chairmanship of the managing director, Mr. Ismay, and a regular consultation and collaboration could thereby be ensured between these authorities and the Corporation. Also it was decided to arrange, under Lord Campbell's chairmanship, an extended annual meeting to include representatives of contiguous authorities. In other matters Lord Campbell reported to the Board on his meetings with the chairmen and members of local authorities. These had proved a useful opportunity to hear of local problems at first hand and, such as Wolverton UDC's appointment of a liaison committee for routine consultation, also to note the welcome arrangements for collaboration with the Corporation. The Board additionally noted the need for the most 'fruitful possible future collaboration' with Fred Pooley, the County Planning Officer and Architect. This was in recognition of his important and valued work and planning carried out during the last decade, and it was agreed the forming of a special relationship with the Board should be discussed as soon as possible with him. (In a statement on Tuesday, July 4th Lord Campbell would announce that Mr. Pooley had accepted the Board's invitation to act as their Special Adviser, and this had been agreed on behalf of Bucks County Council. "Mr. Pooley will undertake this new responsibility in addition to his present responsibilities as County Architect and Planning Officer to the Buckinghamshire County Council. The Board, recognising Mr. Pooley's considerable knowledge of the area, and his imaginative work, suggested this appointment as the best means of combining the personal contribution that he can make to the future of Milton Keynes with the wide experience and the resources of Consultant Planners.") As the conclusion of the meeting it was stated that the 'city' would not be planned 'as a laboratory for new ideas which the inhabitants *might* like. Rather Milton Keynes will be built with the highest possible degree of assurance that the first inhabitants will enjoy living there, yet with provision for future generations to change the features and environment to the needs of their times.' The Board also emphasised their determination that "the views and wishes of those people already living in the area shall be taken into account at all stages." As stated by Lord Campbell, "We do not picture this as someone coming in and producing a once and for all monolithic master plan imposed upon the people. It must be worked out with everybody. It must be for and with people - a city in which people can live." He said people would mostly come from Greater London and South Bucks "but I hope it will be so attractive that we shall have people from all over the world." "We are calling it a city, not a new town. We are not only building the biggest new city ever in great Britain but we are being asked to build it twice as fast as any other new town has been able to achieve." As for any notions of the planning he said "My only pre-conceived idea is not to have any pre-conceived ideas. ... We are not committed to anything whatever about what form the city should take." At the meeting all the members of the Board were present except Mr. J. Cassidy of Bletchley, for his mother had been tragically killed in an accident on June 13th.

For the purpose of choosing a 'Master Planner' for the new city, it was also decided to send to four firms of planning consultants written invitations to forward their proposals to the Corporation. The Master Plan would then be prepared by a process of continuous consultation and collaboration between the Corporation (through its Board and officers), the Master Planners, the Central and Local Government authorities concerned, and possibly others working within this broad field. At their appointment the chosen Master Planners would be asked by the Board to devote priority to the proceeding development plans of local authorities. Also, in order that building might go on during the plan's preparation, to areas where the Corporation could begin development. Prior to completion of the Master Plan importance would additionally be afforded to work considered essential on roads, services and communications. Thus 'the most vigorous possible development' during the early years was the Board's objective, albeit with the consideration that no conflict with the ultimate objectives of the Master Plan must arise. Yet the Corporation stressed this would not be complete for at least two years, and even an interim plan might not be available for a year. Then even after the preparation of the Master Plan it was expected that some 20 years would be needed to build the new city. That was all for the future. The immediate priority was to establish a permanent headquarters, and in consequence subject to planning permission the District Valuer would now undertake the purchase of Wavendon Tower, built around the turn of the century by the then rector of Wavendon as a wedding gift for his son Colonel Henry Burney. He lived there until 1915 with the next occupants being a Mrs. Skinner and her family. After several subsequent owners it was then bought by Major and Mrs. F. Marler in 1934, remaining in this family until succeeded around 1955 by Mr. and Mrs. Barker. Some four years later ownership passed to Mr. E.B. Fernberg, who having built up a prize winning herd of Aberdeen Angus cattle died in November 1966.

With the city now being a certainty, on Monday, June 24th at a special general meeting of the Bletchley Co-operative Society it was unanimously agreed to change the name of the Society to the Milton Keynes Co-operative Society Ltd. Further, the board of directors recommended that a submitted list of rules for the new society should be adopted. The vote was unanimous and the meeting provided a necessary preliminary to the merging of the Bletchley and Wolverton Societies to serve the new town area. By now becoming more acquainted with the area was Mr. Ismay, Deputy Chairman and Managing Director of Milton Keynes Development Corporation, who on Tuesday, July 4th opened the 3,660th post war dwelling to be built by Bletchley Council. As part of a small infill site with separate garages, this was one of the 17 Quikbild Houses in Home Close, off Whalley Drive, and with a ribboned pair of scissors he performed the ceremony by cutting a ribbon across the doorway of the semi detached property. Also becoming more familiar with the area was the Chairman, Lord Campbell, who accompanied by his wife on Saturday, July 8th opened the St. Mary's Church fete at Woughton on the Green. Raising £174 for the church, this was held at the Manor House home of Mr. and Mrs. M. H. Gow, with Mr. Gow saying in his introduction that it was an historic moment for the village. Looking back he had found no record of the village having been visited by anyone like Lord Campbell, who said he hoped the Corporation would see that Woughton church and others would enrich the new city. In addressing a large audience Lord Campbell said that during the two years for the Master Plan to be produced the towns of Bletchley, Stony Stratford and Wolverton would be rapidly built up. However, elsewhere would be left until after then. From living in the country he considered he was well equipped for the task, saying "The advantages of such a chairman should be to see the problems through the rural aspect as well as the urban." "This new city will bring change and disturbance, but we do not intend to change villages completely and we want communities such as this to remain. In planning, there are three things to consider. Firstly we shall plan meetings with the necessary people to keep a regular and frank consultation. Secondly, the clearest possible warning of change. We shall see that the public will know what is to happen as long as possible before it happens. Do not pay any attention to rumour mongers who are talking through their hats when they say they know what is going to be done, here and there. Nobody, not even the Milton Keynes Board, does know what will happen and where until the Master Planners get to work. As soon as that happens the public will know as well as ourselves. The local pub will not become a railway station. We realise there will be hardship and we will try to minimise it. I feel it will be the old people who fear the change, but younger people will welcome it and want to live in the city, so it could be that the gradual development may help to bridge the gap between generations." Concluding he said "I do know the difficulties and changes involved in building a city and I have failed if we cannot increase the sum of human happiness."

Indeed he would soon become aware of some of the difficulties, for during the month from serious misconceptions about the preparation of a Master Plan the secretary to the Development Corporation, Mr. A. R. Wardle, issued a special statement which, released on the morning of July 20th, stated that 'The Board of the Development Corporation have not asked planning consultants to submit plans at this stage; this would be inconceivable in a period of a few weeks. We have simply asked four firms of planning consultants, with Lord Campbell to lead the questioning in the final selection, to let us know whether they would be interested in the commission for the Master Plan for Milton Keynes; what resources they would have available, over the next two years, to tackle the immense responsibility of an environmental and land use study of the whole area; and what work they have already done in this field. It follows that this is in no sense a competition between various plans for Milton Keynes. We are trying to collect information and evidence, from the firms in question, and from elsewhere, so that we may assess which of various well qualified firms is most likely to be able to take on the Milton Keynes assignment at this particular time - taking a whole host of considerations into account. This process of selection will include discussion and interview with representatives of the four firms. It will take some two years to prepare a Master Plan; and it will take twenty years to build the new city. Two final points. The

Board have not at all ruled out architectural competition as a means of proceeding at a later stage with the actual physical development of the City. We hope that one of the hall-marks of Milton Keynes may be planning by consultation. We hope that the Board, and the planning consultants when they are appointed, will undertake a penetrating process of consultation with local government bodies, universities, and other organisations and individuals, in this country and outside it, who may be able to contribute to building a good city."

Also co-operation with the water authorities would be needed, and during the month in his annual report to March 31st Mr. R. Pownall, the engineer and manager of Bucks Water Board, stated that in connection with the new city potential storage sites for service reservoirs, providing day to day storage, had been secured. Upon these sites the distribution system would be ultimately designed and served, and the Board had also secured a 15 acre Depot Site outside the designated area. Regarding the availability of water the Board had arranged to take a temporary supply from the Great Ouse Water Authority's works at Grafham Water but this was limited to 5 million gallons a day, and was only available until 1975. However in the immediate future some of this would be available to meet the new city demands.

By now the Corporation was beginning to attract widespread media attention and on Thursday, July 27th a scrapbook of local and national newspaper cuttings relating to the new city, normally on display at Bletchley Branch Library, was shown by the Bletchley Branch Librarian, Mrs. A.E. Inshaw, to members of the Bletchley Darby and Joan Club. As for the chairman of the NFU Steering Committee, Mr. W. Snook had been disappointed at the failure of their efforts to prevent the arrival of the new city. Yet he had cause for celebration on Saturday, July 29th when his son, Peter Thomas Snook, married Miss Penelope Cripps. In fact there was further reason to celebrate, for Peter, a former pupil of Bletchley Grammar School, had been hailed as the most distinguished student of the year in veterinary science. Having studied the subject at Glasgow University for the past five years he had now gained a degree as Bachelor of Veterinary Medicine and Science, and after his marriage would take up an appointment with a vet at High Wycombe.

Having since its formation been using the 12th floor office in Central London of Booker Bros. McConnell and Co. Ltd., the Corporation now had a headquarters to operate from, for with the purchase of Wavendon

Tower now complete on Tuesday, August 1st despite the heavy rain, which fell throughout most of the afternoon, many buyers attended an auction of the household effects, garden equipment plus the contents of a wine cellar conducted in a marquee by John Foll. The move to the new premises was then made on Wednesday, August 25th, with the telephone number Woburn Sands 3401. Mr. Ismay would be amongst the first to arrive and also Mr. A.R. Wardle who, having until earlier in the year been secretary of the Corby New Town Corporation, would now, until the appointment of an administrative officer, be working for the Development Corporation. Whilst a skeleton staff settled in, during the first week electricians began carrying out certain rewiring of the premises for office use, with this expected to be complete prior to the first meeting of the Board members on September 25th. However, preceding this on Monday, September 11th chaired by Mr. Ismay, and with officers from Bucks County Council as observers, the first meeting of the Milton Keynes Development Corporation Council Liaison Committee took place at the new headquarters, attended by members and officers representing Bletchley, Newport Pagnell and Wolverton Urban District Councils. Also Winslow and Newport Pagnell District Councils, the representatives for the latter being Councillors A. Snaith and J. Goss, who had been appointed at the council's discussion on Wednesday, July 19th. A statement after the meeting read; "The procedure which was being followed to select consultants to prepare a Master Plan for the designated area was outlined and the chairman stated that the Board of the Corporation hoped to be able to announce their first choice following the next Board meeting on September 25th. A number of suggestions were made concerning important points to be considered by the consultants, when appointed, particularly in the field of social development and recreation. The chairman undertook to convey the views expressed to the Board of the Corporation at their next meeting and to keep the consultants fully informed." As regarding the date of the next meeting of the Liaison Committee, this was provisionally arranged for mid December.

In order to meet anticipated pressures caused by the new city, a plan for trebling Winslow's population to 6,500 had now been prepared by the Bucks County Planning Department. This would be considered by the county's development sub committee, Winslow Rural Council, the parish council and other parties, whilst as for other parish councils, at the annual general meeting of the Newport Pagnell and District Association of Parish Councils, to be held at Wavendon Community Centre on October 16th, it was planned that a talk on the 'New City of Milton Keynes' would be given by Lord Campbell. However, before then at the second meeting of the Board of the Corporation, held on Monday, September 25th, he would state that people in Bletchley, Wolverton and Stony Stratford should begin to think of themselves as living in Milton Keynes. At a press conference afterwards he then dispelled fears of a single centred town by saying "There will not be one monolithic centre letting Bletchley, Wolverton and Stony Stratford stagnate, but various centres. We have no preconceived ideas what the functions of the centres will be, but the important thing is for people to begin thinking of themselves as living in Milton Keynes, not as living in Bletchley, Wolverton and Stony Stratford." Also at Monday's meeting the people to be principally concerned with the preparation of the Master Plan were named as Lord Llewelyn-Davies, Walter Bor and Fred Pooley, chief architect and planning officer to Bucks County Council, who in respect of his local knowledge would be regarded as a special adviser. Professor of Architecture at the University of London, Lord Llewelyn-Davies was a member of the Council of the Royal Institute of British Architects and a Member of the Town Planning Institute. He was also chairman of the Board of Governors of the Centre for Environmental Studies, chairman of the Building Research Station's Urban Planning Committee, Fellow of the World Society for Arts and Science, a member of the Ministry of Transport's Urban Research and Planning Group, and a member of the Royal Fine Art Commission. Being from 1962 to 1966 the City Planning Officer for Liverpool, Walter Bor was formerly London County Council deputy Planning Officer, and concerned mostly with housing had been in architectural practice. A member of the Council of the Royal Institute of British Architects and of the Council of the Town Planning Institute, he had also served as a member of the Ministry of Housing and Local Government's Planning Advisory Group, and on the Committee on the Needs of New Communities in New and Expanded Towns.

Indeed the Board were now in the final stages of negotiation with the partnership of Llewelyn-Davies, Weeks, Forrestier-Walker and Bor, who had not only prepared the Master Plan for the new town of Washington in County Durham, but had amongst other major assignments advised on the expansion of Swindon and also on the preparation of a Master Plan for a new city in Venezuela, of population 500,000. As for Milton Keynes, the Master Plan was expected to take two years and take the form not of a detailed physical plan for the city but of an environmental and land use survey, combined with broad recommendations for the development of the designated area. Concerning the phasing of development, control of costs and development control during the process of planning, these latter would consider the fundamental requirements for transport, town centres, housing services, employment and leisure, and operational requirements. Commenting on the Master Plan, Lord Campbell said a main purpose would be to determine the objectives - social, economic, physical - which the new city should achieve. "At an early stage we aim to sit down and look at the immediate requirements and at what Bletchley, Wolverton and Stony Stratford are doing to see whether there are areas within the Master Plan where we could do some building." This would be worked out in close consultation with the Council Liaison Committee and with the County, it being the view of the Board that the new city must avoid dependence upon one monolithic centre. "The existing centres of Bletchley, Wolverton and Stony Stratford must not only be preserved but enhanced in their role in the new city." The aim was to have a new city consisting of various centres, and to avoid the grouping of social, administrative and welfare buildings in any one centre. The possibility of a monorail system for Milton Keynes had also been discussed with the planning consultants. However, "We have no preconceptions about this," adding that the Board had been careful not to ask what specific form of transport they would plan for the new city, but more the considerations which would influence the eventual decision.

Having now been engaged by the Board, a chief engineer and an estates officer would take up their positions on December 1st. The former would be Mr. E. L. Pye, aged 43, who, married with two daughters, was presently the deputy City Engineer at Norwich. Since December 1964 he had been with Norwich City Council, prior to which throughout four years he held the position of deputy Borough Engineer and Planning Officer to the Bedford Borough Council. Born in St. Helens, Lancashire, he obtained the degree of Master of Engineering at Liverpool University, and was a member of the Institute of Civil Engineering, the Institute of Municipal Engineers, and the Town

Planning Institute. Taking up the position of Estates Officer would be Mr. A.G. Ashton, a married man aged 53 year with one daughter. A member of the Royal Institute of Chartered Surveyors, in a position which he had held since 1964 he was presently deputy Chief Estates Officer with the Redditch Development Corporation, having previously been with the Central Electricity Board as Midlands Area valuer and surveyor. Of the other appointments on Monday, 49 year old Mr. G.A.T. Shaw, who had joined the Corporation as administrative officer in late September, would now be appointed Secretary at the end of October. Married with four children he obtained a BA degree at Clare College, Cambridge, and had been Administrative Officer in the Agricultural, Horticultural and Forestry Industrial Training Board in London. For the appointment of a chief finance officer the Board was presently in the process of negotiation. As for that of a chief architect, this was not expected until 'well into the Master Plan,' of which Lord Campbell explained that during the first year of its compilation an 'interim plan' would be issued, with the possibility that during the preparation of both a certain amount of development would be started, such as housing for staff. "People are worrying," he said, "that we are going to go mad, by either having one ghastly traffic snarl or having three Milton Keynes. We do hope to have various centres, but we have no ideas on them yet. But if people in Bletchley say we must have everything in Bletchley and people in Wolverton say we must have everything in Wolverton we are going to get nowhere. I am afraid people are thinking on a different wave-length." Yet he had been astonished by the friendship and co-operation shown towards the Board by the existing local authorities in the area, "and that's not simply for the record, it's true." Local people "should begin to think of themselves as already living in Milton Keynes and not as living in Bletchley, Wolverton or Stony Stratford."

Following a first meeting on Friday, September 29th with the Buckinghamshire Agricultural Executive Committee, during the first week of October an important statement affecting farmers, local landowners and tenants in the designated area of the new city of Milton Keynes was released by the Board of the Milton Keynes Development Corporation. This stated their awareness of the farmers' 'wholly understandable anxiety' but until the master plan was completed in two years' time, or at least until an interim plan was available in perhaps one year, it would be impossible to say what the phasing of the development of the designated area will be, 'and so to say when agricultural land will be requested for other purposes.' Therefore 'The Board could only give farmers the following assurances:

1) That they will be actively and regularly consulted through the Ministry of Agriculture and other appropriate channels of communication, particularly at local level, during the process of preparing the master plan.

2) That through similar channels they will be informed of expected disturbances as far in advance as possible.

3) That if landowners wish to enter into negotiation for the sale of their land in advance of the statutory period of seven years from the date of designation, then the Board will ask the District Valuer to make the necessary arrangements. In appropriate cases the Board would be prepared to consider leasing the land back to the previous owner for agricultural purposes until the Corporation required it.

4) That they are aware of the problems facing tenant farmers and that they are determined to do all within their statutory power and direction to minimise hardship.

5) That arrangements for purchase of land and compensation will, of course, be dealt with through the proper authorities and that officers of the Corporation will ensure that those responsible for negotiation are made fully aware of local and personal problems involved.

6) That the Board are aware of the problems resulting from the present "freeze" on grants for capital improvements, and that this is a strong additional reason for pressing on with the master plan as quickly as possible."

Also on Friday, September 29th, regarding the telephone system of the district Subscriber Trunk Dialling (STD) was introduced, and on the following Monday the Bedford area telecommunications controller Mr. G.C. Goodman, who described himself as "one of the faceless ones - the man responsible for the phone service round here," said with regard to Bletchley's poor service over the past few years "I will try to see that you do not go back where you came from." "We have your big brother Milton Keynes coming along, and it is convenient to use Bletchley as the nucleus for the growth of the new city, as we have nothing at Milton

Keynes itself. But we will see that Bletchley customers do not suffer because of their big neighbour …"

On Wednesday, October 11th at the meeting of Newport Pagnell Rural Council it was reported that the Southern Sports Council was prepared, if asked by the council, to carry out a survey of the social and recreational needs of the new city. Also to take account of the adjacent parts of North Bucks, providing a formal request was made by each constituent local authority as well as by the Corporation. Then on Sunday, October 15th in the early morning 173 youngsters aged from 14 to 21 from Bletchley, Wolverton, Newport and Olney set off from Manor Fields, Bletchley, to walk the 27.6 miles around the perimeter of the new city. This had been organised by North Bucks youth leaders Barrie Field, Mick Arnold, Dave Mosely and Bill Smith, and despite having to sometimes wade through thick mud 125 competitors completed the course and received certificates. Non finishers received silver and bronze certificates, depending on the miles covered, with the trophies for the first three boys and first three girls being presented by Mr. R. Bellchambers, a member of the Corporation Board. He also presented the medals to the winning teams in the team events.

In view of the vastness of the plan for the Milton Keynes new town, on Monday, October 16th Lord Campbell, addressing an evening meeting at Wavendon Community centre of the Newport Pagnell and District Parish Council's Association, said it would be foolish to rush into the project. This was in answer to a question put forward by former Newport Pagnell Rural Councillor Mr. F.T. Hawkins, who enquired why there should be a two years' wait before the Master Plan was ready. In his reply Lord Campbell gave an assurance that no time was being wasted, and that a study of the County Council's plans and previous work was being undertaken; "I feel it would be wrong of us to take this matter too fast. The transport system we decide upon for example, must be in use in hundreds of years time, and we must take into account all sorts of changes. I know two years sounds a long time but really it is short, if you consider the centuries of time it took to build our towns and villages. Two years is an infinitesimal length of time in this sort of thing." On the matter of separate villages in the new town area he said it was the Corporation's intention to enhance these where possible, not to destroy existing life or character. "I shudder at the thought of any habitable dwelling, or any single building of character, being destroyed.

We shall not set out to destroy existing life and character. Where possible we want to add to them." However, "Disturbance, much disturbance, is inescapable. It would be wrong of me to pretend otherwise. But, with imaginative planning, villages and village greens can, to some extent, be embodied in larger districts - gems to be reset, as it were, in city surroundings. Churches and other important and attractive features of local life can be worked into the larger pattern." "Some property may have to suffer through drainage, road or other development, but in such cases we shall give the clearest possible warning of change and disturbance as far ahead as possible." The existing towns of Bletchley, Wolverton and Stony Stratford would be integrated into the new city and "the last thing we would want to do is submerge them."

As for other considerations, the Board had been informed by the Central Council for the Disabled about some of the problems faced by disabled people living in urban surroundings. Discussions had also been held with Miss Marjorie Bucke, Secretary to the National Old People's Welfare Council, who together with her colleagues had offered to advise and assist in the planning for the welfare of old people at Milton Keynes. In recognition of this 'The Board attaches great importance to the contribution made and the stability inspired by old people, and to the responsible and pleasant role they can play in the development of the new city.' 'The Board intends to make certain that architects and engineers concerned in planning the new city provide for old and disabled people to participate to the fullest extent in the life of the community.'

Comprised of representatives from local schools, individual nature lovers, and members of the Workers' Educational Association natural history class, together with their tutor Mr. H. Hill B.Sc., during the month a natural history survey of the Milton Keynes new city area was discussed and planned by a group of 14 enthusiasts. The aim was to ensure that the whole area was 'walked over,' to thereby discover those areas of potentially interesting flora and fauna. These would then be more closely studied, to be put forward as a nature reserve for education if deemed of sufficient interest. The methods of the survey were explained by Miss J. Royston, Assistant Curator of the County Museum, and the meeting also expressed appreciation to Mr. Marvin, of Manor Farm, Milton Keynes, for having allowed the main part of the discussion to be held under cover in one of his farm outbuildings.

Despite the vast amount of development, the new city formed only a part of that alluded to in 'A Strategy for the South East,' for the first report by the Government sponsored South East Economic Planning Council, published on Thursday, November 2nd, contained the recommendation that stretching from just south of Luton to as far north as Northampton a huge corridor of development should be allowed. This type of zone was termed 'a city region' and with the others being at 'Southampton-Portsmouth, Ipswich-Colchester, with possibly the Ashford area and other places' the report favoured several such zones built up throughout the South East. Each city region would be designed to act as a counter magnet to London, and the sectors or corridors leading to them would be based on the main roads and railways. Not that the immediate reaction was locally enthusiastic, with North Bucks being potentially faced with a concrete jungle - 'the one bright spot being the ultra modern city of Milton Keynes in its midst.' However in a counter balance the Economic Planning Council included that for the preservation of certain rural aspects country areas should be set up surrounding, and in some cases within, these city areas, such as Woburn. The report also included that the development of Milton Keynes should be relegated to a secondary importance, with emphasis concentrated on building up a city region around the Southampton area to be known as 'South Hants.' Indeed, commenting on the report William Benyon, the prospective Conservative candidate for North Bucks, said he was afraid the city might turn out to be a second rate community. "It's all very well for the Chairman of the Planning Council to say 'we will remove employment from central London, but have you considered the cost of removing 500,000 jobs. Every single factory has to be purchased at market price. Unless something happens to the contrary we shall not be able to afford the capital expenditure involved in this new city. Something will have to give. ... we shall suddenly find the resources are not there, and have to compromise on a second-rate community, with second-rate architecture and second-rate facilities."

Speaking of the report on the day of its publication Mr. Ismay, as managing director of the Milton Keynes Development Corporation, said this would only stimulate his Board to building an even better city than was planned; "In that way we hope people will want to come to Milton Keynes by choice, rather than to come just because housing is here." Having only read accounts of the publication in the morning papers he declined to commit himself too deeply to any specific comment on the report, and thought it somewhat odd that the Development Corporation had not been informed as early as the previous week, when the Press received their special copies. Yet from his 'limited knowledge' he said it was encouraging that the Government intended to pursue its policy of providing incentives for industry and offices to move out of London, and the report did emphatically state that the drift to the South East had to be stopped. Of his reaction, Ray Furnival, secretary to the Bletchley and Newport branches of the NFU, said "The strategy merely confirms a feeling that the NFU have had all along that Milton Keynes, and now it seems all of North Bucks, will eventually become another suburb of London with a vast loss of farming land. At earlier representations over Milton Keynes with the then Minister of Housing we pointed this out but nobody would listen. ... The main reason why the Steering Committee was not disbanded after the Milton Keynes inquiry was because we could see this sort of thing happening."

At the meeting of the Corporation's Board at Wavendon Tower on Monday, October 30th official confirmation had been announced that Mr. G. A. T. Shaw would be taking over from Mr. A. R. Wardle as secretary to the Milton Keynes Development Corporation, the position to become effective from November 1st. Then on Monday, November 6th in a special statement the Corporation announced that the firm of Llewelyn-Davies, Weeks, Forestier-Walker and Bor were to be the consultants responsible for the Master Plan. With consultations being held with leading sociologists in Britain and from abroad the Board was determined that planning should proceed through a process of continuous consultation, not only with local and central government and the County but also those institutions and individuals in Britain and elsewhere who could contribute knowledge and experience. The determination of the objectives - social, economic and physical - which the new city should achieve was a primary purpose of the Master Plan, and on the news of the selection of the Master Planners, John Cornwall, the prospective Liberal candidate, said "I am delighted with the selection of this quality and breadth of interest. We all hope for a city which will be a model to the world in its provision for the freedom and happiness of the people. ..."

In association with Llewelyn-Davies, Weeks, Forestier-Walker and Bor specialist advice would be sought from a number of consultants:

a) Nathaniel Lichfield and Associates. As experts in the economic aspects of planning and growth of new and expanding towns the firm had surveyed, analysed and reported on many town expansion schemes. Nathaniel Lichfield, B.Sc., Ph.D., M.T.P.I., F.R.I.C.S., A.M.I.Mun.E., was the Professor of the Economics of Town Planning at University College, London, and the Honorary Treasurer and immediate Past President of the Town Planning Institute.

b) Emrys Jones, B.Sc., Ph.D., Professor of Geography at the London School of Economics and Head of the Department of Geography, had charge of the preparation of the Atlas of London and the London Region, sponsored by the Department of Education and Science and the Greater London Council. He had also acted as a consultant to the Government of Venezuela and also for the master plan of Washington New Town.

c) Awarded the Gold Medal of the Royal Institute of British Architects in 1967, Nikolaus Pevsner, C.B.E., M.A., Ph.D., F.S.A., was Professor of the History of Art at Birbeck College, University of London, an Honorary Fellow of the Royal Institute of British Architects, and a member of the Royal Fine Art Commission.

d) A subsidiary of Kates, Peat, Marwick and Company, Traffic Research Corporation Ltd. was a Canadian partnership of management and technical consultants which, together with a sister organisation in the U.S.A., had played a prominent role in the development of land use and transportation studies on both sides of the Atlantic. In Britain they were presently responsible for the Merseyside Area Land Use Transportation Study and the West Yorkshire Transportation Study.

e) Melvin W. Webber, M.C.P., M.A., was currently holder of the Chair of City Planning at the University of California, and lately the senior metropolitan regional planner for the San Francisco Bay Area Rapid Transit Study.

f) Gerald Wibberley, B.Sc., Ph.D., Head of the Department of Economics and Professor of Rural Economy in the University of London at Wye College, was also chairman of the Committee on Rural Land Use (Recreation and Leisure), recently set up by the Ministry of Housing and Local Government.

g) A landscape architect and a past President of the Institute of Landscape Architects, Peter Youngman, M.A., P.P.I.L.A., M.T.P.I., was a member of the Town Planning Institute and since its inception had acted as consultant to the Cumbernauld Development Corporation .

As for other appointments, Kenneth Wren, Fellow of the Institute of Municipal Treasurers and Accountants, and Fellow of the Rating and Valuation Association, had now been appointed Chief Financial Officer. Having served with four local authorities over a period of 20 years, since January 1964 he had been Borough Treasurer of Banbury Borough Council, being prior to this the deputy treasurer. A keen golfer, he was married with a son and daughter, aged respectively 11 and 9.

As announced earlier in the year, during November the new conditions regarding compensation for tenant farmers 'when displaced for non agricultural purposes' were outlined by the Minister of Agriculture, Fred Peart, when he presented the Agriculture Bill to the House of Commons. This was in consequence to his reply on February 21ˢᵗ to the Buckingham MP, Robert Maxwell, who he said "has taken a great interest and my right hon. friend and I are proud to redeem that promise today." Regarding the Bill, landlords would now have to pay tenant farmers additional special re-settlement payments when displacing them for non agricultural purposes. This new extra sum would be four years' rent, and so tenants leaving land destined for development would receive five or possibly six years rent. This said the Minister "is a substantial increase, which is fair not only to tenant farmers but to other interests also." On behalf of the tenant farmers at Milton Keynes Mr. Maxwell thanked the Minister for righting this injustice. He hoped the Government could also give some priority of assistance to finding them alternative farms but the Minister said that was beyond the scope of the present Bill.

Also during the month, on Friday 17ᵗʰ when speaking at the annual dinner of the Wavendon Conservatives the prospective Conservative candidate for North Bucks, William Benyon, said the cost of building the new city could be between £500m and £1,000m. He said the criterion for making the new city a success was the country's economy - "the most vital factor" - and therefore he would be worried about the future of the new development until the economy begin to expand. "I am most anxious that we, as a Party, should identify ourselves with the success of this new city, remembering that it was under a Conservative

Government that the first planning was begun. We started it and it is up to us to finish the job well. ... It is our function to see that in the Master plan for this city the interests of local people and communities are safeguarded and that it provides something which will be in the interests of all of us."

Consequent to the first general seminar on the Milton Keynes development, at a Press Conference in London on Tuesday, December 5th Lord Campbell expressed the view that should money not prove forthcoming to build a balanced new city then the Development Corporation was not prepared to build a second class city. If the Government made any cuts in the finance to provide services, roads, schools and other amenities then to maintain pace with the housing development there would have to be a re-phasing, or even a postponement. Outlining the difficulties of planning a physical environment as a whole - 'when there was a fragmentation of responsibility among the various Government departments' - he said "We will build a balanced city, or no city at all." Emphasising that the Board was not dictating the building of Milton Keynes, he stressed that the city was an experiment, a show piece, and was supposed to set a pattern: "Therefore it must not be badly done simply because of the present (economic) difficulties." If the money did not materialise then there would have to be re-phasing, or alternatively the construction of less than the target figure of 2,000 houses a year; "We are building this city at a time when there are cuts in Government expenditure. The master plan will be produced in two years; if in the meantime it is clear that the money is not forthcoming for all the services then the Board feels that it should not go ahead. ... If there was not full co-operation from the different Ministries, the Board would dig in its toes." Roads were an essential requirement and with the need for a proper system to attract industry the planners wanted to be clear on the transport system within the next six months. If the Minister said there was not enough money for the roads, then the "crunch" would come. Regarding the final cost of the development, in which it was hoped to have a variety of architecture, Lord Campbell estimated this to be in the region of £500 million, with some of the burden on public expenditure to be relieved by bringing private developers and money into the town. Indeed in the new towns it was the wish of the Government to achieve 50% of the development in the private sectors.

Mentioning the unusual amount of agricultural extent in the

designated area, a total of some 7,000 acres, in regard to the farmers he recognised their anxiety from the uncertainty of when their land would be used, and indeed the danger that farms might descend into agricultural slums through farmers being unable to obtain grants. Therefore the Corporation was now prepared to buy agricultural land even in advance of requirements and lease it back to the farmers if necessary. Also the Corporation had asked the master planners to provide as early an indication as possible of when the farm land would be required in the phasing of the building operations. Questioned about existing housing Lord Campbell said "It is against our policy to knock down habitable houses and buildings of quality. Where there is a group of buildings of character and quality we want to try to keep it. But it would be foolish to pretend it will go on being a village. We will try to keep it and re-set it in a city setting." "It is easy to be cynical and to say we are trying to plan Utopia, but it is right to start to look at what is desirable, then consider what is possible and hope there will finally be as narrow a gap as possible." The interim plan should be ready by the end of 1968 and the master plan by the end of 1969 after which, provided the money was available, major building would commence. Meanwhile there would need to be some building to accommodate workers, and already there was an operation in addition to the Bletchley G.L.C. building scheme. As for the purpose of the seminar, held at the Park Lane Hotel, Piccadilly, and attended by Board members, the consultants and their assistants, and representatives of Government and local authorities in the area, Lord Campbell explained this was to try to start planning the city by consultations with all concerned; "We wanted to avoid the planners going away, preparing a master plan, and imposing on the designated area." This seminar was the first meeting at which to discuss some of the main aspects where decisions had to be reached in advance of any planning. Making allowances for the future was of significant concern, regarding which Lord Campbell said "This must not be an open and shut city." The developers had to try and keep options open and leave room for adaptations, and to avoid the mistakes of their predecessors who hadn't foreseen what lay in the future. Lord Llewellyn-Davies said that before actually starting the development the planners were anxious to initially spend a great deal of time examining and discussing the fundamental social goals of the project.

Sites of scientific interest were now also a consideration and a

Milton Keynes Research Committee had been established to make recommendations for their preservation, collect records and specimens, survey sites of archaeological and nature interest, excavate sites and make a general photographic survey of the designated area. At the behest of the Bucks County Council's Museums Sub Committee and the Council of the Bucks Archaeological Society the inaugural meeting had been recently held at County Hall, Aylesbury, with the representation of the local authorities of the area, Bucks County Council, Milton Keynes Development Corporation, local interested societies including Bletchley Archaeological and Historical Society, the North Bucks Historical Committee, The Naturalists Trust, both the historical and natural history sections of the Bucks Archaeological Society, the Council for British Archaeology, the Ministry of Public Building and Works, Nature Conservancy, the consultant planners of the new city and the geography department of University College, London. As chairman Professor W.F. Grimes, director of London University's Institute of Archaeology was elected with County Treasurer Mr. J. R. Worboys as treasurer, and County Museum Curator Mr. C. N. Gowing as secretary. During the meeting it was reported that although now in abeyance due to the outbreak of foot and mouth disease a field survey had been in progress, following the completion of which it would then be possible to recommend those sites suitable as educational reserves or open spaces for use by the general public. Over a long period it was intended to make ecological records in areas of interest, since this would be necessary to obtain funds for the appointment of a field naturalist for at least three years. Also it was hoped that in some areas other surveys would be conducted, particularly by schools. From the archaeological point of view, from the examination of aerial photographs and observations on the ground a list of 35 known sites had already been compiled, of which several were deemed worthy of preservation. However, detailed surveys were needed of all the sites with some needing excavation. No doubt important sites would be discovered during the construction work, and the means to provide for their immediate investigation would have to be found. An industrial archaeology survey was additionally in progress with a general photographic survey of the area also being made.

Despite being formed to counter the Government proposal for the new city, the North Bucks Association was still in existence to now perhaps usefully serve as 'a watchdog,' and to offer constructive help and ideas for the planning and building. Indeed towards this ambition there was encouragement when Lord Campbell and Mr. Ismay recently met the members, who asked questions regarding the current progress and how it was intended to deal with the serious problems of transport, drainage, water supply and the inconvenience to residents and farmers. In answering these concerns Lord Campbell said he appreciated the difficulties faced by those farmers whose land might be required, and although he had no powers outside the designated area liaison arrangements had been made. As for the other matters, the Ministry of Transport and the Ministry of Housing and Local Government were taking the problems very seriously and at high level. Drainage would be planned in consultation with the Ouse River Board, and - 'where it was related to current development, and that there was complete co-operation with County Planning Authority, and no difficulties were expected' - it would be possible for some areas to be developed in advance of the Master Plan. The Board of the Corporation would do everything possible to make Milton Keynes an attractive place to live, and Lord Campbell said he'd been encouraged by the large number of companies interested in establishing factories there.

The first liaison meeting between Milton Keynes Development Corporation and members of the local authorities in the area took place at Milton Keynes Community Centre on Monday, December 11th. Here in his opening address Lord Campbell told a capacity audience that this meeting was 'experimental,' being an opportunity for questions to be asked by members of County Councils and representatives of local authorities in the designated area. Indeed, Lord Llewelyn-Davies, the man principally concerned with the preparation of the Master Plan, would be spending ten days in and around the designated area after Christmas, when it was hoped that he might have time to meet representatives from local authorities and to hear their views. During the afternoon among the many questions put to Lord Campbell, Lord Llewelyn-Davies, and Mr. W. Ismay, was that from Mr. R. Dunbabin, who speaking on behalf of Newport Pagnell RDC, of which he was the clerk, asked if the housing of advance workers had yet been considered. His council had gained some experience of this during the building of the M1 in 1959/60, for the civil engineering contractors involved had lived in caravans. Therefore the council feared that these and the lorries might just be parked anywhere. He said it was common policy to channel the caravans into sites of their own and Mr. J. F. Smithie, Bletchley Town Manager, then suggested that an existing building might serve as a hostel for transitory workers. Agreeing that this was a serious concern Lord Campbell said the problem had already been brought to the attention of the Master Planners, and there were three things that the Corporation must do. Firstly they must ensure full and effective co-operation with local authorities before building. Secondly there must be co-ordination with people throughout the designated area; and thirdly the plans and activities for the new town must be subject to a rigorous control. If there was participation between the local authorities and the Board then this could be effectively controlled and managed. A second question put by Newport Pagnell RDC concerned the arrangements that could best be made for sewage. Also the satisfactory drainage of surface water, and in response Lord Campbell assured the councillors that the Corporation would be meeting engineers regarding these concerns. Members of the Bedfordshire County Council were also worried about the problems of sewage but another of their major anxieties, as with Northamptonshire County Council, was the future of the villages surrounding the new town. Mr. C. M. Jones, deputy clerk of Northamptonshire County Council, said there would be a need to build executive type houses for the low density of people who would not wish to live in the town. Thereby there might be a gradual erosion of existing standards, and "before we know where we are we shall be left with an estate of houses." A member of Beds. County Council confirmed experience of the same sort of problem in their area but in his reply Lord Campbell said this should be stopped by the size of the designated area; "There will always be people who work in the city and want to live outside it, but we do want a green belt in and around the area. We shall have failed in our job unless we do this." From Wolverton UDC, Councillor F. Atter was also concerned about the periphery of the new town. They didn't want to see an urban sprawl extending beyond the designated area but he was assured by Lord Campbell that a green belt would be ensured by stringent measures. The aim, said Lord Llewlyn-Davies, was to meet all the requirements within the designated area, and so remove the pressure from the neighbouring villages; "The whole point of the operation is to stop any sprawling destruction of the towns and villages around the designated area, and the point will be lost if we see people spreading outside."

Stating that the Board's policy was to attract people into better types of houses in the designated area, Lord Campbell said they would be prepared to support the withholding of planning permission for development outside this extent. On a question about the difficulties of a water supply he said it was a problem "which had not yet been solved." Indeed being very much aware of the anxiety expressed at last year's public inquiry he was "trying to get assurances that there will be adequate water supplies (a) to 1995 and (b) to the end of the century!" In fact in conversation with the Bucks Water Board he'd been told there would be water until 1975, and arrangements could be made to supply water after that date. In fact they would not start building until satisfied "that the water will be there." On the subject of transport, Mr. J. F. Smithie suggested that if the Corporation deemed it worthwhile to save the threatened east west branch railway lines then they might consider making representations to the Ministry. However, Lord Campbell had doubts that the Board members were the right people to initiate such representations, but "we have in fact a close working relationship with the Ministry, and this is something we can look at with them." Questioned about plans for communications between the new city and the neighbouring towns of Northampton, Luton, Bedford and Aylesbury, he said the money for roads would have to be committed in an advance programme. "If we are to attract industry, we must have really good communications from the word 'go.'" Fears of speculative building taking place in the villages bordering the designated area were expressed by Mr. Smithie, who of a determination that Bletchley should be a major, and perhaps even the major, centre in the new city of Milton Keynes was now preparing with Bletchley Council a plan of development and road systems for early submission to the Development Corporation. Largely accommodated within the existing urban area this would provide for a population in excess of 70,000, and with the venue being Wilton Hall, Bletchley, some 180 of the town's traders, industrialists and persons of similar interest attended a Monday meeting at which satisfaction with the general aims and ideas was expressed.

Since the first announcement of the new city the Oxford Regional Hospital Board had given special consideration to the provision of its hospital services. Then with informal discussions having taken place for some while, following the appointment of the Development

Corporation an immediate approach was made offering assurance that the three branches of the health service were prepared to put forward one comprehensive scheme. Welcoming this approach the Development Corporation duly promised to take full account of the needs, with it being realised that during the early years of development the general practitioners and local health authority were to be mainly concerned with the provision of a family doctor service, plus domiciliary and community care. A meeting between the Oxford Regional Hospital Board and the chairman of the Development Corporation took place on Friday, December 15th from which as the chair Mrs. Isabel Graham Bryce stated in a subsequent report that the outcome had been most encouraging. This, said Mr. C. Head, of Bletchley, would ease the minds of a lot of people and it was decided to recommend that an honorary contract should be granted to the 'Principal Medical Officer' (to be appointed by Bucks County Council) for work mainly with the Milton Keynes development.

As deputy chairman and managing director of the Development Corporation, Mr. Ismay was now settling into the role although from his previous experience he said when the chief guest at the annual luncheon of the Bletchley Manufacturers' Association, held on Wednesday, December 13th, that he felt very much at home among industrialists. In fact some of his closer 'chums' now accused him of desertion in the face of adversity! However the more he got around the area the more he began to realise the significant contribution they had made.

Index

A

A5 39, 57, 93, 131, 139, 153, 186
Abercrombie, Professor Leslie 1, 2, 83
Adams, Ronald 184
Alexander, Robert Guy 168
Allen, Mrs. S.C.F., Lathbury Park. 137
Architect's Journal 44
Ashford 213
Ashton, A.G., Chief Esates Officer
    MKDC. 209
Aspley Guise 106, 155
Astley, H., County Councillor 17, 137
Astley, Mrs. Margaret 137
Atter, Councillor F., Wolverton UDC.
    21, 82, 108, 112, 147, 195, 196,
    198, 199, 221
Ayers, R.J. 132
Aylesbury 13, 28, 40, 43, 47, 48, 50, 60,
    63, 66, 97, 125, 136, 172, 185,
    219, 222

B

Bains, Councillor A., Clerk, Shenley
    Parish Council 66
Barrett, R. 184
Barron, L., County Secretary NFU. 50
Basildon 127, 176
Bass, A.G. 68
Bates, Councillor R. 58
Baxter, Councillor J. 143
Beachampton 37, 39, 100
Bedford 3, 7, 18, 85, 88, 89, 94, 122,
    124, 152, 156, 208, 210, 222
Bedfordshire County Counci 221
Bedfordshire Water Board 156
Beesley, Walter, County Councillor 14,
    18, 29, 43, 69, 77, 80, 111, 142
Bellchambers, R., Councillor, Newport
    Pagnell RDC. 18, 19, 23, 27, 54,
    57, 69, 72, 87, 98, 103, 104, 105,

106, 107, 109, 110, 111, 112, 120,
    121, 134, 141, 148, 153, 154, 155,
    158, 159, 181, 192, 193, 194, 211
Benson, F. 113
Benyon, William, Conservative Parlia-
    mentary Candidate, Bucking-
    ham. 216
Bevan, Councillor N. 58
Blackmore, T.R. 177
Blakenham, Lord, Chancellor of the
    Duchy of Lancaster 26
Blane, R. Managing Secretary, Bletchley
    Cooperative Society. 143
Bletchley 1, 2, 3, 4, 7, 9, 10, 16, 23, 24,
    25, 26, 27, 30, 31, 32, 33, 34, 35,
    36, 37, 42, 44, 45, 46, 50, 53, 54,
    55, 57, 58, 60, 62, 63, 64, 65, 66,
    67, 70, 73, 74, 75, 78, 79, 80, 82,
    83, 85, 86, 87, 92, 93, 94, 95, 96,
    97, 98, 99, 100, 101, 105, 106,
    109, 110, 111, 112, 116, 117, 118,
    119, 122, 123, 124, 125, 126, 130,
    131, 132, 135, 136, 137, 138, 139,
    140, 141, 142, 143, 144, 145, 146,
    147, 148, 149, 150, 151, 153, 154,
    155, 156, 159, 164, 165, 166, 171,
    172, 174, 175, 176, 179, 180, 185,
    186, 187, 190, 191, 192, 193, 197,
    198, 199, 200, 202, 203, 205, 206,
    207, 208, 209, 210, 211, 212, 214,
    218, 219, 221, 222, 223
Bletchley Chamber of Trade 26, 36,
    143
Bletchley Darby and Joan Club 205
Bletchley G.L.C. building scheme 218
Bletchley UDC 54, 122, 148, 151, 192,
    198, 200
Bodley, D. 144
Bodley, Mrs. O., Shenley Womens'
    Institute 144
Bonham, J., Shenley Farmer. 186
Boulton, D. 27
Bow Brickhill 32, 113, 144, 153, 183
Bowman, Frank 172
Bradshaw, T. Bucks County NFU. 29,
    31, 51, 61, 64, 69, 70, 72, 77, 84,

101, 102, 121, 169

Bradwell 3, 36, 37, 39, 65, 69, 108, 113, 119, 130, 131, 143, 151, 159, 163, 177, 185, 193

Bradwell Abbey 37, 163, 185

Brants Property Co. Ltd 45

Brooke, Henry, Minister of Housing and Local Government. 3

Brookes, Councillor J. 108

Broughton 37, 39, 86, 117, 143, 153, 181, 183, 184, 198

Bucke, Marjorie, Secretary to the National Old People's Welfare Council 212

Buckingham 3, 7, 9, 31, 36, 37, 49, 52, 55, 59, 64, 66, 67, 81, 84, 105, 112, 122, 124, 128, 133, 139, 147, 182, 192, 197, 216

Bucks Archaeological Society 219

Bucks County Council 3, 4, 9, 11, 27, 29, 31, 37, 44, 45, 59, 61, 62, 67, 76, 80, 81, 89, 100, 109, 113, 121, 160, 169, 172, 173, 188, 191, 194, 201, 206, 207, 219, 223

Bucks County Planning Committee 13, 17

Bucks Water Board 7

Bullock, Robert 73

Button, Councillor Aileen 157

C

Caldwell, Councillor W., Bletchley UDC. 33, 78, 79, 97, 105, 185

Calverton 64, 73, 111, 119, 151, 163, 168, 169, 181

Campbell, Lord John, Chairman Milton Keynes Development Corporation 4, 188, 189, 190, 193, 197, 199, 200, 201, 203, 204, 207, 208, 209, 211, 217, 218, 220, 221, 222

Cassidy, Councillor J., Bletchley UDC. 31, 34, 35, 36, 54, 78, 82, 97, 112, 122, 146, 148, 164, 171, 185, 192, 193, 199, 202

Castlethorpe 17, 110, 158

Cater, J., Inspector, Ministry of Housing. 176

Chapman, J. 111

Chase, A., Councillor, Newport Pagnell RDC 18

Cherrington, J. 186

Clarke, G., Councillor, Bletchley UDC. 33

Clay, Dr. A. Chairman, Newport Pagnell UDC. 20, 91, 153, 154, 155

Cockerill, E. 175

College of Aeronautics 51

Colson, Alderman E. 42

Comben, Alderman S. Bucks County Council. 27, 28, 41, 42, 66, 77, 122

Cony, A. 28, 159

Copperad Ltd. 11

Corby New Town Corporation 206

Corfield, F.V., Parliamentray Secretary to Minister of Housing 11

Cornford, Councillor F.W., Chairman Wolverton UDC 89, 107, 108, 175, 196, 199

Cornwall, John, Liberal Party Candidate for Buckingham 144, 169

Cosford, Peter, Councillor, Wolverton UDC. 21, 196, 199

Council for British Archaeology 219

Council for the Preservation of Rural England 116, 128, 137, 153, 159, 168, 190, 195

Country Churchman, The 42

Country Landowners' Association 61, 62, 81, 116, 151, 159, 160, 170, 171, 195

Coventry 18, 107

Cowley, G. 61

Cowley, Reginald 73

Cox, Mrs. W. 44

Cox, R.S., Bucks Water Board 159

Cranfield 51

Cranmer, Robert 117

Craufurd Arms, Wolverton 7

Crawley 20, 80, 176, 185

Crawley, F., Councillor Newport Pagnell UDC. 20

Cripps, Mrs Patricia 58, 205

Crisp, Reverend John, Vicar, Newport Pagnell. 42

Crossman, Richard, Minister of Housing 4, 52, 59, 60, 63, 66, 68, 72, 74, 75, 77, 78, 81, 84, 86, 88, 89, 91, 92, 93, 95, 96, 97, 99, 101, 111, 113, 116, 118, 122, 126, 127, 130, 131, 132, 134, 139, 141, 146, 147, 173

D

Daniels, Councillor E., Loughton 46, 68, 139, 167

Davies, Councillor R. 58

Davis, Mr. J. 144

Denham 127

Dewick, Councillor H. 89

Dormer, D., Club and Institute Union. 52

Dover, Geoffrey, Farmer, Milton Keynes. 117, 122, 185, 186

Drabble, Councillor C. 58

Draft Designation Order 91

Dunbabin, R., Clerk, Newport Pagnell RDC 83, 88, 103, 104, 112, 113, 117, 141, 148, 160, 220

Duncombe, Major P., Secretary County Landowner's Association. 116

Durbridge, Mrs Margaret, County Councillor 192, 193, 194

E

Eley, Councillor A., Newport Pagnell RDC 18

Emberton 35, 58, 158

Engle, Bernard, Engineer. 4, 34

Evans, Councillor Frank 146

F

Farrar, Councillor M., Newport Pagnell RDC. 18

Fenny Stratford 3

Fernberg, E.B. 203

Field, George, Bradwell Abbey Farm 163

Floyd, Brigadier Sir Henry 190

Foxley, D. Loughton Parish Council 44

Fry, Councillor P., Bucks CC. 41, 42

Fuller, Ken 70

Furneaux, Basil, Soil Scientist 135, 163

Furnival, R.P., Secretary, NFU. 57, 86, 88, 99, 135, 140, 149, 156, 173, 185, 187, 214

G

Gadsden, Councillor I., Stoke Hammond 125, 150

Gill, D. 144

Godber, Geoffrey Chapman, Clerk Shropshire County Council. 145, 159

Goodman, G.C., Bedford area telecommunications controller 210

Gowing, C., Curator, County Museum 125, 132, 219

Gow, Mr. and Mrs. M. H. 203

Graham Bryce, Mrs Isabel 223

Grand Union Canal 39, 153, 181

Great Brickhill 31, 149, 150

Greater London Council 4

Great Horwood 37, 73

Great Linford 37, 39, 109, 111, 136, 168

Green Belt 10, 13, 21, 71, 76, 77, 150

Green, Charles 174

Greenwood, Anthony, Minister of Housing, 1967 4, 48, 75, 111, 144, 167, 172, 179, 181, 183, 187, 189, 200

Greenwood, Mrs. J.M. 75

Gregory, Michael, Lead Counsel, County Landowners' Association 151, 160

Gurney, E. 61

Gurney, William 73

H

Hall, Dr. David 119, 146, 196
Hall, F., Clerk to the Newport Pagnell
    UDC. 20, 98, 140, 172
Hanslope 14, 69, 72, 77, 85, 142, 158
Hardmead 69, 84, 101, 121, 169
Harwood, J. Clerk, Wolverton UDC.
    82, 89
Hawkins, Councillor F. 114, 119, 120,
    121
Haydock, Councillor R. 78
Head, Councillor Charles, Bletchley
    UDC. 78, 102
Hedley, Rev. Harry, Rector, Bletchley
    Church 117
Hegan, Keith Van, NFU Organiser 163
Herrington, A. 47
Higgs, Mrs. K. 144
Hill, H., WEA Tutor. 212
Hodges, Councillor, Buckingham RDC
    112
Holdom, E., Councillor Newport
    Pagnell RDC 18, 54, 110, 121,
    148, 157
Hollis, N., Councillor, Newport Pagnell
    UDC. 22, 140
Hootton, G., Chairman, Walton Parish
    Council. 114
Horwood, R.C., County Councillor 14,
    27, 29, 33, 34, 37, 49, 54, 60, 73,
    145
Hoveringham Gravels Ltd. 45

I

Inshaw, Mrs. A.E. 205
Ismay, Walter, Managing Director
    MKDC. 4, 193, 199, 201, 203,
    206, 213, 220, 223

J

Johnson, Councillor E.M. 137
Johnson, W.S., Councillor, Bletchley
    UDC. 30
Jones, Emrys, Professor of Geography
    at LSE. 215
Jones, V., Headmaster, White Spire

    School. 32
Jones, W.J. 169
Joseph, Sir Keith, Minister of Housing
    and Local Government 3, 91, 92

K

Keeble, Lewis Bingham 166
Kellett, Mrs. Elaine, Conservative Party
    Candidate for Buckingham 106,
    127, 128, 131
Kelly, Charles 166
Kessler, David S., Stoke Hammond
    123, 125, 132

L

Lathbury 45, 137, 193
Lay, Edgar 28
Leighton Buzzard 117, 123, 124, 137,
    198
Leighton Buzzard Angling Club 198
Leisure in the Countryside, Govern-
    ment White Paper 168
Lewis, K. 107
Lichfield, Nathaniel, Professor of Eco-
    nomics of Town Planning, Uni-
    versity College, London. 215
Little Brickhill 54, 57, 110, 121, 148
Little Woolstone 111
Llewelyn-Davies, Lord 5, 207, 214, 220
Llewelyn-Davies, Weeks, Forresti-
    er-Walker and Bor, Town Plan-
    ning Consultants 5, 207
London 1, 2, 4, 7, 9, 10, 11, 24, 26, 28,
    32, 33, 34, 36, 38, 39, 44, 45, 47,
    50, 53, 54, 59, 61, 62, 64, 67, 69,
    70, 71, 72, 73, 74, 77, 80, 83, 85,
    86, 93, 97, 102, 110, 124, 127,
    128, 129, 130, 132, 133, 134, 136,
    139, 141, 142, 144, 145, 147, 151,
    152, 159, 160, 162, 164, 165, 166,
    170, 171, 172, 173, 177, 182, 184,
    189, 191, 194, 200, 202, 205, 207,
    209, 213, 214, 215, 217, 219
Loughton 14, 37, 40, 44, 45, 46, 47, 48,
    49, 51, 52, 53, 54, 64, 66, 68, 75,

77, 79, 85, 100, 110, 111, 118, 119, 120, 123, 132, 137, 139, 142, 143, 144, 151, 158, 166, 167, 172, 174, 175, 176, 186

Love, Dr. J., Chairman Wolverton UDC 8, 11, 196

M

M1 24, 26, 39, 57, 80, 85, 93, 94, 106, 122, 131, 139, 140, 142, 143, 183, 198, 220

Macario, John, Aspley Guise 106, 153

Manham, Harold, QC. 156

Mann, Michael 168

Marchant, Andrew 176

Marchant, James 166

Markham, Sir Frank, MP Buckingham 9, 10, 11, 20, 70, 123, 130, 132, 136, 139, 142, 145

Marler, Major and Mrs. F. 203

Maxwell, Robert, MP. Buckingham. 25, 26, 31, 43, 49, 52, 54, 55, 59, 60, 63, 64, 65, 66, 67, 68, 72, 74, 75, 78, 81, 82, 83, 84, 86, 87, 88, 89, 92, 93, 97, 98, 99, 101, 102, 106, 111, 118, 119, 127, 128, 130, 131, 133, 135, 145, 147, 150, 156, 157, 172, 173, 182, 187, 189, 192, 193, 216

Meakin, Rev. M. 106

Mellish, Robert, Joint Parliamentary Secretary 62, 84, 129, 175

Melville, Councillor L., Winslow 196

Menday, F., Bucks County Council. 115

Millard, R., Clerk, Bucks County Council. 34, 40, 71, 191

Milton Keynes 1, 4, 5, 20, 37, 39, 85, 117, 122, 132, 180, 181, 182, 183, 185, 186, 188, 190, 191, 192, 193, 196, 197, 199, 200, 201, 203, 204, 205, 206, 207, 208, 209, 210, 211, 212, 213, 214, 216, 217, 219, 220, 222, 223

Milton Keynes Development Corpora-
tion 4, 188, 190, 199, 200, 203, 206, 209, 213, 214, 219, 220

Milton Keynes village 199

Ministry of Housing and Local Government 23, 32, 35, 52, 85, 87, 129, 138, 144, 145, 149, 157, 172, 177, 179, 197, 207, 215, 220

Ministry of Public Building and Works 219

Moir, Councillor G., Bucks CC. 42, 43

Monk, P. 115

"Monorail City" 3, 13, 14, 15, 16, 18, 20, 22, 25, 27, 35, 36, 37, 38, 41, 47, 51, 52, 54, 59, 86, 97, 110, 131, 208

Morgan, C. 61

Morgan, D.E., Councillor, Wolverton UDC. 21, 89, 195

Moss, Stanley, County Chairman, NFU 51, 61, 63, 65, 67, 73, 91, 92, 138, 173, 174

Moulsoe 31, 37, 54, 106, 142

Myers, Bernard 45, 86, 99, 102, 103, 104, 105

Mynard, D.C. 132

N

Nash 37, 39, 100

National Association of Local Government Officers 175

National Farmers' Union 21, 22, 23, 27, 29, 31, 39, 40, 43, 44, 50, 54, 57, 58, 61, 63, 65, 66, 67, 69, 72, 74, 80, 83, 84, 86, 91, 99, 101, 116, 122, 124, 125, 126, 128, 133, 134, 135, 136, 138, 140, 141, 145, 149, 150, 153, 156, 157, 159, 160, 161, 162, 163, 170, 171, 173, 177, 179, 182, 183, 184, 185, 187, 205, 214

National Union of Agricultural Workers 65, 67, 128, 156, 161, 162

Naturalists Trust 219

New Bradwell 3, 36, 65, 108, 113, 119, 130, 131, 177

Newbury 23, 26, 33, 139

Newport Pagnell 7, 8, 17, 19, 20, 22, 27, 29, 31, 32, 34, 35, 36, 37, 42, 44, 45, 46, 49, 50, 51, 52, 55, 57, 58, 61, 64, 67, 68, 69, 77, 79, 80, 83, 84, 85, 86, 87, 88, 91, 92, 93, 94, 95, 98, 99, 101, 102, 103, 104, 105, 106, 109, 111, 112, 113, 114, 115, 116, 117, 118, 119, 121, 122, 123, 134, 135, 137, 139, 140, 141, 145, 147, 148, 150, 153, 154, 157, 160, 167, 171, 172, 181, 183, 187, 192, 193, 194, 197, 206, 207, 211, 220, 221

Newport Pagnell Conservative Association 20

Newport Pagnell RDC 17, 22, 27, 32, 34, 44, 46, 49, 52, 68, 69, 83, 85, 88, 98, 103, 105, 109, 112, 113, 116, 117, 119, 122, 141, 145, 148, 150, 157, 181, 183, 192, 194, 220, 221

Newport Pagnell Urban Council 17, 19, 20, 22

Newport Pagnell Young Farmers' Club 51

Newton Longville 105, 132, 133, 136, 137

New Towns Act 4, 59, 77, 88, 139, 179

Norman, Professor F., London University. 32

Northampton 59, 62, 85, 88, 89, 94, 152, 213, 222

Northamptonshire County Council 221

North Bucks Association 122, 123, 130, 132, 136, 139, 140, 145, 156, 159, 165, 166, 197, 198, 219

North Bucks Development Corporation 44

North Bucks Licensed Victuallers' Association 172

North Bucks Sports Advisory Council 197

O

Olney 35, 49, 54, 55, 60, 64, 85, 170, 211

Ormerod, Councillor A., Bletchley UDC 164, 171

Ouse, River 2, 7, 28, 78, 80, 124, 132, 136, 137, 139, 142, 156, 163, 171, 198, 205, 220

Ouse River Board 220

Ouzel, River 149, 151, 181, 198

Owen, A. 165

Oxford Regional Hospital Board 222

P

Parsons, R. Councillor Newport Pagnell RDC. 18

Passenham 130, 132, 139

Pevsner, Nikolaus 215

Phillips, V., Chairman, Bletchley NFU. 23, 157

Pilson, Joseph, Chairman, Leighton-on-Linslade UDC. 117

Pooley, Frederick, Chief Architect and Planning Officer, Bucks County Council 3, 4, 8, 16, 18, 20, 21, 22, 23, 24, 25, 26, 27, 28, 29, 32, 34, 35, 37, 38, 40, 41, 43, 44, 45, 47, 48, 49, 51, 55, 59, 60, 61, 62, 71, 72, 73, 74, 78, 84, 86, 88, 92, 96, 98, 106, 109, 115, 116, 191, 201, 207

"Pooley Plan" 32, 35, 43, 47, 48, 49, 59, 60, 84, 86, 88, 96, 98, 115, 116

Pownall, R., Water Board engineer. 50, 205

Price, Harold, Councillor, Bletchley UDC. 25

Pye, E. L., Chief Engineer MKDC. 208

Q

Quarry Hall Farm 45

R

Radcliffe Trust 3, 7, 168

Ramsbotham, J. Councillor, Bletchley UDC. 35, 36, 78, 79, 97

Reading University, Department of
Agricultural Economics. 187
Redbourne 2
Ridgewell, W.M. 144
Risebrow, Michael. NFU Branch Secre-
tary to 1964. 57
Roade 17
Royston, J., Assistant Curator of the
County Museum, 212

S

Scanlon, R., Walton Parish Council
114, 123, 132
Secretary, Joint Parliamentary 62
Sharpe, Councillors R. 110, 142
Shaw, A. 168
Shaw, G. A. T., Secretary to MKDC 214
Shenley 9, 37, 39, 47, 51, 53, 68, 69, 77,
79, 124, 132, 139, 144, 148, 150,
186
Sherington 69, 72, 185
Smithie, J., Engineer and Surveyor,
Bletchley UDC. 33, 34, 62, 164,
221, 222
Snaith, A., Councillor, Newport Pagnell
RDC. 22, 23, 44, 46, 47, 52, 53,
54, 68, 75, 110, 111, 119, 120,
121, 123, 132, 134, 137, 139, 141,
142, 143, 144, 158, 159, 174, 198,
206
Snook, W. Chairman, Bucks NFU. 29,
31, 38, 41, 43, 44, 54, 60, 61, 65,
66, 67, 73, 75, 84, 88, 99, 101,
126, 128, 134, 135, 138, 150, 153,
154, 155, 171, 179, 182, 184, 185,
187, 205
Southampton-Portsmouth area 33
Southern Regional Board for Industry
33
Southern Sports Council 211
Sparling, Rev. H., Chairman Newport
Pagnell RDC. 17, 19, 49, 52, 53,
69, 70, 72, 111, 120, 121
Speed, J. 70
Staniford, Councillor E., Bletchley

UDC 33
Stantonbury 9, 37
Stevenage 2, 8, 81, 158, 186
Stony Stratford 3, 4, 8, 9, 36, 93, 94, 95,
98, 108, 109, 119, 125, 130, 131,
146, 153, 157, 159, 163, 172, 179,
180, 181, 203, 207, 208, 209, 212
Stuff, A. 158
Swindon 208
Sylvester-Evans, A., Ministry of Hous-
ing 159, 160, 170, 171, 173

T

Tattenhoe 37, 132
Taylor, W.T. 169
Timberlake, Councillor J. 43
Tompkins, M. 70
Town and Country Planning Associa-
tion 27
Town Planning Institute 166
Traffic Research Corporation Ltd. 215
Tull, G.K. 132
Twin-city - an aletrenative proposal to
a single large city 130, 147

U

Unwin, Mr. 65
Uthwatt, Miss Stella 168

V

Venn, Mr. E. 61
Verney, Alderman R.B., Bucks County
Council. 42, 66, 100
Verney, Major Ralph, Chairman, Rad-
cliffe Trust 3, 7, 8, 30, 100, 192,
193, 195

W

Waite, H. 114
Wallace, Neville 160
Walton 37, 45, 46, 85, 86, 99, 100, 102,
103, 104, 105, 113, 114, 115, 116,
123, 132, 142
Walton Stud Farm 45, 103

Ward, Alderman A., Bucks CC. 42, 66
Wardle, A. R., Secretary to MKDC 214
Water Eaton 3
Watkiss, F., Woburn Sands Parish
    Council. 32, 141, 148
Wavendon 4, 20, 32, 37, 85, 87, 102,
    106, 113, 114, 116, 119, 183, 201,
    202, 203, 205, 207, 211, 214, 216
Wavendon and District Conservative
    Association 20
Wavendon Tower 4, 201, 202, 205, 214
Weatherhead, H., President, Bletchley
    Chamber of Trade. 26
Webber, Melvin W., Chair of City Plan-
    ning at University of California.
    215
Westminster 52
Whaddon 37, 39, 50, 73, 100, 151, 153,
    169, 197
Whaddon Parish Council 153
Whitchurch 50, 58, 171
Whiteside, Robert, Director, Hovering-
    ham Gravels Ltd. 45
Whiting, Francis, Chairman, Newport
    Pagnell NFU. 84, 102
Wibberley, Gerald, Chairman Comittee
    on Rural Land Use. 215
Willen 37, 39, 110
Williams, Gerald, Brooklands Farm,
    Broughton 183
Wilton Hall 34
Winchendon 50
Wing 112, 150
Wing Rural Council 150
Winslow 7, 36, 37, 58, 59, 93, 95, 99,
    105, 112, 122, 127, 134, 137, 153,
    196, 206
Winslow Rural Council 58, 93, 105,
    122, 137, 196, 206
Woburn Sands 32
Wolverton 3, 4, 7, 8, 9, 10, 11, 16, 17,
    21, 36, 37, 45, 50, 52, 58, 65, 73,
    74, 75, 76, 80, 81, 82, 85, 89, 92,
    93, 94, 95, 96, 97, 98, 100, 106,
    107, 108, 109, 110, 111, 112, 116,
    118, 119, 122, 124, 125, 126, 128,

130, 131, 132, 137, 138, 139, 140,
    141, 143, 146, 147, 151, 153, 154,
    157, 158, 159, 163, 164, 172, 174,
    175, 177, 179, 180, 192, 193, 194,
    195, 196, 198, 201, 203, 206, 207,
    208, 209, 211, 212, 221
Wolverton UDC 8, 11, 21, 58, 76, 82,
    89, 107, 119, 122, 146, 147, 157,
    177, 192, 195, 198, 201, 221
Woollard, F. 23, 42, 51
Woolston 37
Worboys, J. R. 219
Woughton 9, 31, 32, 37, 39, 85, 110,
    131, 132, 185, 203
Wren, Kenneth, Chief Financial Officer
    216

Y

Young, K.F. Clerk, Wing Rural Council.
    150
Young, Major J.D., AldermanBucks CC.
    42, 50
Youngman, Peter, Landscape Architect
    216

Books by John Taylor

All aspects of life in North Bucks during the 1914-1918 war, detailed in 6 volumes:

Stony Stratford during the First World War ISBN: 9781909054127

Newport Pagnell during the First World War ISBN: 9781909054134

Bletchley during the First World War ISBN: 9781909054264

North Bucks during the First World War ISBN: 9781909054202

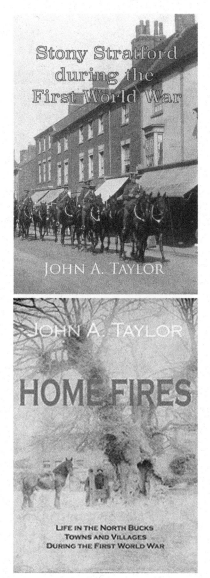

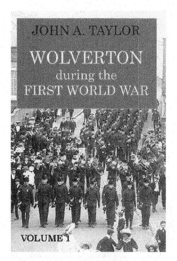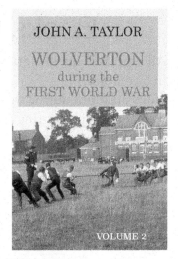

Wolverton During the First World War - published in two volumes
ISBN: 9781909054233 and 9781909054301

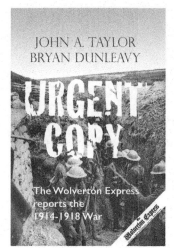

Urgent Copy: The First
World War reorted
through the letters of
seving soldiers, and pub-
lished in the Wolverton
Express.
ISBN: 9781909054165

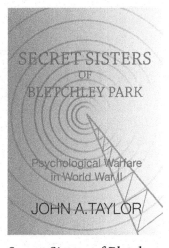

Secret Sisters of Bletch-
ley Park
The lesser-known story
of the secret war that
was conducted from
various locations near
Blatchley during WWII.
ISBN: 9781909054288

Other Local Books of Interest

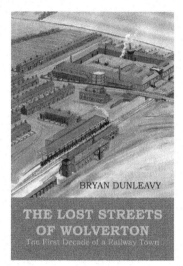

The Lost Streets of Wolverton
Bryan Dunleavy
ISBN: 9781909054004

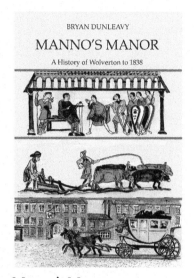

Manno's Manor
Bryan Dunleavy
ISBN: 9781909054059

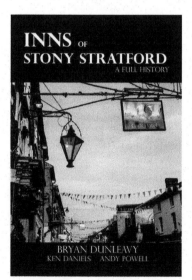

Inns of Stony Stratford
Bryan Dunleavy, Ken Daniels, Andy
Powell
ISBN: 9781909054080

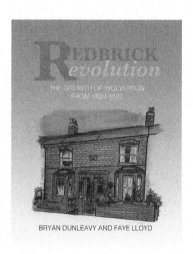

Redbrick Revolution
Bryan Dunleavy, Faye Lloyd
ISBN: 9781909054172

Lightning Source UK Ltd.
Milton Keynes UK
UKOW05n1343240117
292774UK00002B/3/P